ROUTLEDGE LIBRARY EDITIONS:
INDUSTRIAL ECONOMICS

Volume 2

T0362050

COMPETITION IN
BRITISH INDUSTRY

COMPETITION IN BRITISH INDUSTRY

Restrictive Practices Legislation in Theory and Practice

DENNIS SWANN, DENIS P. O'BRIEN, W. PETER J. MAUNDER AND W. STEWART HOWE

Routledge
Taylor & Francis Group

LONDON AND NEW YORK

First published in 1974 by George Allen & Unwin Ltd

This edition first published in 2018
by Routledge
2 Park Square, Milton Park, Abingdon, Oxon OX14 4RN

and by Routledge
711 Third Avenue, New York, NY 10017

Routledge is an imprint of the Taylor & Francis Group, an informa business

British Library Cataloguing in Publication Data
A catalogue record for this book is available from the British Library

ISBN: 978-1-138-30830-5 (Set)
ISBN: 978-1-351-21102-4 (Set) (ebk)
ISBN: 978-1-138-57229-4 (Volume 2) (hbk)
ISBN: 978-1-138-57245-4 (Volume 2) (pbk)
ISBN: 978-0-203-70207-9 (Volume 2) (ebk)

Publisher's Note
The publisher has gone to great lengths to ensure the quality of this reprint but points out that some imperfections in the original copies may be apparent.

Disclaimer
The publisher has made every effort to trace copyright holders and would welcome correspondence from those they have been unable to trace.

COMPETITION IN BRITISH INDUSTRY

RESTRICTIVE PRACTICES LEGISLATION IN
THEORY AND PRACTICE

Dennis Swann

Denis P. O'Brien

W. Peter J. Maunder

W. Stewart Howe

London · George Allen & Unwin Ltd
Ruskin House   Museum Street

ISBN 0 04 338066 2 hardback
     0 04 338067 0 paperback

Printed in Great Britain
in 10 point Times Roman
by Unwin Brothers Limited
Old Woking, Surrey

To competitors everywhere

Acknowledgements

The research upon which this book is based was carried out with the aid of a grant from the Social Science Research Council. The cost of extensive industrial visiting being what it is we could not have carried out the project without substantial financial aid and we are therefore most grateful to the Council for its support. We must also record our debt of thanks to Sir Rupert Sich, Registrar of Restrictive Trading Agreements, and members of his staff at Chancery Lane, who helped us in discussions and by enabling us to consult registered agreements and transcripts of cases. We must also thank a host of people in industry. It would not be possible to mention the names of all those who have helped and in any case many would prefer to remain anonymous. We have had fruitful discussions with many directors, managers and trade association secretaries. We have been greatly impressed by their willingness to give up time to talk to us and we are extremely grateful to them. On the buying side we have talked not only to people in private industry but to purchasing officers in nationalised industries, local authorities and hospital boards. Again we have enjoyed much co-operation and this has often extended to the provision of valuable data. Again we must record our gratitude.

We owe a great debt to our secretaries Brenda Moore, Pam Thirlwell and Beth Skepper who with their usual courtesy and efficiency have helped us to put our findings into final shape.

D.S.
D.P.O'B.
W.P.J.M.
W.S.H.

April 1973

Contents

Contents

Introduction

The purpose of this book is to present the findings of a research project and to consider their implications for public policy. The project was designed to find out what effect the 1956 Restrictive Trade Practices Act (and the subsequent legislation of 1968) had on British industry. The project itself had a twofold origin. It was a logical extension of our study of information agreements[1] and embodied techniques developed in that study. But equally important was a feeling of some dissatisfaction with the way in which studies of restrictive practices policy in the United Kingdom had developed. To a considerable degree economists had been involved in what may be termed 'case-mongering'. That is to say both books and articles had concerned themselves with two main topics: (a) the evolution and present nature of the law and (b) the Judgements of the Court. Judgements had been mulled over, errors of economic logic had been exposed and inconsistencies between one finding and another had been highlighted. (A similar approach had often been evident in the case of monopolies and mergers.) It was no part of our argument that this kind of activity was without value. Clearly it was important that scholars should be concerned with assessing how well-conceived legislation was and in this respect the economist had much to offer. Equally the industrial economist in particular was concerned with the way in which the Court had approached individual cases. We should further point out that we could hardly object to this kind of activity in view of the fact that in our separately published case studies we have indulged in it ourselves. What did, however, disturb the authors was the incompleteness of much of this activity. Incompleteness in this context refers to the failure to follow out the effects of Judgements. Clearly this is crucial to any assessment of policy. In case this charge of neglect appears to be all-inclusive we would readily admit that there have been honourable exceptions – the most notable being J. B. Heath whose early investigation, the results of which were published in the *Manchester School*,[2] must be regarded as a pioneering piece of work within the U.K. context. Another most important exception is those economists who have been directly associated with the work of the Monopolies Commission and the Restrictive Practices Court. Clearly they have been involved in the anti-trust field in the most practical way and the results, even if sometimes unadvertised, have been extremely important.

When the Conservative government passed the 1956 Restrictive Trade Practices Act it was opting, although somewhat hesitantly, in favour of competition against a background of well-entrenched and widespread restrictive agreements. On the face of it the Act was an initial success. In the majority of contested cases agreements were struck down. More important much of industry voluntarily chose to abandon agreements rather than go before the Court. The purpose of this study has been to probe behind this initial impact. Our basic question has been–how effective was the Act, not just on the surface and immediately but in terms of business behaviour over a period of years?

In order to find an answer to this basic question we selected eighteen industries and studied each in depth.[3] (The resultant case studies are published separately and are available from the Department of Economics, Loughborough University. The results derived from these help to form the broad conclusions contained in Chapter 4 of this book.) The word 'industry' has been interpreted broadly–thus the study of woven carpets also took account of the tufted variety and it was recognised that cast iron baths had to compete with steel and plastic varieties. The critic may say that eighteen industries was a limited sample upon which to base any firm conclusions about the effectiveness of the legislation on *industry as a whole*. We would reply that eighteen case studies are better than none. The list of industries was deliberately chosen in order to give a wide coverage of industrial situations. Capital goods (i.e. transformers) and consumer goods (i.e. bread) were both included. Relatively capital intensive industries (i.e. cement) and relatively labour intensive industries (i.e. sanitary ware) were involved. Although price agreements were in a majority (and were in practice by far the most important form of restriction), other forms of practice were included (i.e. the Tyre Trade Register). We would also point out that case studies involve a great deal of time, effort and indeed mileage, and the desire to produce a book which is up-to-date sets a limit to the number of cases which can be dealt with. To be absolutely certain of producing quickly a result which inescapably answers our question in respect of *industry as a whole* would have required a multitude of workers and a small fortune. In practice we believe the results obtained in respect of eighteen industries are a good guide to industry as a whole. We are reinforced in this view by the fact that side by side with the eighteen major case studies we carried out another twenty-two minor studies.[4] These have not been written up as case studies but they inform the broad conclusions of Chapter 4 of this book. It follows that the Chapter 4 analysis is based on forty case studies.

Since the Act did in some cases lead to the upholding of agreements, we thought it worthwhile to inquire into the reasons for so doing, the arrangements which were sanctioned and the subsequent course of events. The first four of our separately published major case studies deal with this topic. But since the overwhelming majority of registered agreements were struck down or abandoned we concentrated on such instances and fourteen of the major case studies fell into this general category. Within the latter abandonment was the most important consequence of the 1956 and 1968 Acts and so eight of the fourteen studies related thereto.[5]

Where agreements were struck down or voluntarily abandoned we asked a whole series of questions. Did competition *in fact* emerge? If so, could the causes be identified? Was it due to the onset of rivalry between erstwhile collaborators? Was it due to the removal of barriers to entry? Or was competition dependent on the emergence of a new technology, i.e. the Schumpeterian factor? Was the latter independent of the legislation or did previous agreements hold it back? What form did competition take–did it centre on price, product design or what? How long did it take for competition to emerge and how long did it last? Did buyers take advantage of the new situation to stimulate more competition? (Where cases were fought before the Court and the Respondents and Registrar pointed to the likely effects of competition it was instructive to compare prognostications with actual events.)

The above questions related to the causes and nature of competition. The other equally important category of questions were concerned with effects. Did the consumer enjoy a price fall or abatement of price increases? What happened to profit margins and return on capital? Did competition enforce greater efficiency? If excess capacity previously existed did competition lead to its elimination? Was technological progress stimulated or retarded? Was there any evidence that competition was not always the most desirable state of affairs? For example, did competition ever give rise to a damaging degree of instability?

Alternatively did industry seek ways of avoiding competition? Was this by means of information agreements? How effective were such arrangements? Alternatively did some form of price leadership arise? Or did industry resort to secret collusion? Were mergers and takeovers a way of eliminating inconvenient competitors and creating a more 'manageable' industrial structure?

How did industry react to competition? Was the merger a more comfortable way of increasing market shares than price competition with an added bonus of more control over the market? This in turn raised the whole question of whether laxness of the Board of Trade and its successor, or fundamental inadequacies of the legislation in respect of mergers, frustrated the Registrar and Court. Then again did legislation such as that establishing the Industrial Reorganisation Corporation and prices and incomes machinery run counter to the ends envisaged by the legislators of 1956?

From ends we turn to means. Initially we had a series of interviews with bodies generally involved in competition policy. These included staff at the Office of the Registrar, the then Board of Trade, the then Consumer Council, the C.B.I., the N.E.D.C. and the I.R.C. This enabled us to derive some initial impressions, although in the case of the I.R.C. it was one of mystification. Thereafter we turned to specific case studies. Our approach was as follows. Clearly at the outset some background information was desirable and in respect of the cases which came before the Court this was available in the form of law reports and case transcripts (this was additional to the registered agreements). In other cases we had the advantage of other sources of information such as those provided by the reports of the Monopolies Commission and the National Board for Prices and Incomes. We did not, however, allow our choice of industries to be dictated by such considerations and in a number of instances apart from registered documents we started from scratch. This was true, for example, in the cases of roadstone, sanitary ware and baths. It is of course obvious that the kind of questions we asked can only be answered by a direct approach to those involved in particular industries. The second stage therefore usually consisted of a series of intensive interviews with firms on the production side together with relevant trade association secretaries. Ideally we sought those whose experience stretched back to 1956 or before. Directors and managers proved to be remarkably co-operative. In only one industry–permanent magnets–did we encounter a widespread refusal to co-operate and fortunately some firms came to our rescue. We always sought a wide coverage of firms so that we could obtain as firm a basis as possible upon which to found our conclusions. Thus in the case of carpets we interviewed all the important woven carpet producers in the Kidderminster and Yorkshire sections and this also brought us in contact with tufted carpets.

Interviewing is essentially a detective game. A wide variety of facts and impressions are collected (sometimes these conflict) and the ultimate aim is to piece them together to produce a coherent picture of what happened over the period of time since agreements were terminated and what is the current industrial structure and pattern of behaviour. Witnesses vary in the willingness to volunteer information. Some proved reticent, which is hardly surprising given the nature of the subject, but gratifyingly most proved forthcoming and occasionally we sat back and had the lid taken off completely. Such a contingency would have been totally improbable had we not been operating as research workers independent of the anti-trust authorities. One of the problems encountered in interviewing was the variation in the ability of those interviewed to analyse their own actions and the structure and workings of their industry. It is also important to guard against pet hunches on the part of businessmen which are not founded on fact. Memories tend to be imprecise and it was important not to rely too heavily on recollections of, for example, how far or how quickly prices fell. Documentary evidence was therefore desirable and the cross-checking of what one interviewee said against what another had said was imperative. A healthy scepticism was also important. For example, in one industry the uniform movement of prices was frequently ascribed to oligopolistic awareness until at last an extrovert revealed that it was all simply the product of collusion!

In an earlier study of information agreements it became obvious that too much reliance should not be placed on producers. When it came to the movement of prices they were somewhat reticent. Then again in a situation where tendering was operative, if competition existed producers would not know the prices tendered by other firms and if there was collusion they would be doubly careful to avoid giving any impression that they knew what their 'rivals' were intending to offer. The alternative was to approach the consumer who was in a unique position to reveal the pattern of price offers and the movement over time and had little to lose by discussing the matter. This proved successful in the case of information agreements and we adopted it here. The third stage in each study therefore consisted of the identification of a wide range of buyers. These were interviewed. They proved extremely helpful, in some cases providing series of tender prices going back over the period to 1956. Following interviews with customers it was in some cases possible to devise questionnaires which would cover a much wider range of buyers.

The basic technique adopted in this study was then that of interview, supplemented where appropriate by questionnaire. While

B

there may have been other ways of conducting a study such as this, it was the technique which we felt most appropriate and which two of us had operated with success in investigating information agreements. Nevertheless it is desirable to say why we felt it appropriate. The main alternative approach to that adopted in this study was a statistical one, with various levels of aggregation being possible. Thus it might be argued that examination of rates of change and productivity in *sectors* generally affected by competition policy as compared with sectors unaffected, would be instructive. It might have been, but we doubt it. The defects of the data when used in broad aggregates alone make this unlikely; but in addition there was the fundamental problem that in a non-static world *ceteris* are hardly ever *paribus*, and it seems likely that any conclusions reached on this basis would have been highly misleading.[6]

At a more disaggregated level it should, in principle, be possible to obtain data about output, investment and labour productivity. (Some comparison of the rate of innovation is also conceptually possible, although without knowing what proportion of relevant opportunities the innovations represent, which is something that statistical investigation alone will not reveal, it is not clear what significance can be attached to this information.) Such data, obtained for each one of a broad sample of industries which had been affected by competition policy, could then be compared with a similarly sized group which was untouched by such policy. But the problem of unequal other things remains; and as soon as it is found necessary to allow for changes in underlying data, particularly as a result of technical change, it is necessary to dismount the statistical horse.

But in any case, the data required for such studies is rarely available. To obtain the data on labour productivity in any of the industries at which we looked in this study would have been a major undertaking, and indeed would have been impossible in secretive industries such as the magnet makers. Data on output and investment are not a great deal easier to come by because of problems of defining 'the industry': the only satisfactory data relates to a specified group of firms and though trade associations have access to this, it is not always available to outsiders–indeed rarely so.

On the whole we found a micro-economic technique, taking interviews as a starting point, to be wholly satisfactory. It often gave us access to data which would not normally have been available, and we are grateful for the co-operation we received from the vast majority of industries. We found that our interviewees were usually coherent and articulate–and, as in intelligence work, the collation of interviews was a satisfactory method of sifting the wheat from the chaff. We certainly would not subscribe to the view that our respondents were in a perpetual fog as a result of 'spending . . . many hours in . . . smoke-filled rooms'[7] so that they were unable to tell what they were doing or why they were doing it. In any case if this were to be accepted as a valid argument against micro-studies of the kind we have undertaken (and at times it seems to be offered as such)[8] it should be noted that not only does it rule out trying to find out how firms operate (which is necessary enough) but also to rule out useful *a priori* theorising since the motivation and methods of the firm do not apparently give rise to any predictable conclusions.

We did not ask questions designed to produce the answers we wanted[9] but allowed the interviewees to give us the picture of events as they saw it. This is not to imply that we did not cross-question; we certainly did. But we did not seek to read our views into the answers we were given, nor to ask questions which would produce answers which supported our particular prejudices. Rather this was an exercise in the venture, still all too rare amongst academic writers on industry, of getting off the seat and into the boots.

Chapter 1 reviews the evidence relating to the emergence of restrictive agreements and traces the involvement of the government which culminated in the 1948 Monopolies and Restrictive Practices (Inquiry and Control) Act. Emphasis is laid on the impotence of the common law before 1948 and the essentially informational role of the 1948 Act. Restrictive agreements did not come under attack until 1956. Chapter 2 reviews the contents of the 1956 Act. It provides evidence of the initial impact of the Act and indicates the loopholes of which information agreements were a prime example. Although the Court was able to attack these arrangements under the provisions of the 1956 Act it was not until the 1968 Act that express requirements concerning registration were introduced. The period from 1965 onwards indicates some retreat as a result of the then new philosophies of economic planning and incomes policy. Chapter 3 presents the theoretical background to competition just as Chapter 2 provides a legal backdrop. Here we review what economic theory has to say about the effects of competition and the factors which influence its nature. Following on from this we examine the implications which restrictive agreements have for the operation of competition. In Chapter 4 we review the evidence of the eighteen major case studies, in conjunction with that derived from the twenty-two minor studies. We ask how the legislation affected industry and how effective it was, what was the effect on resource allocation and what were the policy implications. In Chapter 5 we examine the content of the new Fair Trading legislation in the light of the recommendations arising from our study.

REFERENCES

1 See D. P. O'Brien and D. Swann, *Information Agreements, Competition and Efficiency* (London, 1968).
2 'Restrictive Practices and After', *Manchester School of Economic and Social Studies*, Vol. 29, May 1961, pp. 173–202.
3 These are as follows: cement, standard metal windows, permanent magnets, glazed tiles, (all upheld); transformers, carpets, glass containers, wire rope, tyre distribution, bread (all struck down); roadstone, sanitary ware, electric motors, surgical dressings, electric cables, baths, automotive batteries and steel drums (all abandoned).
4 These are as follows: pipes (sewage and drainage); galvanised tanks; wire mesh; Leavers' lace; switchgear (sold to Area Boards); chocolate and sweets; sand and gravel; electric meters; hard fibre rope and twine; aluminium castings; files and hacksaws; polythene film; black bolts and nuts; silica and general firebricks; tyre mileage; metal bedsteads; electric lamps (filament exceeding 28 volts, discharge and fluorescent); gas meters; jute spinning and weaving; paper bags; steel arches and light rails (for mining); watertube boilers.
5 Within the forty cases abandonments clearly dominate since the twenty-two minor studies include only two upheld cases (black bolts and nuts and watertube boilers) and one struck down case (jute spinning and weaving). It is true that the cases of galvanised tanks, tyre mileage and electric meters were the subjects of cases but these occurred well after formal abandonment. Leavers' lace was a special case of an industry which avoided the legislation for a considerable period. Thus about two-thirds of *all* cases considered fall into the abandoned category.
6 The same may well be said of macro-economic studies which purport to test the existence or otherwise of marginalist behaviour by firms. Thus the conclusion that profit margins are influenced by elasticity of demand has been drawn by some writers from data which showed a different mark up from direct cost; which could, however, merely be the result of inadequate information on costs (highly likely in the particular industries studied) or (also highly likely) the result of oligopolistic pressures and estimates of likely retaliation which is not, however, casuistically interpreted, support for marginalism.
7 A. Silberston, 'Price Behaviour of Firms', *Economic Journal*, Vol. 80, 1970, pp. 511–82, 555.
8 *Ibid.*, pp. 556, 574.

9 For an example of a study which may well be considered to have relied upon leading questions, see J. S. Earley, 'Marginal Policies of "Excellently Managed Companies"', *American Economic Review*, Vol. 46, 1956, pp. 44–70. For criticism of this, see especially H. A. Simon, 'Theories of Decision-making in Economics and Behaviour Science', *op. cit.*, Vol. 49, 1959, pp. 253–83, 264.

A monopoly is where in any Realme there is a setled trade of any one nedfull Comoditie, ether wrought or unwrought, By which many do rayse ther Lyvinges, as in wolle, tyne, Lede, Clothe, Corne, wine, wood, alam, mader, thred, paper, Canves, and suche Like; yf any one suche Comoditie be by graunt from the prince Brought to one mans hand, so that none shall have the transportinge out, The bringinge in, or the servinge of the state, of any suche nedfull Comodities, But that vnder payne of Confyscacion the same must passe that one mans hand, The same is said to be monopoly and very preiudiciall to the state.

For the makinge of paper and monopolyes, 1586.

Chapter 1

COMBINATION AND THE STATE

The day of the fixed price has come, and such a develop-
ment must be considered as a real condition of social and
economic progress.
British Electrical and Allied Manufacturers' Association, 1930.

I. EARLY COMBINATION

Although in the nineteenth century the dominant economic philosophy was one of free competition this does not mean that restrictive agreements and arrangements of various kinds were not to be found. As Clapham observed,

> There had been in various industries a good deal of quiet price fixing without formal association all through the nineteenth century. 'Free and open competition' had never been perfectly attained, or even universally and sincerely desired.[1]

Ashworth maintains that despite the stress on the virtues of un-restricted competition, associations of producers in the same industry or district were common in the 1840s. They may, however, have become less common the next quarter of a century.[2] This view concurs with that of Clapham who observed,

> The prosperity and the economic outlook of the third quarter of the century had reduced the occasions for such co-operation; and there is some reason to think that there was less of it in the middle 'seventies than there had been before 1850.[3]

Several studies have thrown light on the existence of combinations in the first half of the nineteenth century. The coal owners of the Tyne and Wear had 'limited the vend' but were eventually thwarted by the competition of rail-borne coal. Barker and Harris in their study of St Helens throw light on price-fixing associations, local in character, in salt and coal production during the first three decades of the century.[4] Flint glass producers too had their local associations and as early as 1812 representations were made to the government on matters relating to the excise duty. As Barker and Harris observe,

> Although the minutes are chiefly concerned with the excise talks, the question of price regulation cropped up with regularity.[5]

For example, in 1831 the flint glass trade held a meeting at Lichfield and the various deputations agreed on a net minimum price list. Later the Warrington district producers agreed to adhere to it.[6] Bottle glass producers too are recorded in 1845 as fixing the price of their product.[7] Window glass was a fertile field for restrictive activity. Barker in his study of Pilkingtons traces understandings back to the seventeenth century. He points out that

> There were relatively few units of production and it was, therefore, easy for the handful of manufacturers to join together to prevent cut-throat competition by fixing the selling prices of their goods. They could also, if they so wished, unite to prevent any interloper from breaking into their circle.[8]

The St Helens Crown Glass Company was indeed a member of the Crown Glass Association and there is evidence to suggest that the latter came into existence about 1825. Direct price-fixing in respect of sales to merchants and dealers was followed in 1838 by output restriction by means of quotas. Those who sold below Association levels were in turn undersold by the Association and driven out of business. Barker and Harris also show that alkali and soda producers were getting together at least as early as 1838–the Alkali Association itself dating from 1860.[9]

Soap makers too exhibited an early taste for consensus as opposed to the ruthless individualism we have been led to expect. There was a London and Country Association of Soap Manufacturers in the late 1830s although local associations had existed previously. In the 1850s there is clear evidence concerning the activities of a North of England Soap Association–this was purely concerned with price-fixing in a period when war was interfering with tallow supplies from Russia and causing the raw material price to rise. In 1867 the United Kingdom Soap Makers' Association came into being and it continued in one form or another for upwards of sixty years. The Association was, however, dominated by London producers–the northern producers therefore also participated in their own Northern Soap Makers' Association. In respect of prices an extremely uneasy alliance existed between the two. However, Musson's verdict is that, despite the constant accusations and counter-accusations of treachery, double-dealing, fraud and evasion of agreed rules, the national Association did reduce, even though it could not abolish, cut-throat competition, and agreed changes in price were sometimes achieved.[10]

II. THE COMBINATION MOVEMENT 1880–1914

Although the third quarter of the century may have witnessed a diminution of restrictive activity, the last two decades of the century were quite different. The growth of combination in the shape of formal trade associations and informal agreements as well as mergers (the latter were then termed trusts) were cardinal features of the period. By the middle of the 1880s, according to Clapham,

> A network of trade associations, more or less formal, more or less efficient, covered a good part of the industrial field.[11]

Associations were indeed sufficiently numerous in the 1880s for Joseph Chamberlain as president of the Board of Trade to instruct his officials to open direct personal contacts with them and chambers of commerce on all important matters of policy and day to day administration.[12] The movement towards combination continued in the earlier years of the present century and gained a real impetus during the First World War. As a result, when in 1919 the Committee on Trusts reported it observed,

> We find that there is at the present time in every important branch of industry in the United Kingdom, an increasing tendency to the formation of trade associations and combinations, having for their purpose the restriction of competition and the control of prices.
>
> Many of the organisations which have been brought to our notice have been created in the last few years and by far the greater part of them appear to have come into existence since the end of the nineteenth century. . . . There has been a great increase in the creation of trade associations during the period of the war.[13]

Professor John Hilton, in a memorandum to the Committee, estimated that there were at least 500 industrial trade associations in existence.

During the period 1880–1914 a wide range of industries were cartelised. Prominent among these was iron and steel. Pig iron producers in various regions of Britain were organised into local associations. According to Macrosty,

> The ironmasters or their representatives also meet regularly in the daily or weekly pig iron markets, held at the local Metal Exchanges, and at the quarterly trade meetings at Birmingham, where they have opportunities of discussing the condition of the trade and exchanging views. In this way they informally thresh out a common price, for in a restricted market each man's business is easily known. When any attempt is made to regulate production it is usually done through the local pig iron trade associations, and not by the formation of any special kartell; this flexibility of constitution is particularly English.[14]

Such arrangements are reported by Macrosty as existing as early as 1881. Malleable iron was also organised. There was an informal ring producing marked bar iron and in 1895 an Unmarked Bar Association was formed. The latter was an arrangement between Midlands and Northern Counties producers[15] but in addition combinations among Scottish malleable iron producers also date at least from the 1880s. The rail trade was highly organised–in 1883 British producers joined German and Belgian firms in forming the International Rail Syndicate. The decade 1878–1887 marked the transition from the use of iron to that of steel in ship construction and as early as 1885 there are reports of a combination of Scottish producers of boiler plate and ship plate. Production of this product in Scotland was indeed organised on a rigorous basis. By the end of the century the Scots had separate boiler plate and ship plate associations whilst in 1898 a Boiler Plate Association was also organised in Lancashire and the North East had its own Plate Association. Tube production was also cartelised. In 1898 English boiler-tube producers attempted to form an association. By 1901 there were both Scottish and English associations working in alliance. Relations were soon severed but in 1902 a truly British effort to advance prices was successfully manifested. Galvanised sheet was also organised. As early as 1883 a Galvanised Iron Trade Association–a largely Midlands organisation–was fixing prices. In 1905 a step forwards was taken when a national association was formed–the National Galvanised Sheet Association–to which 95 per cent of producers in the Midlands, Lancashire, London, the North-East, Scotland and Wales were parties. By the turn of the century a wide variety of metal trades–particularly in the Midlands–were regulating prices. There were associations concerned with axles, tinned sheet, hoops, gas strip, galvanised holloware, galvanised wire netting, as well as brass founding and nail making.[16] These were merely the tip of the iceberg. There was also considerable activity in the iron founding trade. The Monopolies Commission report on cast iron rainwater goods for example indicates that in 1911 foundries in various parts of the kingdom came together to form the National Light Castings' Association – the forerunner of the British Iron Founders' Association. The Commission, however, observed that there had been in existence for many years previously local and sectional associations but none of them was effective for the purpose of trade regulation.[17] This tendency towards the formation of national in place of local organisations has already been noted in the case of galvanised sheet.

Trade association price-fixing – in the language of the times 'terminable agreements' – were also evident in the textile industry to a limited degree but generally where they existed they were predecessors of permanent amalgamations. For example, the amalgamations in 1895 and 1896 which established a dominant position for J. & P. Coats were preceded by a sales association – the Central Thread Agency. Likewise the amalgamation of 1897 which led to the English Sewing Cotton Company grew out of the Association of English Sewing Cotton Makers founded in 1888. Again the Bleachers' Association – an amalgamation dating from 1900 – was an outgrowth of trade association activity. The amalgamation prospectus observed,

> For a great number of years past, there have existed in the Manchester bleaching trade voluntary associations for the regulation of prices in different branches of the business, and for other purposes, and these have worked in harmony with the merchants as well as to the advantage of the trade; but it has been realised that the full advantages of co-operation can be secured only by amalgamation, for the success of which the existence and organisation of these associations give exceptional facilities. The present amalgamation has secured the adhesion of many firms who were not previously members of any price association.[18]

The year 1899 also witnessed an amalgamation which created the Yorkshire Woolcombers' Association. The latter, however, had been preceded by an association of firms in the Bradford district, formed in or about 1893, for the purpose of preventing price cutting. In 1894 the Yorkshire dyeing trade entered into an alliance for regulating prices – this in turn was followed by two amalgamations–one in 1899 which created the Bradford Dyers' Association and another in 1900 which led to the formation of the British Cotton and Wool Dyers' Association. In the light of the above, it is perhaps worth noting that the remark made to the Select Committee on Labour in 1890 to the effect that in the woollen trade of the West Riding there was 'not a single particle' of organisation amongst employers was wearing thin by 1900, although it is true that spinning and weaving, as opposed to combing and dyeing, were notably absent from the list of 'organised' activities.

The electrical industry was subject to price-fixing at a relatively early stage in its development. The industry, which emerged in the 1880s and 1890s, provided itself with a national organisation in 1902 in the shape of National Electrical Manufacturers' Association and in 1911 this was replaced by the British Electrical and Allied Manufacturers' Association (B.E.A.M.A.). A Steam Turbine Manufacturers' Association came into existence in 1909 and price agreements were introduced in the 1911–1912 period. The B.E.A.M.A. group concerned with the production of small motors and generators introduced a price agreement in 1913.[19] Cable making was also cartelised from an early date. The Cable Makers' Association was formed in 1898 and the Telephone Cable Makers' Association came into existence in 1904.[20]

The chemical industry was another sphere of cartel activity. In 1885 manufacturers who had grown weary of competitive warfare came together to form a voluntary agreement to raise the price of bleaching powder and caustic soda. The agreement was terminated at the end of 1889 and in 1890 a merger which gave rise to the creation of United Alkali Limited followed. The latter was not a success as a means of stabilising the market and according to Macrosty in the early years of the present century resort had to be made to international agreements in order to achieve this end. Macrosty's account is reinforced by Musson's historical study of Crosfields which confirms the existence of national and international agreements to regulate the markets for caustic soda and silicate of soda. The latter study indicates that in respect of silicate of soda Crosfields and Gossages (who had themselves arrived at a *modus vivendi*) collaborated with continental (mainly German) manufacturers and agreed the division of markets and the regulation of prices–an International Silicate Association was established in 1900. This collapsed in 1903 but was revived in 1907. Arrangements also existed with United Alkali although the latter was not party to the Association. The history of Crosfields confirms that the formation of United Alkali did not solve the problem of regulating the domestic caustic soda market either. From 1900 on Crosfields discussed prices with a number of producers including United Alkali and Brunner–Mond. There was also an international agreement for caustic soda similar to that in respect of the silicate. Glycerine was another area of restrictive activity. In 1889 the Soap Makers' Association attempted to get a minimum price agreement but failed. However, in 1898 representatives of Levers, Crosfields, and Thoms decided to form a Glycerine Association. The latter was subsequently joined by firms in London and Bristol but failed largely because non-members took advantage of the minimum price agreement to undersell. The Association was revived in 1901. It broke up in 1905, mainly because of competition from continental firms outside the agreement, but was revived in 1907 although for how long it is not known.[21]

Grain milling was another area where price-fixing gained considerable ground during the period under consideration. The National Association of British and Irish Millers dated back to 1878. But neither it nor the local associations it sought to inspire and federate proved capable of controlling competition. In 1900 a national conference resolved to establish local associations which would be responsible for price-fixing. In some areas price-fixing bodies already existed (as was the case in the London Flour Millers' Association and the North Eastern Millers' Association where the membership included a gentleman called Rank) but undoubtedly during the next few years association formation proceeded at a brisk pace.[22]

In linoleum a loose organisation was formed in 1906.[23] In rubber an Association of British Rubber Manufacturers was formed in 1898 and quickly addressed itself to the task of regulating price and output.[24] Matches was another product where competition gave way to regulation. In the nineteenth century there was considerable competition between producers. There were fourteen manufacturers in East London alone and supplies from Sweden and Eastern Europe added to a basically lively situation. However, in 1905 seven of the principal U.K. producers formed the British Match Makers' Association. A quota system was adopted and those who overproduced paid a fine whilst those who underproduced were rewarded. In its early years the Association also fixed manufacturers' prices and discount and rebate terms to different classes of buyer.[25]

In retailing the maintenance of resale prices was a powerful impulse behind the formation of associations. The oldest of these were the Proprietary Articles Trade Association (in the drug trade) and the Publishers' Association (in the book trade). Both were formed in 1896 although the latter did not concern itself with resale prices until 1900. A whole procession of associations followed: the National Federation of Agricultural Implement Dealers in 1899, the Ironmongers' Federated Association in 1900, the Retailers' Sugar Association (London and Suburban) in 1904, the Saddlers' and Harness Makers' together with the Stationers' Association in 1905, and the Motor Trade Association in 1913–to mention just a random selection. Little was to escape the attention of the association movement–a London Coffee House Restaurant Keepers' Trade Society was formed in 1900 and quickly decided that a 4d plate of meat should cost 5d and that no $\frac{1}{2}$d cup of tea, coffee or cocoa should be sold after 7.30 pm.[26]

From what has gone before it is apparent that not only did the period after 1880 witness the growth of 'terminable associations' but also saw a very considerable amalgamation or trust movement. The latter is not central to the theme of this book and its progress will not be discussed in detail although there are several aspects of it which are worthy of attention. The first is the reason for choosing the trust as opposed to the 'terminable association'. Undoubtedly the main reason was the extreme difficulty encountered in securing widespread initial agreement to a price-fixing scheme not to mention the subsequent difficulties encountered in ensuring that it was honoured. Large numbers, together with an ingrained individualism, often precluded effective organisation. Perhaps individualism is the wrong word–rather it was secretiveness, suspicion, together with a disposition to take advantage of opportunities to break the rules when times were hard which may more accurately describe the problem. Difficulties were, for example, acute in the case of calico printing. About the 1890s there were probably between seventy and ninety firms in the trade. Competition was intense and numerous attempts at co-operation were tried but in vain. It should be added that to the number problem was added the intrinsic difficulty of fixing prices in respect of printing. As one commentator has observed,

> The product varied too much, the process varied, quality could not be defined and the amount of service given by the printer varied.[27]

The problem was equally acute in the case of cement. About the turn of the century there were a surprisingly large number of producers in the Thames and Medway valleys and added to this was the problem that the population of firms was constantly changing as some went out of business and other hopefuls came in to take their place. There was also the problem of attitudes. According to Macrosty, firms in the cement industry always 'kept themselves to themselves'[28] while H. O. O'Hagan, who was later to be an important figure in the amalgamation which formed Associated Portland Cement Manufacturers Limited in 1900, put it more strongly when he observed, 'Cement manufacturers had always shown hostility to each other and entertained unfounded suspicions of their neighbours.'[29]

The fact that in the eyes of those who wished to 'organise' industry trusts were preferable to associations throws important light on the nature of the latter. The history of associations in the late nineteenth and early twentieth centuries indicates considerable instability. In some industries there was a procession of associations. When an association continued in existence for a number of years periods when prices were maintained alternated with those when arrangements had to go by default partly because of backsliding on the part of members, but also because of undercutting from outsiders and by virtue of foreign competition. The chairman of the United Kingdom Soap Makers' Association no doubt spoke with feeling when in 1893 he observed, 'The history of our association is a history of exploded agreements.'[30] Because of this it is a great mistake to overestimate the strength of the associations which came into existence in the 1880s and after. However, it is important to note that from the 1920s and 1930s onwards there is evidence that the associations which already existed, or came into existence, were more permanent and more powerful in their control over the market. There are indeed a number of factors which explain this change. One is that they were introduced in a period when the climate of public and official opinion was definitely favourable to them. Secondly, tariffs were a powerful factor in buttressing their position in the market. By contrast the associations of the later nineteenth century were always limited in their power to raise prices by the possibility of free importation.[31] Thirdly, by the 1930s competition had knocked out many competitors and the amalgamation movement had swallowed up many others. As a result numbers had declined and the possibility of organisation was all that much better. The cement industry is a case *par excellence*. Fourthly, whereas in earlier days the membership of an industry was constantly changing, by the 1930s this was becoming a relatively less important factor and to that extent the organisation of trade was easier. Finally, the tendency

C

to produce national associations reduced the incidence of local associations undercutting each other.

The trust movement itself was confined largely to the period about 1897–1902. Some of the impetus for its emergence in 1897 was probably the cheap money conditions which existed in the years immediately preceding, whilst the tendency for it to peter out after about 1902 may have been due to a failure on the part of some of the more important schemes. Undoubtedly some of them proved to be less financially worthwhile than had been anticipated largely because of the inflated capital values paid when firms were brought into the amalgamation. It should also be noted that these combinations did not always rule out the need for agreements–both in the case of salt and sewing cotton arrangements were still necessary in order to regulate the trade as between rival trusts or between the trust itself and those who stayed outside it. Finally, one point of some importance is the lack of official reaction to the large-scale amalgamations. Some of the trusts were alarming in terms of the degree of concentration to which they gave rise. For example, the Calico Printers' Association Limited brought within its scope 85 per cent of the capacity of the industry. It is, therefore, significant that there appears to have been no great official reaction to such developments. That is not to say that there was no hostility at all. For example, the soap trust, which was proposed by Lever in 1906, was effectively prevented by virtue of a vigorous propaganda campaign on the part of the Northcliffe press.

Inevitably the intriguing question arises as to what forces gave rise to the combination movement which was so obviously in progress by the 1880s. Economic instability, and particularly instability of price levels, suggests itself as an obvious major cause.[32] Undoubtedly deficiencies of demand in relation to productive capacity, which provoked price cutting, were a potent cause. Mains cable production provides a good example. Around 1900 the demand for this kind of cable expanded rapidly. Capital raised for the expansion of the electricity supply system amounted to £2·4 million in 1896 but was £11·5 million in 1900. With the well-publicised ending of patent protection in respect of paper insulated cable new firms began to enter the industry and capital was built up in the 1897–1901 period to cope with the expansion of electricity supply. But in 1902 the rate of expansion of electricity supply fell quite dramatically and the excess of productive capacity among cable makers led to severe competition. Mergers followed but failed to cure the problem and so the Mains' Cable Council was formed (within the ambit of the Cable Makers' Association) and price and quota agreements were introduced.[33] The National Light Castings' Association of 1911 had a similar origin. During the last decade of the nineteenth century there was a rapid rise in house construction which reached a peak of 140,000 in 1899 and the light castings industry was expanded appropriately. A progressive decline in building then ensued and during the four years 1910–1913, a particularly bad period in the eyes of the trade, the average annual number of houses built numbered only 62,000. As a result it is reported that there was severe competition, low wages and an inadequate return on, and depletion of, capital.[34]

But this factor, although undoubtedly a potent cause of association, was not unique to the late nineteenth and early twentieth centuries. The question, therefore, remains as to what were the *new* factors at work during this period. Undoubtedly one was intense foreign competition. In the industrial field competition grew as other economies began to industrialise. This competition began to manifest itself not only in the U.K. market but also in foreign markets which had previously been a largely British preserve. In the heavy electrical industry competition from Germany and the United States led to excessive manufacturing capacity and price cutting. Between 1900 and 1914 more than a quarter of the subscribed capital of heavy plant producers failed to achieve a dividend. Foreign competition drove British manufacturers together to salvage collectively what they could. This was undoubtedly an important motive behind the formation of the National Electrical Manufacturers' Association of 1902 and B.E.A.M.A. in 1911.[35] In the agricultural products sector competition was also important – one of the chief reasons for the formation of the National Association of British and Irish Millers in 1878 was the alarm over the increased importation of foreign flour. Further evidence that foreign competition was a causal factor of the association formation was provided by the 1919 report of the Committee on Trusts. It indicated that to a significant extent the agreements it investigated required domestic dealers and purchasers to deal exclusively with home producers and thus to exclude imports.

Producers were also driven together by increased state interference at home and abroad. There was, for example, a growth of protectionism in Europe after the Franco-Prussian war and because of this British producers were driven to protect by joint action their interests in the rest of the world and to press for reciprocal protection at home.

The growth of trade unions was an important factor. The need for collective action on the labour front brought producers together. More specifically the rise of mass trade unionism increased stickiness of wages and profit margins could no longer be protected by depressing wages in the event of a shortfall of demand. The most obvious alternative course would seem to be a price agreement. In some cases what were originally employers' associations broadened their activity to cover trade regulations. In others the practice of collaboration in respect of labour suggested, and gave rise to, separate bodies to deal with production and marketing problems.[36]

Emulation of the trust and cartel movements in Germany and the United States (which in terms of time preceded development in the United Kingdom and were of more far-reaching significance) should also not be ignored. Also active apostles of combination were at work. Perhaps the most famous was E. J. Smith whose book *The New Trades Combination Movement*[37] extolled common costing and price-fixing and attracted a good deal of attention when it was published.

The final and perhaps the most important factor has yet to be mentioned—namely the great depression and the general trend in the economy manifested after about 1870. Undoubtedly after the latter date there was a retardation of economic growth in the British economy. It could be argued that during the period of rapid growth which characterised the British economy in the first three-quarters of the nineteenth century, with its continuously expanding demand, agreements to fix prices and share markets were less relevant[38] than was the case when the rate of economic growth began to slow down. Then there was the great price fall which extended from about 1875 to 1895. It seems reasonable to suppose that this was accompanied by a narrowing of profit margins[39] since fixed charges would by definition not be readjustable downwards except in the longer term. Whether in the mature economy of the last quarter of the nineteenth century the narrowing of profit margins arose also from more intensive competition stemming in turn from the accumulation of capital is an open question. It is noticeable that in the 1880s, particularly, foreign investment was high and not surprisingly the explanation which has been afforded is that capital went abroad because it could not be profitably employed at home.[40]

III. EFFECTS OF THE 1914–1918 WAR

In modern times wars have always tended to stimulate collective action in industry and the First World War was no exception.[41]

During the war there was, as the Committee on Trusts observed 'a great increase in the creation of trade associations'.[42] The basic reason was simple: the problem of shortages and the need to channel resources in particular directions led the government progressively to impose stricter control over industry. This in turn required that there should be some body which could speak on behalf of particular industries and could act as a government agent for the purpose of seeing that government controls were properly implemented. Thus in the case of oils and fats,

> ... impelled by a mixture of motives, strategic, economic and political, the government proceeded towards the logical completion of their policy. They set up the Soap Makers' Federation, which though in form a voluntary association of manufacturers was in fact an engine of official compulsion. It contemplated activities including the distribution of raw material, the fixing of prices, and the 'rationalisation' of productive capacity. It was hardly born before the armistice brought about its premature death, but its very inception demonstrated the change brought about by four years of war in Englishmen's notions of the functions proper to their government.[43]

Another instance arose in connection with sulphuric acid. During the war a great deal of acid manufacturing plant was created specifically for war purposes. It was realised that when hostilities ceased this could lead to an embarrassing problem in respect of market outlets. A departmental committee of the Ministry of Munitions was therefore set up in 1917 to consider the problem. It recommended the formation of a comprehensive association of acid producers to co-operate in solving the postwar problem. The result was the National Sulphuric Acid Association Limited of 1919.[44] Where the government did not itself compel action the habit of working together acted as a catalyst. Thus the Monopolies Commission observed,

> When the 1914–1918 wartime controls ended the established petrol companies, having become accustomed to a certain amount of co-operation with each other during the war, continued to act together on such matters as agreeing wholesale and retail selling prices and the general conditions of trading and relations with retailers and with the public.[45]

Towards the end of the war various official bodies, not to mention associations themselves, began to consider the shape and role of trade bodies in the postwar world. The general conclusion was that associations should be encouraged and their role *vis-à-vis* government confirmed. There was also a tendency to look favourably on price-fixing activities. A departmental committee on textiles came down firmly in favour of each textile trade having an association to consult on all matters of mutual interest and to be regarded by government departments as the authoritative and accredited medium for communication with various parts of the industry.[46] The Committee on Commercial and Industrial Policy after the War also reported in 1918. Within its membership industrial knights were well in evidence and in retrospect its conclusions are predictable. Its basic conclusion was as follows:

> We approve of combinations among manufacturers. All such combinations should, where necessary, be legalised, so as to be enforceable between members.[47]

The Committee briefly reviewed policy abroad. It disliked the U.S. approach but looked with more favour on that of Canada, presumably because its main weapon was publicity. The Committee did feel that in respect of combinations adequate information should be made available to the government and the possibility of investigation in special cases should be provided for. However, one of the virtues of this machinery was that it would give those who wished to combine a free hand since public fears would tend to be allayed. The Committee explicitly recommended that it should be possible for agreements to be registered with the Board of Trade. But there was a sting in all this–having been registered, they would then be enforceable at law.

IV. OFFICIAL ATTITUDES 1919–1948

(i) *The Postwar Price Problem*

This period witnessed a movement of official opinion in the direction of a policy for controlling trade associations and the restrictive agreements to which they often gave rise. But movement was not all in one direction. Immediately after the 1914–1918 war the phenomenon of rising prices and the spectre of profiteering led to a shift in official and public opinion in favour of control. But with the financial collapse of 1921 and the emergence of the interwar structural and unemployment problems there was a shift in the opposite direction. It was only in the Second World War that official opinion moved back towards control and in so doing paved the way for the present machinery.

The first manifestation of concern after the First World War was the appointment by the Ministry of Reconstruction of the Committee on Trusts which reported in 1919. The Committee noted the growth of trade associations and the strengthening which had occurred during the war. Although no evidence of excessive prices was put in evidence, and government departments praised the usefulness of associations during the war, the Committee observed,

> We are unable to share the optimism of those representatives of associations who thought that under no circumstances was there any danger of their operations leading to excessive prices or to the detriment of the public. While fully recognising the honesty with which the great bulk of business in the country is conducted, it is obvious that a system which creates virtual monopolies and controls prices is always in danger of abuse.[48]

The Committee unanimously took the view that it would be desirable to institute machinery of investigation, particularly as it felt that in due course combinations and trade associations would exercise a paramount influence in all important branches of trade. The Committee envisaged a tribunal consisting of a person of legal qualifications plus two to seven members to be selected by him from a Board of Trade panel. The power of instituting investigations would lie with the Board of Trade. The Board, working from complaints, would be responsible for the preliminary enquiries. If it considered that there was a *prima facie* case that activity contrary to the public interest existed, then the case would be referred to the tribunal for investigation and report. Remedial action was, however, to rest with the Board.[49] The parallel with the role of the Monopolies and Restrictive Practices Commission and the Board of Trade under the 1948 legislation is striking.

The Lloyd-George coalition appears to have been impressed by the Report of the Committee on Trusts and in 1919 and 1920 it introduced Profiteering Acts. Basically the Board of Trade had the power to investigate costs, prices and profits. It could declare what was a reasonable price and legal proceedings could be initiated against those who deviated – i.e. those who were profiteering. Where profiteering was proved a producer could be required to reimburse a complainant. In order to implement these powers a series of committees were established by the Board to investigate various trades and thirty reports followed. In 1921, with a depressed economy on its hands, the government allowed the legislation to lapse. There is some reason for regarding the Profiteering Acts as one of the earliest attempts at formulating an anti-trust policy in Britain. Their emphasis was of course upon control of abuse in the sense that where, for example, trade associations were guilty of charging unduly high prices the government would seek to bring about a reduction. It did not seek to change industrial structures or behaviour by breaking up combinations or declaring agreements illegal. Commentators tend to regard its impact upon price determination as having been very limited.[50] The early 1920s also saw some abortive attempts to reduce anti-trust legislation. In 1920 the Board of Trade drafted a Trading and Monopolies Bill but it was not introduced. Private members' Bills were also introduced in 1923 and 1925. The 1925 Royal Commission report on food prices was also hostile,[51] but thereafter the postwar drive for control of restrictive activity was a spent force.

(ii) *New Bearings—Rationalisation and Restriction*

One of the immediate consequences of the 1921 crisis, and the doldrums into which the economy subsequently settled, was in some cases the collapse and in others the weakening of trade association agreements. According to G. C. Allen,

> Some of the wartime consolidations were broken up in the early 'twenties, and many of the attempts to create effective cartels in the more seriously depressed industries were unsuccessful . . . It was not, indeed, until the very end of the decade that the competitive organisation of the great staple industries was substantially modified.[52]

Prominent among the cartelisation failures were the American Cotton Yarn Association in cotton spinning and the Five Counties Scheme in coal mining. The iron and steel industry suffered a similar fate. According to Fitzgerald,

> During the postwar boom associations found no difficulty in fixing minimum prices, but the depression completely changed the situation, and by the middle of 1922 most of the associations had either been dissolved or had ceased to exercise any control over prices. They were revived during the trade recovery of 1922–1923, but foreign competition soon reasserted itself, and price control in most branches of the industry became largely nominal.[53]

The lace industry is yet another example. It reflected both the effects of the depression and also the change in fashion. In 1915 producers of Leavers' lace, who have been described as being 'secretive almost to the point of hermitry',[54] came together to form the Midland Counties' Lace Manufacturers' Association and quickly devised a scheme of minimum prices. But in the early 1920s the trade was in desperate straits. Competition became cut-throat as merchant converters refused to take delivery at the postwar boom prices. Half the trade went bankrupt–a process which was hastened by the fact that machine holders were in the grip of yarn producers who held contracts negotiated at boom price levels. Members of the Association resigned rather than face the consequence of being detected as price cutters and the Association never succeeded in restoring control over prices until about 1941 when wartime controls began to operate.

In the 1920s there were indeed many signs which pointed to a growing disenchantment with free competition. One was the growth of tariff protection. During the First World War the government had interrupted a long-established free trade tradition by imposing the McKenna duties in 1915.[55] They were abandoned in 1924 by the minority Labour administration but were quickly re-imposed in 1925 by the new Conservative government. The British dyestuffs' industry was afforded protection in 1920 and in 1921 *ad valorem* duties were imposed on a selected range of goods under the Safeguarding of Industry Act. The culmination of the protection movement occurred in 1932 with the passage of the Import Duties Act which imposed a general 10 per cent *ad valorem* tariff. Undoubtedly this protection provided a fertile ground for more effective regulation of industry by trade associations.

An anti-competitive tendency of the time was also evident in the attitude of the government towards business concentration. According to Rowley,

> During the interwar period the governments of the day retained a largely paternalistic interest over developments within the business unit. In general the State encouraged the expansion in the size of the firm.[56]

He goes on to point out that,

> The government made use of fiscal policy to this end. The Trade Facilities Act 1921 empowered the Treasury to underwrite loans made to private firms from private sources provided that the loans were raised for aims that would promote employment. This facility encouraged the provision of expansion finance to firms. In 1926 the government allowed the remission of stamp duties on capital issues made consequent upon an amalgamation. In addition the banks, in close association with the Bank

of England, were encouraged to assist rationalisation schemes involving amalgamations.[57]

Indeed a number of significant concentrations took place in the 1920s. Thus in 1925 the Distillers Company was formed. In 1926 I.C.I. came into being by virtue of the fusion of Brunner–Mond, Nobel Industries, United Alkali and the British Dyestuffs' Corporation.[58] In 1927 the British Match Corporation made its bow.

It is also highly relevant that official reports did not come down in favour of an active competition policy. First, there was the Balfour Committee on Industry and Trade which was appointed in 1924 and reported in 1929. It extolled the virtues of combinations as a means of achieving specialisation of plant–on the whole in this respect mergers were regarded as being better than terminable agreements. The latter, however, had the virtue that they were often the first step on the road to a complete consolidation. As far as elimination of the inefficient was concerned the Committee observed,

> It seems unquestionable that this operation can often be performed more speedily and 'rationally' and with less suffering through the mechanism of consolidation or agreement than by the unaided play of competition.[59]

On the question of control of monopoly and restrictive practices it debated the relative merits of, on the one hand, greater publicity by requiring companies to divulge more information and, on the other, the creation of a tribunal to investigate abuses of economic power. On balance it preferred the latter but was not in favour of the creation of powers to rectify any abuses which were uncovered. It then considered the subject further and finally concluded,

> On the whole, and on balance, we feel that, in the circumstances of the present industrial situation, the case for immediate legislation for the restraint of such abuses as may result from combinations cannot be said to be an urgent one. Should, however, undesirable features develop in the future to the detriment of the general public, we recommend that any action by the State by way of inquiry and publicity should be on the lines already indicated.[60]

Reading this and other reports during the interwar period the reader is bound to find it difficult to resist the observation by Alex Hunter that,

There was to be observed among the reports and recommendations of all the numerous commissions and committees of enquiry during the interwar period hesitancy and disinclination to reach definite conclusions. Monopoly and restrictive practices, it was agreed, *potentially* were dangerous. But they did appear to offer stability, security and certain economies of scale to business people during a period of great economic stress. Consequently rather than recommendations for legislation there emanated from the committees only suggestions for departmental surveillance and investigatory tribunals–an attitude of mind to the problem which was to persist into the postwar years.[61]

The 1931 Greene Committee report on resale price maintenance was equally conservative. It did not regard the system as free from disadvantages from the public point of view but did not consider that if law was changed the interests of the public would be better served.[62] In 1931 the Macmillan Committee reported, and it added its voice to industry's call for organisation and association. The Committee observed,

It has been represented to us strongly in evidence that a great deal remains to be done in more than one important industry in overcoming sectional and individual opposition to desirable amalgamations and reconstructions designed to eliminate waste and cheapen costs. It was stated to us that very important economies and much greater efficiency are possible if there are concerted movements to that end. We believe this to be the case . . .[63]

Political opinion too showed a general tolerance of restrictions of competition. As Pollard has pointed out, Labour members of the 1919 Committee on Trusts emphasised their belief that the evolution towards combination and monopoly was both inevitable and desirable, provided it was controlled in the public interest.[64] Labour thinking in the 1920s did not put anti-trust at the head of its list of priorities for dealing with the monopoly problem. One example of Labour thought on this subject is indicated by the report of the parliamentary committee of the Trades Union Congress, published in 1921, which regarded the extension of public ownership as priority number one. Conservative opinion showed a predisposition to favour regulation and controls as opposed to free enterprise and competition. In 1932 Harold Macmillan, himself in favour of industrial planning, observed

Production cannot be planned in relation to established demand while industries are organised on competitive lines.[65]

Even the Liberal Party exhibited a degree of conformity with the new thinking. Thus the Liberal Industrial Enquiry of 1928, whilst recognising that in some industries private enterprise was superior, was elsewhere averse to restoring

... the old conditions of competition, which involve waste and effort, the uneconomic duplication of plant or equipment, and the impossibility of adopting the full advantages of large-scale production. In modern conditions a tendency towards some degree of monopoly in an increasing number of industries is, in our opinion, inevitable and even, quite often, desirable in the interest of efficiency. It is, therefore no longer useful to treat trusts, cartels, combinations, holding companies and trade associations as inexpedient abnormalities in the economic system to be prevented checked and harried ... We believe there is still room ... for large-scale enterprises of semi-monopolistic character which are run for private profit and controlled by individuals.

As for trade associations it stated

... we think that cases may arise in which it is in the legitimate interests of trade or industry that a small minority shall be required to conform to the rules which the majority have decided to impose upon themselves ... we suggest, therefore, that, where an Incorporated Association can show that 75 per cent of those affected are in favour of a trade rule or instruction ... The Association shall have the right to apply for powers to issue an order enforcing the rule in question on all members of the trade or industry or of the appropriate section of it, whether within the Association or not.[66]

During the 1920s the staple industries in particular were depressed and competition did not succeed in removing the surplus capacity which existed. With the onset of the great depression the excess capacity became even more acute, and the need for rationalisation schemes aimed at removing this surplus was pressed vigorously. From the late 1920s onwards the State took an active role in their promotion. Not surprisingly they were often accompanied by price and quota restrictions. In 1929 the Lancashire Cotton Corporation was formed to acquire ten million spindles (about one-fifth of the total) and it was proposed that one-half of these should be scrapped. In 1936 the Spindles Act gave statutory power to organise the elimination of surplus spindle capacity and thus to remove the possibility of excessive competition. This was followed in 1939 by the Cotton Industry (Reorganisation) Act which conferred upon cotton spinners powers to purchase and scrap plant and to fix legal minimum prices. (The outbreak of the Second World War, however, prevented this scheme from being implemented.) In coal mining there was a similar element of State involvement. The Coal Mines' Act of 1930 established the Coal Mines' Reorganisation Commission to promote amalgamations and concentrate production. However, due to the determined opposition of industry it was unable to carry out its task and under the Coal Act of 1938 the vote was passed to the newly created Coal Commission. The 1930 Act also involved a compulsory cartel system. A Central Council representing coal owners was required to allocate sales quotas to seventeen districts into which the country had been divided and the districts were in turn to allocate quotas to collieries. The system was not perfect–not all districts set up common selling agencies and price competition between districts continued. However, in 1936, due to official pressure, there was a further tightening up. In 1930 the shipbuilders formed the National Shipbuilders' Security Limited, which represented 96 per cent of total production capacity in the industry. The intention was to buy up and scrap capacity. Joint agreements about tendering followed. Iron and steel is probably the most interesting case of government sponsorship of cartelisation. The Import Duties Advisory Committee (I.D.A.C.) made protection contingent upon satisfactory schemes of reorganisation being brought forward by the industry. The result was a strengthening of the central organisation of the industry by means of the formation of the British Iron and Steel Federation (B.I.S.F.). Prices were thereafter determined by the B.I.S.F. in collaboration with the I.D.A.C. The government also backed the B.I.S.F. in its negotiations with the European Steel Cartel for the limitation of imports into the United Kingdom; the government raised tariffs against European producers until they accepted the importation limitation.[67]

It was not of course merely in the staple industries that restrictive activity took on a new lease of life.[68] Some of the restrictive agreements which survived to face the 1956 Act, and in some cases to be upheld under it, effectively date from this period. Price stability under the Cement Makers' Federation Agreement–an arrangement which survived the 1956 Act–dates from 1934. The

Heavy Steel Makers' Agreement had its origins in the formation of the B.I.S.F. in 1934. The Associated Transformer Manufacturers' Agreement emerged in 1932 and remained intact until struck down by the Restrictive Trade Practices Court in 1961. The Metal Windows Association was formed in 1933. The Watertube Boiler Makers' Association began life in 1933 and lived on to find favour with the Court. These are but a few random examples.

V. ATTITUDES AND INFLUENCES—WAR AND POSTWAR

The war had two effects in the context of the previous discussion. As on the previous occasion it called into being new trade associations and strengthened the grip of existing ones. For example, in 1942 the Mica Trade Association was formed to negotiate with the government on controls.[69] Then again the British Insulin Manufacturers held its first meeting on 25 February 1941 in order to discuss common problems created by the war, but when the war ended they passed a resolution confirming 'the members' intention to continue the collaboration so successfully carried out during the war years'.[70] Where associations already existed wartime controls increased their power over prices. For example, the impotence of the Midland Counties' Lace Manufacturers' Association during the interwar years has already been referred to, but when the Association was given the task of allocating raw materials during the war lapsed members began to rejoin and the Association was able to reassert itself in respect of prices. Concentration led to a central selling organisation—Lace Productions (1944) Limited—which survived the war. In 1948 another central selling organisation—Lace Productions (1948) Limited—came into existence and the trade was able to continue this arrangement, and escape the consequences of the 1956 Act, until 1971.

The other effect of the war was to focus attention on the need for better economic management when the conflict was over. In particular the impact of Keynesian thinking led the government to produce the 1944 White Paper on Employment Policy. This marked a major turning point in policy, not only in committing postwar governments to the maintenance of full employment, but also because it represented a distinct change in anti-trust policy when compared with both the doubts and hesitancies of previous official enquiries and the government policy in the interwar period. The White Paper noted that

... an undue increase in prices due to causes other than

increased wages might . . . frustrate action taken by the government to maintain full employment.

It went on to observe,

> There has in recent years been a growing tendency towards
> combines and towards agreements, both national and inter-
> national, by which manufacturers have sought to control prices
> and output, divide markets and to fix conditions of sale. Such
> agreements or combines do not necessarily operate against the
> public interest; but the power to do so is there. The government
> will therefore seek power to inform themselves of the extent and
> effect of restrictive agreements, and of the effect of combines–
> and to take appropriate action and to check practices which may
> bring advantages to sectional producing interests but work to
> the detriment of the country as a whole.[71]

The apparent philosophy was that restrictive practices might make
the attainment of full employment more difficult–in other words,
extra demand might give rise to higher prices rather than greater
output and employment. Also in a longer-term sense such practices
could militate against the achievement of a rapidly expanding
output; the problem of the future was to be one not of avoiding
cut-throat competition but of increasing productivity. It is
probable that Hugh Dalton was responsible for this aspect of the
White Paper. He was president of the Board of Trade at the time
and had drafted out the heads of a Restrictive Practices Bill but it
was never introduced.[72] This increasing awareness of the possible
dangers of monopoly and restrictive practices was supported by
the reports of a number of committees which the government
appointed during the immediate postwar period. Whilst they did
not all come down against restrictive practices, they at least helped
to indicate the widespread nature of the phenomenon. The Simon
Committee was appointed by the Ministry of Works in 1946 'to
examine the organisation and methods of distribution of building
materials and components with particular reference to cost and
efficiency, and to make recommendations'. The Committee's
conclusions included the following:

> We find . . . that restrictive arrangements affecting the distribu-
> tion of building materials and components exist on a wide scale:
> indeed, it may fairly be said that in this field monopoly, quasi-
> monopoly, and restrictive practices have reigned almost un-
> challenged for many years. These arrangements, whether
> embodied in formal agreements between manufacturers and

merchants, in tacit agreements or in analogous arrangements, and whether or not the merchant is party to them, permeate virtually the whole field. The broad pattern of the manufacturer/ merchant agreement is an exchange of pledges whereby the manufacturer undertakes to supply the merchant on specially advantageous terms, and the merchant in return agrees to maintain resale prices and not to buy outside the ring. There are a number of effective sanctions behind these arrangements. This does not mean that at different times and in different circumstances formal arrangements are not freely broken, but there is no doubt that in general such agreements are effective. These practices are profitable to the associated manufacturers and also to the majority of merchants. In our view they are not in the national interest. In particular they have tended to lead to a higher level of prices than would have obtained in their absence; to an inflation of gross and net distributive margins; to the consumer being deprived of improvements, actual or potential, in the efficiency of distribution; to an over-elaboration of services provided in the field of distribution and therefore to a waste of manpower and other resources; to there being too many merchants; and to consumers being unable to obtain the precise materials they want from whatever source they prefer.[73]

It recommended that immediate action should be taken to control distributive margins and that in the long run restrictive practices should be eliminated. Noting a statement by the Lord President of the Council in July 1946 that legislation on the lines of the 1944 White Paper would be introduced, the Committee observed,

We have no information as to details of the proposed legislation, but on the assumption that it would be sufficiently widely framed to deal with the whole field of industry and trade, we make no recommendation that special legislation should be introduced in the field of building materials. In this field, however, we recommend that after specific enquiry by an appropriate body there should be power:

(a) To require the registration of all agreements relating to trade practices;
(b) To declare individual agreements or types of agreement between manufacturer and merchant to be in restraint of trade and illegal;
(c) To prohibit either a manufacturer or a merchant from

exercising price discrimination between customers in accepting orders;

(d) To control prices and margins.[74]

The Central Price Regulation Committee also reported in 1946 on the prices of radio valves. The producers established the prices of initial equipment independently but agreed collectively on replacement equipment prices. The report did not condemn the arrangements. However, although it noted that profitability was reasonable, it also pointed out that

> ... prices may well have been too high because costs were inflated through the adoption of restrictive practices by the manufacturers. This question needs some consideration. It would appear that some producers have lower costs than others. If there were competition in the trade throughout, therefore, high cost producers might give up production of valves and the supply might then be produced on a larger scale and therefore more cheaply by the producer whose costs are already lower than the average.[75]

The fforde Committee on the cement industry did not produce any dramatic proposals but it did indicate that the industry was tightly organised. The price agreement operated by the Cement Makers' Federation was accompanied by market sharing, exclusive dealing and a deferred rebate system.[76]

It is apparent that by 1946 the Labour government was proposing to take legislative action. There is also no doubt that there was growing all-party support for such developments. Winston Churchill in a speech in 1947 said,

> Instead of attacking capital we will attack monopoly, instead of imposing restrictions and controls we will attack restrictive practices of all kinds.[77]

The Conservative Industrial Charter of 1947 condemned out of hand

> ... any price agreement designed to keep prices above the cost of the most efficient producers, or levies on the most efficient to keep the least efficient in business.[78]

VI. THE IMPOTENCE OF THE LAW

One good reason why parliamentary action was necessary was the impotent state of the common law when it came to dealing with

D

the problem of restrictive practices. There were in fact three common-law doctrines which might in principle have been applied to remedy the restrictive practices problem; they were the doctrines of monopoly, conspiracy (both civil and criminal) and contracts in restraint of trade.

Monopoly, however, tends to have a very restrictive meaning: in effect a monopoly exists when an individual controls the total supply of a product–a highly unlikely situation–and in practice the doctrine has proved of little use.[79]

The doctrine of conspiracy proved of little greater utility. Generally speaking conspiracy is an act which is otherwise lawful but which becomes unlawful if two persons combine to take action with intent to do injury to another. The modern doctrine of conspiracy was laid down in a trilogy of cases[80] at the end of the nineteenth century, of which the *Mogul* case is the most celebrated, and was summed up by Lord Cave in the case of *Sorrel* v. *Smith*.[81] The upshot of these cases was that however severe the effect upon a third party of the actions of a combination in forwarding or defending their trade interests, no legal liability attaches. Only if the object of the combination is to wilfully and maliciously damage a third party is the case actionable. As Lord Bowen observed in the *Mogul* case,

> The substance of my view is this; that competition, however severe and egotistical, if unattended by circumstances of dishonesty, intimidation, molestation, or such illegalities as I have above referred to, gives rise to no action at common law.[82]

The result of the Judgements leading up to *Sorrel* v. *Smith* was thus highly favourable to combinations. It was relatively easy for the parties to them to prove that the purpose of their association was to further their own interests; whilst for plaintiffs to argue that their motive was really malicious was altogether more difficult.

The doctrine of restraint of trade on the face of it appeared more promising. The modern doctrine was laid down by Lord Macnaghten in the *Nordenfelt* case.[83] He maintained that all restraints were void. But there were exceptions to this rule where such restraints were held to be reasonable–'reasonable that is, in the interests of the parties and reasonable in the interests of the public . . .'. On the face of it this seemed to provide for the possibility of regulating restrictive agreements since the second limb took explicit account of the public interest. In practice this did not prove to be the case. The balance was loaded very much in favour of the parties to the agreement since, whilst it was easy to prove reasonableness *inter-partes*, the onus of proving that the agreement was injurious to the public interest, which lay with the person making the allegation, was altogether a more difficult task. As the Privy Council observed in the *Adelaide* case,[84] 'this onus will be no light one'. Indeed it was not, since it was ruled that evidence of the actual or likely consequences of an agreement by trade, technical or other expert witnesses was not admissible.[85] Moreover, as two perceptive critics of the courts have observed,

> . . . by equating the public interest with reasonableness between the parties to the contract, they excluded the judges from any serious concern with the economic impact of such contracts.[86]

Thus the law afforded no effective means of dealing with restrictive agreements. Moreover, it should be added that the judges themselves showed considerable scepticism of the value of competition and, like their American brethren, felt that decisions about the public interest would involve them being dragged into the field of public policy. This they were reluctant to allow.

VII. THE 1948 MONOPOLIES AND RESTRICTIVE PRACTICES (INQUIRY AND CONTROL) ACT

This was a milestone–it was the first specific piece of anti-trust legislation introduced by a U.K. government in modern times. It was, however, a modest step. It did not condemn monopoly or restrictive practices outright–there was no parallel with the *per se* approach which characterises American anti-trust. Instead it embodied a case by case approach. Each situation was to be judged on its merits–the Act did not proscribe certain forms of restrictive activity. There was therefore no question of fines or imprisonment by virtue of past misdemeanours.

The Act related to the supply of goods of any description, to the application of a particular process to goods of any description and to exports of any particular type of goods from the United Kingdom. A monopoly was defined as a situation in which at least one-third of such goods, such processing or such exports was supplied either by one person, by two or more persons being interconnected bodies corporate or by two or more persons who restricted competition either by agreement or otherwise. The restrictive activity of trade associations was therefore covered–provided the one-third rule was satisfied.

Where one of the situations described above appeared to exist, the Board of Trade could refer the case to the Monopolies and

Restrictive Practices Commission for investigation. The Commission was to consist of not less than four, and not more than ten members, appointed by the Board. It was neither a judicial body nor a group of civil servants but consisted of persons who, by their experience, were considered capable of making unbiased and informed Judgements about complicated industrial situations. In practice the Commission consisted largely of economists, lawyers, accountants and businessmen. The Board, in referring a case to the Commission, could merely require it to state whether a monopoly, as defined by the Act, existed, and if so, what the enterprise or enterprises involved did by virtue of, or to preserve, their monopoly. In addition the Board might require the Commission to state whether the conditions found to exist operated against the public interest. The latter was defined as the need to achieve

(a) production and distribution of goods by the most efficient and economic means so as to ensure that the volume of goods produced and their prices were such as would best meet the requirements of home and overseas markets;
(b) an organisation of industry and trade which would ensure that efficiency was increased and new enterprise encouraged;
(c) fullest use of labour, materials and productive capacity;
(d) development of technical progress, the expansion of existing markets and the opening up of new ones.

Where a reference included the requirement to consider the effect of monopoly conditions and practices upon the public interest, the Commission could also state what remedial action should be taken. General powers were conferred upon the Commission to enable it to require persons to attend and give evidence. The reports of the Commission were to be submitted to the Board of Trade; the latter was required to lay them before Parliament, although parts could be deleted in the public interest or in order to safeguard legitimate business interests.

As has already been implied, the Act provided for remedial action if it was thought necessary. Such action was to be taken by any competent authority, which included the relevant ministries as well as the Board.

In terms of its immediate effect on the restrictive practices problem the impact of the Act was very limited. There were several reasons for this. The first was speed, or rather the lack of it. Between 1948 and 1956 the Commission produced seventeen reports of which fifteen were essentially concerned with trade association activities. In other words, it took about nine years to produce fifteen reports, whereas the later Restrictive Practices Court produced its first fifteen Judgements by the beginning of 1961, that is to say, in about five years. In only about half of the fifteen reports did the government secure redress either by voluntary agreement or statutory order. Considering that in 1944 the P.E.P. report on trade associations in the United Kingdom estimated the number at 2,500[87] and bearing in mind that 2,240 agreements had been registered with the Registrar of Restrictive Trading Agreements by the end of 1959, it was not difficult to see that the Commission procedure was not likely to produce a traumatic impact on British industry.

The second reason lay in the fact that under the 1948 Act, as we have already observed, no practice was regarded as illegal *per se*, or even initially presumed contrary to the public interest as was to be the case in the 1956 Act. Under the latter an adverse Judgement automatically implied that the practice was void whereas the application of remedies was not automatic under the 1948 Act and was a matter for the discretion of the Board of Trade and other departments.

Thirdly, even when the Commission found against a restrictive practice, and even if the government decided to act, the latter did not automatically call for abandonment. Rather what happened in some cases was that an objectionable agreement was replaced by a more acceptable variety, or was subject to government surveillance. For example, the common price systems of the Cable Makers' Association, and the Covered Conductors' Association, were both keenly criticised by the Monopolies Commission.[88] The Ministry of Supply in general accepted the Commission's conclusions, but did not call for the termination of the agreements relating to mains cables and rubber cables, requiring instead that the common price be replaced by a minimum price scheme offering reasonable profits to the lowest cost producers.[89] The industry accepted this. Then again in the case of the price system operated by the British Insulin Manufacturers,[90] the solution adopted was to institute a system of supervision of insulin prices and profits.[91]

Fourthly, the Commission lacked the impact of a court of law. The latter, working through the system of precedent, can make a large impact, since when key cases have been decided, parties to other similar agreements are likely to abandon them rather than to incur the expense and publicity of a court appearance. In addition the desire not to be found in contempt of Court is a potent influence dissuading trade associations from resurrecting

agreements struck down or voluntarily abandoned. In the case
of the Monopolies Commission, however, there is some evidence
that industry was not over-awed by the prospects of what might
happen if voluntary undertakings were ignored. Thus, following
the report on Imported Timber[92] (where it was revealed that an
approved list system existed in which agents on behalf of shippers
sold only to importers, and importers only bought from the agents)
the Timber Trades' Federation gave a voluntary undertaking to
abrogate these arrangements,[93] but in 1955 complaints were lodged
by certain persons to the effect that they had been precluded from
importing because their names were not on an approved list. A
follow-up investigation was called for, which indicated that in the
hardwood and softwood sectors of the trade the abrogated agreements had been replaced by new agreements similar in effect.[94]

Finally, the 1948 procedure contrasted with that under the 1956
Restrictive Trade Practices Act whereby publicity was given to
agreements. The latter had to be registered and were open to
inspection by the public. In the pre-1956 days no such provision
applied and trade associations could carry on their activities behind
the mantle of business secrecy, secure in the knowledge that, with
luck, the Commission would take a long time to reach them.

There is indeed little evidence of the Commission having any
impact beyond the bounds of its own investigations and more
particularly beyond the bounds of any subsequent government
action. In the case of the Commission report on Rubber Footwear,
made in 1956, it is true that whereas prior to 1948 minutes of the
meetings recording discussion of prices included the word 'agreed',
thereafter the word was absent.[95] The Commission, however, had
little difficulty in demonstrating that the absence of the word had
not affected the results of the collective deliberations.[96] In support
of this view it should be added that during the process of the
research project upon which this book is based virtually no cases
have come to light of agreements being significantly modified, let
alone abandoned, because the 1948 Act was in force.[97]

VIII. THE COMING OF THE 1956 ACT

It has been pointed out that the 1948 Act had no great immediate
impact upon the restrictive practices problem, but in another sense
its effect was quite profound. The Act has been described by Alex
Hunter as a reconnaissance and this undoubtedly highlights its
main contribution. The series of reports produced by the Commission helped to indicate how widespread and deeply entrenched

restrictive practices were. One report in particular–that on Collective Discrimination[98]–was extremely influential.

Under the 1948 legislation the Board of Trade had the power to make references relating to general types of practice as opposed to monopoly situations in particular industries. By 1952 the Conservative government was increasingly aware of the need to make use of this procedure. Several reports had revealed the existence of certain common types of practice and it was felt that a general report was desirable in order to discover if certain conclusions reached in these earlier reports were applicable to industry as a whole. This decision to make a general reference should be set against a background of mounting pressure for a more effective policy, particularly in the light of the slow rate of progress which the Monopolies Commission was inevitably forced to make.[99]

The Collective Discrimination reference covered a variety of practices. For example, it related to arrangements whereby a group of producers undertook collectively to maintain resale prices. X and Y would agree that if Z sold the goods of either below the required level then they would collectively cut off supplies to Z. It covered the arrangements whereby buyers and sellers agreed reciprocally to deal exclusively with each other. Dealers who dealt exclusively might attract a special discount. It also included arrangements whereby the rebate paid to a buyer was determined not by his purchases from one firm but from the whole group of producing firms party to the arrangement. One of the frequent effects of the latter two types of arrangement was the exclusion of new entrants and imported supplies.

At the end of its deliberations the Commission concluded,

> Because they involve collective obligations which in some way limit freedom of the parties in the conduct of their businesses, all the arrangements within our reference in some degree restrict competition. . . . we do not say that in every individual case this restriction is necessarily against the public interest, but we are satisfied that all the types of agreements which we have examined do adversely affect the public interest, some to a considerably greater degree than others.[100]

It also expressed views as to the way in which the restrictive practice problem should be dealt with. Within the Commission there was, however, a split. The majority took the view that the practices in question should be generally prohibited and they proposed that the legislation should create a new criminal offence. There would be provision for exceptional treatment and the

Commission specified examples of the reasons it thought might be the basis of such an exemption. Applications for exceptional treatment would be referred to an independent body and the Minister responsible should only issue an Order granting an exemption (to be laid before Parliament) after obtaining the advice of that body. It follows that the majority did not envisage this body as being the final arbiter. The minority, on the other hand, took the view that the correct procedure would be to call for the registration of agreements (publicity itself would have a salutary effect) and to combine with this the possibility of individual examination of cases. They also felt that collective enforcement of resale prices was not against the public interest.

A further factor which contributed to the eventual enactment of restrictive practices legislation was the publicity which trade association activity attracted in the press.[101] The latter, ever aware of the human aspect, seized upon the more dramatic cases – particularly those where dealers were disciplined by private courts. A typical case was that of a Mr Mendelsohn, a motor accessory dealer from Stockport, who had to appear before such a private court – the title 'Star Chamber' sprang readily to hand – because he sold below the list price level. He fought back and the press took up the cause. Stockport appears to have had a more than ordinary share of free spirits since more or less simultaneously the national press was reporting the case of the Stockport barber who was tried for cutting hair for less than the association rate. The case of the Birmingham trader whose supplies of tea were withheld because he cut the price thereof to old-age pensioners was bound to provoke public indignation. Indeed the general public was being treated to an interesting spectacle – whilst ministers of the Crown were crying out for price stability, those who offered lower prices were being privately harried for their pains. Added to all this was considerable press publicity concerning the practice of level tendering to local authorities.[102] The government taking note of the latter decided to refer the general practice of level tendering and common pricing to the Commission[103]. Subsequent legislative developments, however, precluded a report from being produced.

Meanwhile the political parties were becoming increasingly aware of the need for an advance on the 1948 position. But they were not without division within their own ranks when the subject of legislation was raised; indeed the passing of the 1956 Act involved the same internal dissensions within Conservative ranks as occurred in 1964 when Edward Heath piloted the Resale Prices Bill through Parliament. Labour too had its objectors – particularly on the union wing. For example, the Lloyd Jacob report[104] of 1949 recommended the continuance of individual resale price maintenance but came out against the collective variety. The Labour government however went further and in a White Paper[105] in 1951 proposed to ban both. But at a Labour Party conference in 1952 it was obvious that some unions, particularly those concerned with distribution, were unhappy with these proposals. Union unease was also evident in respect of some Monopolies Commission reports, for example that on Calico Printing.

By 1955 both main parties were pledged to take action and in 1956 the Conservative government introduced the Restrictive Practices Bill. During the period of the drafting of the Bill considerable speculation arose as to the nature of the legislation; was it to take a *per se* line, or was there to be a general presumption against restrictive practices with the possibility of exemption; was the process to be administrative or judicial, and so forth? It is clear that the interested parties–such as the Federation of British Industry–were bringing pressure to bear on the Board of Trade, possibly before publication of the Collective Discrimination report and certainly in the period after its publication and before the Bill was in its final form. On the government side the main protagonists were Peter Thorneycroft, then president of the Board of Trade, and Lord Kilmuir (formerly Sir David Maxwell Fyfe), then Lord Chancellor.

One of the important issues was the nature of the body to be responsible for implementing the new legislation. In the debate on the Collective Discrimination report Thorneycroft revealed himself to be undecided. But Maxwell Fyfe, in a book on monopoly published in 1948, was against placing legislation in the hands of the Court since such an approach involved

> ... treating as a matter of law many questions which ... are primarily matters for economic judgement.[106]

However, by the time the Bill was introduced the judicial approach had been adopted. As Lord Kilmuir he recollected in his subsequent memoirs that,

> Peter Thorneycroft and I had come to the conclusion that the Commission was unpopular with industry. Ministers, even with all departmental assistance, had not time to give full consideration to its reports, and the House of Commons would neither be able to grasp the full facts, nor come to a decision unbiased by party prejudice. We wanted, therefore, to give the problem

back to the courts, who had seisin of it in the nineteenth century, but somehow let it slip from their hands.[107]

There were indeed a number of forces pushing in the direction of a judicial solution. One was the Board of Trade which undoubtedly found the responsibility of enforcement under the 1948 Act an embarrassment in view of its need to retain good relations with industry and trade associations. Not only that but the delays involved in obtaining industry's agreement to the termination or modification of agreements led to criticism of the Board in the press.[108] Industry itself was overwhelmingly in favour of a judicial solution.[109] The Monopolies Commission was unpopular being regarded as prosecutor, judge and jury all rolled into one. Given this constellation of forces it was not therefore surprising that when the Bill emerged it was firmly based on a judicial foundation.

The other main area of conflict was the onus of proof. Industry objected to the reversal of the normal order of things; under the Bill agreements were deemed contrary to the public interest unless the parties satisfied at least one of the specified tests or gateways. In addition the respondents had to show that the agreements did not operate to an unreasonable extent to the detriment of the public. Great pressure was applied by rebel Conservative M.P.s – they were dubbed 'Trade association Tories' – to secure an amendment of this aspect of the Bill. In response Thorneycroft introduced an amendment which required the respondents to show that an agreement was not unreasonable, having regard to the balance between the satisfaction of one or more gateways and any detriment to the public. Concessions such as this, together with the fact that the Labour opposition was basically in favour of the new legislation, was sufficient to secure the final passage of the Act. The detailed contents of the statute, the Judgements and abandonments to which it gave rise, together with the subsequent 1968 Act, will be discussed in Chapter 2.

REFERENCES

1 J. H. Clapham, *An Economic History of Modern Britain* (London, 1938) Vol. III, p. 302.
2 W. Ashworth, *An Economic History of England 1870–1939* (London, 1960) p. 100.
3 Clapham, *op. cit.*, p. 213.

4 T. C. Barker and J. R. Harris, *A Merseyside Town in the Industrial Revolution, St Helens 1750–1900* (London, 1969) pp. 246–9.
5 *Ibid.*, p. 250.
6 *Ibid.*, p. 251.
7 *Ibid.*, pp. 251–2.
8 T. C. Barker, *Pilkington Brothers and the Glass Industry* (London, 1960) p. 70.
9 Barker and Harris, *op. cit.*, pp. 253–4.
10 For an illuminating account of soap association activity see A. E. Musson, *Enterprise in Soap and Chemicals Joseph Crosfield & Sons, Limited 1815–1965* (Manchester, 1945) Ch. 9.
11 Clapham, *op. cit.*, p. 213.
12 J. W. Grove, *Government and Industry in Great Britain* (London, 1962) p. 24.
13 Committee on Trusts, 1919, Cd. 9236, p. 2.
14 H. W. Macrosty, *The Trust Movement in British Industry* (London, 1907) p. 57. In fact, combination in the iron industry dates from at least the 1820s.
15 In 1904 there were reports of bar iron associations in South Yorkshire and the North of England.
16 This account of association activity in the metal trades is based on Macrosty, *op. cit.*, Ch. 3.
17 Monopolies and Restrictive Practices Commission, *Report on the Supply of Cast Iron Rainwater Goods*, 1951, p. 19. The weakness of a local association structure was undoubtedly in part a result of the tendency for outside associations to undermine the local price agreements.
18 Quoted in Macrosty, *op. cit.*, pp. 141–2.
19 See Monopolies and Restrictive Practices Commission, *The Supply and Exports of Electrical and Allied Machinery and Plant*, 1957, pp. 13, 59, 114.
20 *Idem.*, *The Supply of Electric Wires and Cables*, 1952, p. 16.
21 Activity in regulating the silicate of soda, caustic soda and glycerine markets is dealt with in Musson, *op. cit.*, Ch. 9.
22 Macrosty, *op. cit.*, Ch. 8.
23 *Reports of Restrictive Practices Cases*, L.R.2 R.P., p. 401.
24 Macrosty, *op. cit.*, p. 313.
25 Monopolies and Restrictive Practices Commission, *Report on the Supply and Export of Matches and the Supply of Match-Making Machinery*, 1953, p. 12.
26 For an account of associations concerned with distribution see Board of Trade, *Restraint of Trade Report of Committee appointed by the Lord Chancellor and the President of the Board of Trade to consider certain trade practices* (The Greene Committee) 1931, p. 11; and Macrosty, *op. cit.*, Ch. 10, 11.
27 P. L. Cook, 'The Calico Printing Industry' in P. L. Cook (ed.), *Effects of Mergers* (London, 1958) p. 146.
28 Macrosty, *op. cit.*, p. 30.
29 P. L. Cook, 'The Cement Industry' in Cook, *Effects of Mergers*, p. 30.
30 C. Wilson, *The History of Unilever* (London, 1954) Vol. I, p. 59.
31 Thus a contemporary observer noted 'none of the English trusts or cartels has been shown to have succeeded in raising . . . prices above the natural level. It is impossible for any English combination to raise English prices above the level of international prices, for if they tried to do so, the goods

would be immediately undersold by importations from abroad. An English trust, if it is to dictate prices and destroy competition must be an international trust . . .'–F. W. Hirst, *Trusts and Cartels* (London, 1905) p. 12.

32 The upward movement of raw material prices was probably another factor. A price agreement was the most efficacious mechanism for achieving a simultaneous and uniform price increase in a trade.

33 K. Grossfield, 'The Origin of Restrictive Practices in the Cable Industry', *Journal of Industrial Economics*, Vol. 7, No. 1, October 1958, pp. 22-7.

34 Monopolies and Restrictive Practices Commission, *Report on Cast Iron Rainwater Goods*, p. 19. Significantly other building materials were organised about the same time for similar reasons; a greystone mortar association was formed in 1911 and the Midland Pipe Association in 1912; see P. Fitzgerald, *Industrial Combination in England* (London, 1927) pp. 109–14.

35 Monopolies and Restrictive Practices Commission, *Report on Electrical and Allied Machinery and Plant*, p. 13.

36 P.E.P., *Industrial Trade Associations* (London, 1957) p. 8. The growth of trade unions as a causal factor in the development of trade associations is also stressed by Ashworth, *op. cit.*, p. 100 and Grove, *op. cit.*, p. 20.

37 E. J. Smith, *The New Trades Combination Movement* (London, 1899).

38 Except in the relatively infrequent spells of contraction.

39 See D. H. Aldcroft and H. W. Richardson, *The British Economy 1870–1939* (London, 1969) p. 187.

40 See L. H. Jenks, 'Migration of British Capital' quoted in A. Cairncross, *Home and Foreign Investment 1870–1913* (Cambridge, 1953) p. 233.

41 Apart from trade associations, this period also witnessed the creation of the Federation of British Industries (F.B.I.) in 1916 (it remained responsible for union–employer relations until 1919 when the British Employers' Confederation was formed) and the British Manufacturers' Association in 1915 (which became the National Union of Manufacturers in 1917). Both the F.B.I. and N.U.M. were to be important vehicles for the exertion of industrial influence on the shape of future restrictive practices legislation – see below.

42 Committee on Trusts, *op. cit.*, p. 2.

43 Wilson, *op. cit.*, pp. 221–2.

44 Monopolies Commission, *The Supply of Chemical Fertilisers*, 1959, p. 19.

45 *Idem.*, *A Report on the Supply of Petrol to Retailers in the United Kingdom*, 1965, p. 15.

46 *Report of the Departmental Committee appointed by the Board of Trade to Consider the Position of the Textile Trades after the War*, Cd. 9070, 1918, p. 113.

47 *Final Report of the Committee on Commercial and Industrial Policy after the War*, Cd. 9035, 1918, p. 40. The report reflected contemporary fear that cartels gave German industry a competitive edge and that the advantages of size arising from trusts were equally important.

48 Committee on Trusts, *op. cit.*, p. 4.

49 A minority of the Committee was in favour of more radical action including public ownership of offenders.

50 C. K. Rowley, *The British Monopolies Commission* (London, 1966) p. 22, and A. C. Pigou, *Aspects of British Economic History 1918–1925* (London, 1947) p. 130.

51 *Report of the Royal Commission on Food Prices*, Cmd. 2390, 1925, p. 139. It expressed the view that 'the time has come to equip somebody with power to deal with monopolies, trusts and combines which charge unduly high prices for the service they render to the public or suppress competition merely in order to maintain or expand their profits'.

52 G. C. Allen, 'Monopoly and Competition in the United Kingdom' in E. H. Chamberlin (ed.), *Monopoly, Competition and their Regulation* (London, 1954) p. 89.

53 Fitzgerald, *op. cit.*, p. 41.

54 D. Varley, *A History of the Midlands Counties' Lace Manufacturers' Association 1915–1958* (Long Eaton, 1959) p. 95.

55 These were non-revenue duties imposed on selected commodities.

56 Rowley, *op. cit.*, p. 27.

57 *Ibid.*

58 For further details of the factors leading to this merger see W. J. Reader, *Imperial Chemical Industries: the Forerunners 1870–1926* (London, 1970) Vol. I.

59 *Final Report of the Committee on Industry and Trade*, Cmd. 3282, 1929, p. 179.

60 *Ibid.*, p. 192.

61 A. Hunter, *Competition and the Law* (London, 1966) p. 76.

62 Greene Committee Report, p. 34.

63 *Report of the Committee on Finance and Industry*, Cmd. 3897, para. 385.

64 S. Pollard, *The Development of the British Economy 1914–1967* (London, 1969) p. 170.

65 H. Macmillan, *Reconstruction, A Plea for a National Policy* (London, 1933) pp. 9–10.

66 Liberal Industrial Inquiry, *Britain's Industrial Future* (London, 1928) pp. 77, 93–4, 99. The proposal that the majority should be able to coerce the minority was paralleled in the 1930s by bills, sponsored by Lord Melchett on behalf of the Industrial Reorganisation League, aimed at enforcing schemes of reorganisation.

67 For further details of these rationalisations see G. C. Allen, *British Industries and their Organisation* (London, 1959) pp. 74–81, 118–19, 236–7.

68 During the 1930s there was also official action to regulate agricultural markets.

69 D. H. Aldcroft, 'Government Control and the Origin of Restrictive Trade Practices in Great Britain', *The Accountants Magazine*, September 1962, p. 682.

70 *Ibid.*, p. 685.

71 Cmd. 6527.

72 H. Dalton, *The Fateful Years: Memoirs 1931–1945* (London, 1957) p. 447.

73 Simon Committee, *The Distribution of Building Materials and Components* 1948, p. 50.

74 *Ibid.*, p. 52.

75 Central Price Regulation Committee, *Prices of Radio Valves*, 1946, p. 8.

76 fforde Committee, *Cement Costs*, 1947. (It is perhaps worth noting that the Anglo-American Council on Productivity teams also drew attention to the existence of cartels in the United Kingdom in contrast with the United States.)

77 A broadcast speech on 16 August 1947 cited in *The Economist*, 20 September 1947, p. 475.
78 P. 67.
79 This is a simplification of the legal position; for further details see R. Wilberforce, A. Campbell and N. Elles, *The Law of Restrictive Trade Practices and Monopolies* (London, 1966) pp. 23–44, 47.
80 *Mogul S.S. Company* v. *McGregor, Gow*, [1892] A.C.25; *Allen* v. *Flood*, [1898] A.C.1; *Quinn* v. *Leathem*, [1901] A.C.495.
81 [1925] A.C.700, pp. 711–12.
82 [1892] A.C.25.
83 *Nordenfelt* v. *Maxim Nordenfelt Guns and Ammunition Company*, [1894] A.C.535, 565.
84 *Attorney General of the Commonwealth of Australia* v. *Adelaide S.S. Company*, [1913] A.C.781, 796.
85 Hunter, *op. cit.*, p. 71.
86 R. B. Stevens and B. S. Yamey, *The Restrictive Practices Court* (London, 1965) p. 29.
87 P.E.P., *op. cit.*, p. 1.
88 Monopolies and Restrictive Practices Commission, *Report on Cables*, pp. 76–92.
89 Board of Trade, *Monopolies and Restrictive Practices Acts, 1948 and 1953, Annual Report for the year ending 31 December 1954*, p. 5.
90 Monopolies and Restrictive Practices Commission, *Report on the Supply of Insulin*, 1952, pp. 20–6.
91 Board of Trade, *Monopolies and Restrictive Practices (Inquiry and Control) Act, 1948, Annual Report for the period ending 31 December 1952*, p. 6.
92 Monopolies and Restrictive Practices Commission, *Report on the Supply of Imported Timber*, 1953, pp. 26–51, discusses the approved list system.
93 Board of Trade, *Monopolies and Restrictive Practices Acts, 1948 and 1953, Annual Report for the year ending 31 December 1954*, p. 5.
94 Monopolies Commission, *Imported Timber: Report on whether and to what extent the Recommendation of the Commission has been complied with*, 1958, p. 57.
95 Monopolies and Restrictive Practices Commission, *Report on the Supply of Certain Rubber Footwear*, 1956, p. 73.
96 *Ibid.*, pp. 73–5.
97 The only substantive exception occurred in the case of the Metal Window Association where quotas were abandoned in 1949–see the discussion of the *Metal Windows* case in the separately published case studies.
98 Monopolies and Restrictive Practices Commission, *Collective Discrimination: A Report on Exclusive Dealing, Collective Boycotts, Aggregated Rebates and other Discriminatory Trade Practices*, 1955.
99 The Commission was initially hampered by being limited in size and not able to work in groups.
100 *Report*, pp. 81–2.
101 The motor trade, and in particular the tyre trade, received a good deal of attention from the press.
102 See for instance *The Times*, 18 and 21 February 1956. The Association of Municipal Corporations also felt moved to investigate the problem and collected a considerable amount of evidence of level tendering–see *The Builder*, 29 April 1955, pp. 719–20.

103 Some commentators took the view that the common price reference should have preceded that on collective discrimination.
104 *Report of the Committee on Resale Price Maintenance*, 1949, Cmd. 7696.
105 *A Statement on Resale Price Maintenance—being a trade practice which prevents shopkeepers from reducing certain prices to the public*, 1951, Cmd. 8274.
106 Sir D. M. Fyfe (Lord Kilmuir), *Monopoly* (London, 1948) p. 50.
107 *Idem., Political Adventure* (London, 1964) pp. 261–2.
108 This case is argued by J. J. Richardson, *The Making of the Restrictive Trade Practices Act, 1956* (Manchester University M.A. Thesis, 1965) pp. 110–35. This is a valuable study of the forces shaping the 1956 Act.
109 Industry was to regret this. By 1967 the C.B.I. was calling for a return to the Commission approach!

Chapter 2

LEGAL BACKGROUND

I believe that the law, although deeply rooted in the history of the institutions of our country is not an heirloom which is to be taken down, dusted, reverently considered and placed back. I believe that the law is as effective a dynamic force in modern problems as it is soundly based on these historical roots. Therefore I believe that the law should be brought in to help in the solution of the great problems of a modern State. This is one of the great problems, and therefore the solution which I advance to your Lordships is one which provides for those affected the best machinery for arriving at the truth and reaching justice which the world has so far devised.

Lord Kilmuir, House of Lords, 1956

I. THE 1956 ACT–BASIC PROVISIONS

The 1956 Restrictive Trade Practices Act has a threefold element, only one of which is of immediate relevance to the central theme of this book. Firstly, in view of the fact that Parliament had decided to pass the restrictive practices remit of the Monopolies and Restrictive Practices Commission to another body, Part III of the Act provided for the retitling of the Commission as the Monopolies Commission. It was reduced to a maximum membership of ten and left with the investigation of single-firm[1] monopolies.[2] Groups of firms (collectively constituting a monopoly) who restricted competition other than through the medium of an agreement also continued to fall within the ambit of the Commission.[3] Secondly, Part II dealt with resale price maintenance. It declared that agreements between two or more persons to collectively enforce resale prices were *per se* illegal. Thus agreements concerning stop lists and other discriminatory devices designed to force dealers to maintain resale prices were illegal as they stood. On the other hand it also strengthened the position of suppliers in respect of individual resale price maintenance by introducing a non-signer provision. Provided a dealer had notice of the resale terms his position *vis-à-vis* the supplier was similar to what it would have been had he been bound in a contractual relationship. Thirdly, as has already been intimated in the previous chapter, Part I of the Act created a new body of law and new institutions for dealing with restrictive agreements.

All agreements between two or more persons carrying on business in the United Kingdom in the production of, supply of, or application of processes of manufacture to, goods were to be registered with a newly created Crown Officer, the Registrar of Restrictive Trading Agreements. An agreement was defined as the acceptance by two or more parties of restrictions relating to such things as prices to be charged, terms or conditions on which goods were to be supplied, quantities to be supplied, processes of manufacture to be applied and persons and areas to be supplied.[4] (When trade associations made recommendations it was assumed that the members accepted a restriction on their activity.) The Registrar of Agreements was open to public inspection; this idea had been canvassed by the Monopolies and Restrictive Practices Commission in the Collective Discrimination report. It was not, however, the fact of registration but the legal status of agreements which represented a fundamentally new departure. These were initially presumed contrary to the public interest.[5] However, had the matter rested there then the position in U.K. law of, for example, price agreements would have resembled the *per se* rules developed in the United States through a long line of cases of which *Addystone Pipe* and *Trenton Potteries* are among the most famous. In fact the basic presumption concerning the public interest does not hold if (a) the Court can be satisfied that certain advantages arise from the operation of an agreement (to put it another way certain disadvantages would arise were the agreements to be terminated) and (b) the advantage (or avoidance of disadvantage) so proved outweighs the presumed detriment. The Act did not allow parties to agreements to range freely in seeking advantages but delineated seven types of pleading. These have come to be known as the 'gateways' and are shown in full below:

(a) that the restriction is reasonably necessary, having regard to the character of the goods to which it applies, to protect the public against injury (whether to persons or to premises) in connection with the consumption, installation or use of those goods;

(b) that the removal of the restriction would deny to the public as purchasers, consumers or users of any goods other specific and substantial benefits or advantages enjoyed or likely to be enjoyed by them as such, whether by virtue of

E

the restriction itself or of any arrangements or operations resulting therefrom;

(c) that the restriction is reasonably necessary to counteract measures taken by any one person not party to the agreement with a view to preventing or restricting competition in or in relation to the trade or business in which the persons party thereto are engaged;

(d) that the restriction is reasonably necessary to enable the persons party to the agreement to negotiate fair terms for the supply of goods to, or the acquisition of goods from, any one person not party thereto who controls a preponderant part of the trade or business of acquiring or supplying such goods, or for the supply of goods to any person not party to the agreement and not carrying on such a trade or business who, either alone or in combination with any other such person, controls a preponderant part of the market for such goods;

(e) that, having regard to the conditions actually obtaining or reasonably foreseen at the time of the application, the removal of the restriction would be likely to have a serious and persistent adverse effect on the general level of unemployment in an area, or in areas taken together, in which a substantial proportion of the trade or industry to which the agreement relates is situated;

(f) that having regard to the conditions actually obtaining or reasonably foreseen at the time of the application, the removal of the restriction would be likely to cause a reduction in the volume or earnings of the export business which is substantial either in relation to the whole export business of the United Kingdom or in relation to the whole business (including export business) of the said trade or industry; or

(g) that the restriction is reasonably required for purposes connected with the maintenance of any other restriction accepted by the parties, whether under the same agreement or under any other agreement between them, being a restriction which is found by the Court not to be contrary to the public interest upon grounds other than those specified in this paragraph, or has been so found in previous proceedings before the Court.

The setting of detriment against advantage is usually referred to as the 'tailpiece' balancing provision.[6]

The position of an agreement under the Act can therefore be

summarised as follows. If the parties can pass through no gateway, the initial presumption against their agreement holds. The agreement is then declared against the public interest, is void and must be terminated. The law was therefore 'biased' against agreements in the sense that it could have taken the view that only if agreements involved an abuse would they be declared illegal. Such a posture would have implied legality in the absence of proven abuse. Clearly this is not the stance which was adopted in the Act. If, however, the parties can pass through one or more gateways then the balancing procedure comes into play. The more restrictive and damaging the agreement is in any of its aspects, the more persuasive the counterbalancing advantageous aspects have got to be. If the advantage established by passing through one or more gateways is large enough the agreement can be upheld. Otherwise it becomes void.[7]

It is apparent that all this required a body to arbitrate and this was the newly created Restrictive Practices Court. This is a branch of the High Court consisting of lay members qualified by their knowledge of, or experience in, industry, commerce or public affairs, as well as High Court judges. A High Court judge always presides and any decision on a point of law is made by the judges although on points of fact the Court decides by simple majority. Appeal to higher authority is possible but only on matters of law and not fact.

The role of the Registrar was of course more than merely one of keeping a Register of Agreements. It was also his role to refer agreements to the Court and to present the Crown case. The Crown seeks to point out the detriment to the public interest inherent in an agreement. The Respondents for their part must, if they are to hope to succeed, pass through one or more gateways. The Crown must therefore also engage in rebutting the Respondent's gateway pleadings. The Court, having heard Counsel for both sides, having listened to the examination and cross-examination of witnesses[8] and having studied the documents submitted in evidence, finally has to pronounce for or against. This did not exhaust the Registrar's role. What has been described so far may be termed prosecution. In addition there is enforcement. If an agreement is terminated, whether by being struck down or by voluntary abandonment, it is clearly important that the parties to it do not resurrect it somehow or other.[9] The Registrar had also got to ensure that all agreements were brought on to the Register.

The rigour of the legislation is further emphasised when it is compared with the regime relating to monopolies. Under the latter there is discretion on the part of the government both in referring cases and in deciding what action to take following a report. This has to be contrasted with the fact that under the Act agreements must be registered. Having been registered they have to be referred.[10] Judgement then follows which must be adhered to if contempt proceedings are to be avoided.

It is also worth noting that the Act prescribed certain exemptions. For example, standardisation agreements fall within this category provided that the producers are agreeing to abide by standards set by the British Standards Institute.[11] Then again agreements which were purely related to exports were not registrable but had to be notified to the Board of Trade (as it then was).[12] However, agreements which covered both domestic and export trade had to be registered.[13] Not surprisingly when the 1956 Act came on to the Statute Book many associations rewrote their agreements and severed the home from the export restrictions.[14] Only the former went on to the Register–the latter were notified to the Board of Trade who could refer them in certain circumstances to the Monopolies Commission.

II. CRITIQUES OF THE ACT

Criticisms of the Act centred originally on three aspects: the basic posture, detailed drafting of parts of the Act (notably the gateways) and the general and fundamental question of justiciability.

On the question of basic posture a prominent critic, Alex Hunter, has maintained that despite the initial presumption concerning the public interest, the Act is too negative and ought to have embraced a more positive view of the advantages of competition.[15] There is much to be said for this view since when one or more gateways have been satisfied the 'tailpiece' is curiously negative. In the light of the evidence revealed by the Commission, and the attitude of the majority in the Collective Discrimination report, a more positive attitude was probably justified. Such a posture would have had the additional benefit of giving clearer guidance to the Court–a point which will be relevant when the issue of justiciability is considered.

The gateways have attracted a certain amount of criticism. Gateway (a) could be said to be redundant. It can be argued that a potentiality of injury to the public should attract specific legislation rather than be the basis of trade association restrictions.[16]

The Court took such a view in its first case which related to chemists' goods. In this case the Chemists' Federation Agreement, which had the effect of confining the sale of proprietary medicines to chemists' shops, was defended on the grounds that it was reasonably necessary if the public was to be protected against injury. In point of fact the case failed since chemists' goods were sometimes sold by unqualified assistants and the goods in question included many which were entirely innocuous.[17]

It has been pointed out by several commentators that gateway (b) is unduly accommodating. As Hunter pointed out, 'Without doubt it is the most "open" and vulnerable of the gateways.'[18] (Moreover it has been argued that this gateway is a good example of Parliament not making up its mind and therefore preferring to leave it to the Court to make policy decisions. Clearly the question of justiciability arises here and this will be dealt with below.) Hunter was of the view that the basic idea of gateway (b) is good in the sense that, as opposed to the *per se* view, there may be justifications for agreements. However, he pointed out that experience in judicial review has led to the identification of the kind of specific arguments which could be accepted under such a gateway. He suggested the following:

> . . . the removal of the restriction would deny to the public, or purchasers, consumers or users, the advantages of *substantially lower prices, superior technology and/or its rapid dissemination* or a *substantial convenience* or *valuable personal service.*[19]

Gateways (c) and (d) have also attracted some criticism. In the case of (c) Hunter argued that it assumes a pattern of behaviour on the part of single large firms which is not often borne out in reality and it may well be redundant.[20] In practice it has rarely been employed. In the case of (d) the main problem is lack of precision. It refers to a 'preponderant part' of a trade but no indication is given as to what proportion constitutes a preponderant share.

Major criticisms have been levelled at gateways (e) and (f), especially the latter. In the case of (e) the main problem is the lack of guidance which is given to the Court as to the likely response of the government to a serious and persistent level of unemployment in an area. Should the Court proceed on the assumption that the government will take action or should it assume that nothing will be done? J. B. Heath is of the opinion that

> . . . some co-ordination of policies, for which the Restrictive

Practices Act does not provide, would render this Section 21 (1) (e) redundant.[21]

In the case of gateway (f) a whole series of criticisms can be levelled. Stevens and Yamey point out that assuming the underlying argument behind gateway (f) to be the possibility of contributing towards a favourable balance of payments, it is odd that exports are singled out and that imports are ignored. The gateway also relates to the gross contribution of exports to the balance of payments and ignores the fact that exports may have an import content which should be taken into account. Then again one form of export may preclude either another or the production of goods which would be substitutes for imports. There is also a reference to the volume of export business when clearly it is value which is important. The relativity included in the gateway can also lead to discrimination in favour of small industries and against large ones.[22] Hunter also drew attention to the unfortunate effect of allowing justifications relating to exports to support restrictions in the domestic market. In his view the Court should be able to sever the home from the export aspect of an agreement.[23]

A good deal of controversy has surrounded the issue of justiciability. The latter is generally defined as the aptness of an issue for determination by the Court. Whether a matter is justiciable or not appears to depend upon (at least) two matters. One is the nature of the law which the Court is armed with. The other is the appropriateness of the Court system for dealing with this kind of problem.

The first matter raises the question of the proper role of the judiciary. Generally it is argued that Parliament makes the laws and the judiciary applies them. An essential element in this arrangement is that the laws should be clear-cut so that the judiciary is not left with a degree of leeway which in effect confers upon them the role of policy maker. Clearly Parliament never entirely precludes the judiciary from some policy making–thus in matters of tax law the Court has had to decide what was capital and what was income. The arguments of the critics of the 1956 Act was that Parliament failed to be sufficiently precise in its attitude to competition. It failed to come down sufficiently clearly either in favour of or against competition, and gateway (b) in particular left the Court with considerable latitude. In effect it was argued that Parliament had shuffled off the problem of policy making in respect of competition on to the Court and had presented the judiciary with a task which their American brethren would regard as beyond theco mpetence of a judge. A number of critics have indeed argued that those who pursued the justiciability argument had logic on their side. Thus as we have seen, Hunter in effect argued (after dallying with the attractions of the *per se* approach) that the Act could have been improved if a firmer presumption in favour of competition had been included and he also points out that experience has proved that a tighter gateway (b) is feasible.

Intermingled with the above line of criticism were two other points. One, already referred to above, is the question of the appropriateness of the court procedure. Given that the judges had some room for manoeuvre, were they really capable of comprehending the subtleties of economic logic and carrying out the economic forecasting which the 1956 Act undoubtedly calls for? Some of the oddities and inconsistencies of economic logic, particularly in cases where agreements were upheld, give some grounds for disquiet.[24] Then again was the adversary procedure the best way of carrying out the complicated process of economic analysis which is called for? It is indeed doubtful whether witnesses were always able to put their points adequately when faced with Counsel well skilled in the art and hurly-burly of cross-examination.[25] Added to this is the impression that in some instances Counsel with the best will in the world found the intricacies of economic analysis beyond their comprehension.

So much for the essence of the justiciability argument,[26] but whether it was in practice of great significance is open to doubt. If the 1956 Act had taken a completely neutral view of the pros and cons of competition it could be argued that the leeway given to the judges combined with their not always happy excursions into economic analysis could have led to ill-founded Judgements. The nature of Judgements has undoubtedly influenced industries in their decisions as to whether to abandon or not and in practice some of these decisions may therefore have been ill-founded. However, the Act was not so conceived. In an admittedly hesitant way it opted for competition. In practice therefore there is much to be said for the argument that the leeway left to the judges could only be said to have led to inappropriate results if the majority of agreements had been allowed to continue. In practice the majority of those defended were struck down and there followed a wholesale abandonment. In practice therefore whatever the shortcomings of the drafting of the Act, the course of events mirrored, even if imperfectly, the views of the Monopolies Commission, the press, informed academics and, so far as we can judge, the government.

III. INITIAL IMPACT

There can be no doubt that on the face of it the initial impact of the Act was almost wholly favourable if a favourable impact is defined as being the general termination of agreements. The Act had a more or less immediate effect in that some agreements (just how many is not known) were abandoned before registration.[27] In other cases agreements were redrafted so that they were, or appeared to be, less restrictive.[28] (Much redrafting activity was also directed towards severing the home from the export aspects of agreements[29] and in other cases it was hoped that a revised version would be more likely to satisfy technically one of the gateways.)[30] The early abandonments and redraftings were, however, almost certainly less significant than what happened after registration.

In April 1957 the Registrar began to institute proceedings against registered agreements. The first agreement to come before the Court was that of the Chemists' Federation. Given the relatively unimpressive pleadings in its favour,[31] the fact that it was struck down was not likely to influence business thinking. The second case, however, was an entirely different matter. It concerned the Yarn Spinners' Agreement. Here was one of the most important (if not the most important) agreements in the Lancashire cotton industry. Moreover, the size and historical significance of the industry was bound to render the Court's conclusions of considerable significance for industry generally. In practice the Registrar, ably assisted by his economist witness Professor S. R. Dennison, was able to persuade the Court: (a) that the minimum price agreement kept prices higher than would be the case under free competition (and contributed to inefficiency by keeping high cost producers in existence); (b) that in a contracting industry the agreement kept excess capacity in existence whereas a more compact industry was called for; (c) that there was some consequent loss to the export trade. On the other hand the Respondents were able to persuade the Court that the agreement passed through gateway (e). It accepted, although somewhat hesitantly, that in areas where collectively about 70 per cent of the workforce was employed there would be a serious adverse effect on the general level of unemployment. With greater doubt and hesitation it felt that this effect would be persistent. Despite this it found against the agreement.[32] The impact of this was very considerable. Industry generally asked itself whether there was much point in incurring the considerable expense of a Court hearing if this was a sample of how the Court intended to proceed. There can be little doubt that this single determination was one of the most important steps towards the establishment of a more competitive economy. It was reinforced by the next case which concerned the Blanket Manufacturers' Agreement. Here it was accepted that the agreed minimum (stop loss) price was not effective in practice but yet the agreement was struck down.[33] Thus it appeared that mere harmlessness was no defence.

Some commentators have taken the view that during the first eighteen months (whilst Lord Devlin presided) the Court interpreted the basic intention of the Act as being the promotion of competition. Undoubtedly it was stringent–seven of the first eight agreements went down.[34] Thereafter it is argued a subtle modification took place in which a less clear-cut approach was adopted.[35] Nevertheless between 1958 and 1968, out of thirty-three cases where agreements were defended for the first time, twenty-three went down and only ten were upheld.[36]

The effect of all this was to induce many industries to voluntarily terminate their agreements. This they could do by abandoning them (or letting them lapse if they were of limited duration) or by removing from them all restrictions to which the Act applied. The latter is termed 'varying' or 'filleting'. The growth in the number of registered agreements and also of terminations is shown in Table 2.1.

TABLE 2.1 Statistics Relating to Registration of Agreements

Date	Total Agreements Registered	Voluntary Terminations		
		Abandoned	Varied	Lapsed by effluxion of time
28 November 1957	1,200	—	—	—
31 December 1959	2,240	300	320	60
30 June 1961	2,350	590	475	60
30 June 1963	2,430	1,000	525	60
30 June 1966	2,550	1,135	840	75
30 June 1969	2,660	1,240	960	90

Source: Registrar of Restrictive Trading Agreements, *Report for the Period 7 August 1956 to 31 December 1959* (1960, Cmnd. 1273); *Report for the Period 1 January 1960 to 30 June 1961* (1962, Cmnd. 1063); *Report for the Period 1 July 1961 to 30 June 1963* (1964, Cmnd. 2246); *Restrictive Trading Agreements, Report of the Registrar for the Period 1 July 1963 to 30 June 1966* (1966, Cmnd. 3188); *Restrictive Trading Agreements, Report of the Registrar for the Period 1 July 1966 to 30 June 1969* (1970, Cmnd. 4303).

IV. LEGAL LOOPHOLES

One of the earliest investigations of the effect of the Act was carried out by J. B. Heath.[37] It related to the period up to mid-1959 and was concerned with tracing largely by means of a questionnaire the course of events following abandonment. The results were only moderately encouraging. For example, analysing response by agreement: 67 per cent felt the degree of competition was about the same as would have been the case if agreements had *not* been cancelled; only 32 per cent felt that there would have been less competition (and, interestingly, 2 per cent felt there would have been more).[38] The effect on prices was also only moderately encouraging: 64 per cent felt that the cancellation had left prices more or less untouched; only 32 per cent felt they were lower (and 5 per cent that they were actually higher as a result).[39] Why, it may be asked, wasn't the response more positive in terms of competition? One possibility is that firms were still being guided by the terms of abandoned agreements and that only the passage of time and changing cost and market conditions would induce a more individualistic response. But the other possibility was that there were other factors at work. One was price leadership and 41 per cent of the responses analysed by agreement admitted to recognising a price leader.[40] Another was information agreements – that is to say, agreements to exchange information about price lists, discounts, prices to be tendered and so forth. Here Heath revealed that eighty-three agreements involved arrangements of this kind.[41] Another alternative was for firms to merge with competitors or take over awkward individualists. But according to Heath,

> Although there is some support for the hypothesis that if the security a price agreement is said to provide is removed, firms will find the alternative of increased concentration through merger, it is certainly less than commentators expected, and provides less than adequate confirmation of the hypothesis.[42]

(The final possibility was secret collusion. This was not on the face of it a loophole *in the law* since the Act had enforcement provisions designed to assist the Registrar in detecting such transgressions; whether, however, they were inadequate and therefore technically a loophole did exist will be discussed later.)

It was quite apparent that at least one potential loophole existed, namely informational arrangements (these could, of course, be a vehicle for price leadership). As early as 1960 the

Registrar in his second report explicitly noted the emergence of this phenomenon. Thus he observed,

> Not infrequently on the ending of a price agreement the parties enter into an information agreement under which they send to their trade association or to a central agency their price lists or the prices at which they have entered into contracts.[43]

Provided the obligations of the parties under the agreement related purely to the sending of information these agreements were not registrable. But it was always possible that matters might go further and that either tacit arrangements would arise or that the agreements would act as a forum for explicit collusion. In his third report the Registrar again returned to the problem and suggested that such agreements might be made subject to registration. There was obviously much to be said for such a move. Although it was not necessary that registration should automatically imply contrariness to the public interest, the possibility of restrictions arising from such agreements was great and it was desirable in the interests of effective surveillance that the Registrar be fully informed as to which industries had adopted the device and in what form. The Registrar's suggestion was indeed taken up by the then Conservative government which in 1964 issued a White Paper entitled *Monopolies, Mergers and Restrictive Practices*.[44] In it the government announced its intention to amend the 1956 Act so as to make information agreements registrable. It also proposed plugging other loopholes. Thus it observed,

> Another way of circumventing the Act is by means of a series of bilateral agreements which are apparently unconnected. They can be used by a trade association to operate a price ring or a central selling scheme. The association enters into a separate agreement with each of its members, under which only the member accepts a registrable restriction. Such agreements would therefore be outside the scope of the Act, because it covers only agreements in which at least two parties accept restrictions.
> The government propose to amend the Act to make subject to registration agreements under which only one of the parties accepts a registrable restriction, that is to say, a restriction of the kind specified in Section 6 (1) of the Act. The present safeguards in the Act, which prevent ordinary commercial transactions, i.e. ordinary contracts for sale, sole agencies etc., being brought within the Act, would have to be suitably extended.[45]

It is also pointed out that,

> There is another type of case which must be covered in order to strengthen the operation of the Act. Experience has shown that it is possible to reproduce the restrictive effect of an agreement which the Court has already condemned, by making another agreement which is restrictive in somewhat different terms. This is not within the scope of the Order already made by the Court because it is not technically an agreement 'to the like effect'. For instance, when the Court condemns a common or minimum price agreement, the parties could replace it by a maximum price agreement which could be operated as a device to achieve the same result. The consequence is that parties to an agreement condemned by the Court can enter into another restrictive agreement which would produce the same results and which, though registrable, can be operated by the parties until it in turn is dealt with by the Court.[46]

The White Paper also proposed to strengthen the law relating to monopolies, mergers and services. Then in 1964 there was a change of government. The new Labour administration proceeded in 1965 to deal with the latter matters but regarded a change in the law relating to restrictive practices as being of lower priority. It was therefore not until 1968 that legislative action was taken to deal with information agreements.

Meanwhile the Registrar began to take his own steps to deal with the information agreement problem by applying the law as it stood. The attack really centred on the word 'arrangement'. Section 6 of the 1956 Act, which deals with registration, refers not only to 'agreements' but also to 'arrangements'. But the exact meaning of 'arrangement', and its possibilities for the Registrar, only became clear in 1962 and 1963 with the Judgements in the *Basic Slag* case.[47] Basic slag, a by-product of steel manufacture which was used as a fertiliser, was sold by steel companies through a common marketing company, British Basic Slag Limited, which the steel companies themselves had formed. Each steel company not only held shares in the concern but also entered into a ten-year agreement with Basic Slag about the terms on which it supplied it with fertilisers. In 1954 the member firms all signed identical arrangements with Basic Slag. Each steel firm agreed to the arrangement independently, on its own judgement, without its course being conditional on that followed by the other firms. But none of them would have agreed to Basic Slag, of which each steel firm had part control through its shareholding and the nomination of a director, entering into an agreement with one of the other controlling firms which was different from the one it itself had entered into. By these identical agreements each firm undertook to sell the whole of its fertiliser output to Basic Slag and not to sell it to anyone else without the consent of that company. The latter in turn agreed to buy as much of the members' output as it could sell, to try to sell the whole output, and to buy from the parent companies in an equitable manner.

Now on the face of it this was a series of bi-partite agreements of the kind which had been absolved in the previous *Austin Motor* case.[48] Basic Slag and the steel companies held that the agreements did not therefore come within the Act. Basic Slag was free to buy from any firm and there was then thought to be no restriction under Section 6 (1) of the Act; and the separate agreements did not constitute an 'arrangement' under Section 6 (2).

The Court held that Basic Slag had been deprived of freedom to buy from any other than its parent companies and, because it had agreed to buy from them proportionately, it had restricted its buying even from them.

But, far more importantly from the point of view of the general discussion, the Court held that the steel firms had been party to an 'arrangement' within Section 6 (3) of the Act. To quote the words of Justice Cross:

> As I see it, all that is required to constitute an arrangement not enforceable in law is that the parties to it shall have communicated with one another in some way, and that as a result of the communication each has intentionally aroused in the other an expectation that he will act in a certain way. If that be right, then, as it seems to me, the member companies made an arrangement that they would each of them execute the relevant agreement with Basic.[49]

The case went to appeal but the initial Judgement was upheld. Most significantly too, the meaning of the word 'arrangement' was further clarified. Lord Justice Diplock, said

> No necessary or useful purpose would be served by attempting an expanded and comprehensive definition of the word 'arrangement' in Section 6 (3) of the Act . . . I think that I am only expressing the same concept (as Justice Cross) in slightly different terms if I say, without attempting an exhaustive definition for there are many ways in which arrangements may be made, that it is sufficient to constitute an 'arrangement' between A and B, if

1. A makes a representation as to his future conduct with the expectation and intention that such conduct on his part will operate as an inducement to B to act in a particular way;
2. such representation is communicated to B, who has knowledge that A so expected and intended; and
3. such representation or A's conduct in fulfilment of it operates as an inducement, whether among other inducements or not, to B to act in that particular way.[50]

This was of very great significance. The term 'arrangement' had not only received definition, but it had received definition of the most comprehensive and all-embracing character. This was to prove of great significance in the treatment of information agreements. (It also meant that bilateral agreements no longer circumvented the Act.)

The attack by the Registrar was also partly based on another legal development—the clarification of the meaning of 'to the like effect'. Guidance on this matter had been given in the second *Black Bolts and Nuts* case.[51] Lord Evershed then propounded two alternative tests:

1. the Court should look at the terms of the agreement or arrangement and ask itself whether it would achieve the same things as the former agreement;
2. did the agreement in practice operate to achieve the same things despite the fact that its terms were not apt to achieve the same result?

The second test was to prove of particular relevance in assault on information agreements. Also relevant was the dictum of Lord Justice Pearce, (in relation to a different part of the Act) in which he sought to point out,

> That . . . it is not likely that Parliament was intending to create for the enforcement of its purpose a jurisdiction that could so easily be evaded.[52]

As a result of all this agreements which for technical reasons had circumvented the 1956 Act were no longer able to do so.

The Registrar then took advantage of these developments in his attack on information agreements. The first assault arose in the *Galvanised Tanks* case.[53] This case concerned the Galvanised Tank Manufacturers' Association (G.T.M.A.) which voluntarily abandoned a common selling price agreement on 16 July 1959. Prior to the abandonment, to be precise on 1 May 1959, the Association entered into an information agreement the basic features of which was that each party to it would inform the secretary of the Association of his current price list and within two days would notify the secretary of any changes therein. However, in practice notification took place before changes. In other words the agreement was of the pre-notification variety.[54] The Registrar invited the Court to construe the behaviour of the firms concerned (and it gave rise to a remarkable degree of price parallelism) as an arrangement which was to the like effect of the one which had been abandoned. (It should be noted at this point that when it abandoned its original agreement the G.T.M.A. had given an undertaking not to operate an agreement to the like effect.) In other words the Registrar was inviting the Court, in the light of what Justice Cross, and Lord Justice Diplock, had said, to construe the notifying of proposed changes by each firm to all the others as a device which was designed to, and in fact did, arouse an identity of action—in other words it was an arrangement. In fact the Court failed to come to any decision on the arrangement issue having apparently been somewhat impressed by the firms' legal innocence. They were not guilty of contempt on this issue although an accompanying stern warning implied that next time things might be different. The Court did, however, deal with a number of instances of explicit collusion and for that a collective fine of £102,000 was imposed.

In 1966 the Registrar returned to the attack in the *Tyre Mileage* case.[55] Here again a price agreement (relating to tendering for the maintenance of local authority bus tyres) was abandoned and the usual undertaking given. Again a new agreement came into existence before the old one was abandoned. Post-notification was mandatory. Pre-notification was provided for but it was merely permissive. In practice the parties chose to operate the permissive part. What usually happened was that when a tyre company was intending to quote a rate it notified the rate to the group[56] secretary who circulated it to all other members. All other companies who were interested in the business did likewise. If a tyre company, in the light of other intended quotations, proposed to quote below the lowest rate notified, it submitted a revised quotation which was in turn circulated. The upshot of the arrangement was that, if operated honourably, each firm was aware of the rate (i.e. the lowest notified) which it had to match to be on a par, but no more than on a par, with the most aggressive competitor. The system gave rise to a remarkable degree of level tendering. Again the Registrar invited the Court to consider this as an arrangement to the like effect of the one abandoned. This time the Court could not fall back on explicit collusion since none was alleged. In fact the Court accepted the Registrar's invitation and fines of £10,000 were imposed on each of the parties. The main implication of this was that those operating pre-notification agreements were in considerable danger of contempt. The effect which this had on industry will be made apparent in the case studies and conclusion.

Two legislative developments are also worthy of mention. One was the 1964 Resale Prices Act. This was not conceived as a means of dealing with a loophole in the attack on horizontal agreements. That it would, however, have an impact on horizontal agreements will be evident in the case studies. Then in 1965 the Labour government enacted the Monopolies and Mergers Act. We have noted the observation by J. B. Heath that some commentators expected mergers to be employed as a device for evading the full impact of the 1956 Act but that in his study there was little evidence of such a trend. It will therefore hardly be surprising to note that when the mergers' legislation was introduced into Parliament the idea that mergers could undermine the restrictive practices provisions of the 1956 Act was not mentioned.[57] The problem was largely seen as preventing undesirable monopolies (the one-third criterion was applicable here) from coming about rather than as preventing competitive structures from dissolving into oligopoly. The fact that in the longer-term mergers have been a loophole is clear from examination of our case studies which, as indicated earlier, are published separately.

V. THE ANTI-COMPETITIVE TIDE

The Resale Prices Act and the Monopolies and Mergers Act, although outside the central theme of this book, represent a high water mark in postwar anti-trust policy. Thereafter anti-competitive forces began to exert an influence and these undoubtedly had an impact in the restrictive practices sphere.

Pressure was exerted from four points: bodies representing industry generally, national planning institutions, those organs responsible for prices and incomes policy and the government itself. This pressure really began to mount after the Labour Party came to power in 1964. However, there is little doubt that as far as industry was concerned the 1956 Act began to become unpopular well before then. In February 1962 the Conservative government announced that the Board of Trade was to put in hand a comprehensive study of the then existing monopolies and restrictive practices policy. The National Association of British Manufacturers[58] responded by issuing its views[59] in June of that year. It took the view that the presumption that restrictive practices were against the public interest unfairly prejudged the issue. However, it also recognised that this 'presumption of guilt' was by then firmly built into the legislation and it would not be realistic to press for its removal. It therefore concentrated its attention on redrawing the gateways. It suggested that in gateway (b) the word 'and' in 'other specific and substantial benefits' should be replaced by 'or'. This would place a less onerous burden on Respondents. Then again in gateway (d) it suggested that 'preponderant' should be replaced by 'large'. It also proposed that 'persistent' should be removed from 'a serious and persistent adverse effect' in gateway (e). The Association also suggested that a new gateway should be added to the following effect:

> That the removal of the restriction would deny to the industry, and especially to those employed in the industry, specific or substantial benefits or advantages enjoyed or likely to be enjoyed by that industry, whether by virtue of the restriction itself or of any arrangements or operations resulting therefrom.

In this connection it was pointed out that,

> Under the existing legislation, it is virtually impossible to submit any evidence concerned with labour conditions or the wider issue of industrial relations in general. This is particularly regrettable since, in the N.A.B.M.'s view, there are some industries in which employees have benefited materially from the existence of stable prices, resulting from price agreements. It is not relevant to show that an agreement is harmless or does good, nor that it is beneficial to the health, efficiency and strength of the industry. The suggested amendment would meet this objection.

However, by 1966 the views of industry were more radical than this. In that year the C.B.I. let its views be known. It drew attention on the one hand to the national need for rationalisation agreements but on the other to the substantial deterrents to anyone engaging in such activity. The main obstacle was the adversary procedure before the Court which might involve direct and indirect costs amounting to as much as £100,000. There was also the delay to any investment involved in a rationalisation scheme since cases might take three to four years to settle. The experience of the Engineering Equipment Users' Association (E.E.U.A.) was also drawn upon. This body existed to work out and publicise

F

standards where B.S.I. norms did not exist or were inappropriate. The E.E.U.A. had been attempting to obtain for itself the same privileged position which applied under the Act in respect of B.S.I. standards. This it had sought to do under the provisions of Section 12 but it had been unsuccessful. The C.B.I. pointed out that in the unlikely event of the E.E.U.A. obtaining a favourable verdict under Section 12, every time it issued a new handbook it would have to seek exemption afresh. If a Section 12 exemption failed to materialise it would either have to cease to recommend standards or face the rigours of a Court appearance.

The C.B.I. therefore recommended that the Board of Trade and the Department of Economic Affairs should have the power to exempt from registration agreements which they certified were in the national interest. This was a short-term recommendation. In the longer term it was proposed that the supervision of restrictive practices and monopolies should be unified under an administrative tribunal.[60] Students of anti-trust will detect a certain irony in this proposal when it is recollected that in 1956 industry was anxious to escape from the 'judge, jury and prosecution all rolled into one' system said to be inherent in a Monopolies and Restrictive Practices Commission reference. Now having experienced the excellence of Lord Kilmuir's machinery, industry was anxious to put the clock back. The curious student may wonder why.

A certain sympathy can nonetheless be reserved for industry for by this time economic policy had invoked the process of planning to supplement the forces of competition.[61] Industry found itself caught between official exhortations collectively to improve efficiency and the requirements of the law. The journal of the C.B.I. put it thus:

> Industry is urged to rationalise, to specialise, to standardise, to form itself into larger, more efficient units to meet the challenge of foreign competition. All involve an element of agreement and co-operation between firms. Yet to do so, runs the constant risk of coming up against existing legislation.[62]

Apart from the government, the National Economic Development Council was centrally involved in exerting pressure for more scope for collective action. The Council was surrounded by a series of Economic Development Committees (E.D.C.s) for particular industrial sectors ('Little Neddies'). The ideas which the Council put forward filtered up from these bodies upon which sat, amongst others, industrialists. It soon became apparent that the N.E.D.C. was in the vanguard of the movement to modify the 1956 Act. Any doubts about this can be quickly disposed of by reference to a statement by the president of the Board of Trade in Parliament in 1967. Answering a question on the possibility of amendments to the 1956 Act, Mr Douglas Jay replied,

> I shall take this opportunity to seek powers which would enable me to grant temporary exemption from registration under the 1956 Act of agreements which can be shown to be positively beneficial to the national economy. The National Economic Development Council has suggested action on these lines.[63]

The philosophy of the N.E.D.C. had a twofold aspect. Firstly, following the general opinion of the period that British (and indeed West European) firms were often too small by comparison with U.S. rivals (the creation of the Industrial Reorganisation Corporation reflected this thinking), it supported rationalisation agreements as a first step towards mergers. Secondly, the general posture of the 1956 Act and the cost of fighting cases hindered efficiency. It was argued that,

> The experience of a number of E.D.C.s has revealed that the strong bias in the Restrictive Trade Practices Act against all forms of restrictive agreements and its rigid interpretation in the Restrictive Practices Court can frustrate co-operative action which would be in the national interest. In certain circumstances unlimited competition may serve to increase costs and prices, e.g. where a powerful buyer is able in the absence of restrictive agreements to insist on special features which prevent desirable standardisation in manufacturing, or where competition is extended throughout a product range in conditions where specialisation could produce longer production runs. Standardisation of equipment and procedures in fragmented industries such as building and distribution can offer large economies but their introduction is dependent on the assistance of trade associations whose activities are severely curtailed by the Act. Agreements involving rationalisation and the elimination of over-capacity or co-operation and marketing or research, can similarly reduce manufacturing costs and promote technical innovation. In a capital intensive industry such as chemicals agreements on investments can economise scarce capital resources and encourage the construction of import-saving capacity.[64]

The latter instance referred to the Chemical Industry Association which found that the 1956 Act acted as a deterrent to discussions about investment projects which had the object of preventing unnecessary duplications of plant. A report in *The Financial Times* underlined the problem as follows:

> The chemicals' Little Neddy, for example, reported two years ago that the industry could cut £30m. off its import bill in various ways. The most obvious is the manufacture in this country of some of the imported products. But who is to build the new plant? Some agreement is obviously necessary. Company A agrees not to manufacture a certain product in order to leave for company B a market large enough to justify investment on a scale that would make its manufacturing costs internationally competitive. Perhaps company B is able to return the compliment. Over this, the industrial advisers, Neddy and the Department of Economic Affairs stand benevolently–in theory. But, in fact, few if any, companies have been able to bring themselves to make such arrangements because of the spectre of the Restrictive Practices Court, statutorily bound to examine them.[65]

The problem of the E.E.U.A. was also alluded to. Another case cited was the paper industry which had sought to give effect to recommendations made by the Paper and Board E.D.C. The basic idea was to save pulp imports by increasing the supply of waste paper from local authorities. But partly because of a previous ruling of the Court in the end the industry decided it could not pursue a line of co-operative action.

These inhibitions on co-operative rationalisation achieved a not inconsiderable publicity–a fact which is surprising when it is borne in mind that even the N.E.D.C. employed the words 'not numerous' and 'paucity' in describing the number of cases which had been encountered. The possibility that anti-competitive forces were 'muscling in' on the planning process cannot be easily dismissed.

The other force was prices and incomes policy. The reports of the National Board for Prices and Incomes had a limited undermining effect. Thus in a report on the prices of bread and flour the Board took the view that competition in bread distribution was uneconomic and benefit would accrue from abandoning it in favour of a parcelling out amongst competitors of districts within particular towns.[66] Then in its report on aluminium semi-manufactures, the Board was anxious to secure increases in productivity as a means of absorbing further increases in factor costs. It noted that there was a tendency for purchasers to place relatively small orders and for there to be a marked lack of standardisation in production. The Board felt that this problem could be dealt with if the manufacturers could come together and exchange information on costs. The costs of production of small lots and non-standard products could be ascertained. Price differentials which would favour large as opposed to small lots and standard as opposed to non-standard products could then be agreed. However, the Board recognised that whilst an exchange of information on costs might not itself contravene the 1956 Act, any agreement about the price changes consequent upon such an exchange would be a contravention.[67] Again the 1956 Act was presented as an obstacle to greater efficiency. In practice the prices and incomes policy did give rise to a modification of the legislation. Under Section 24 of the 1966 Prices and Incomes Act the government could (for a period of two years) exclude from the ambit of the 1956 Act agreements and trade association recommendations relating to prices arising in connection with reports by the Board.

Significant as this power undoubtedly was, in anti-competitive terms it was almost certainly less significant than the early warning system. The need to give such warning undoubtedly forced firms to collectively negotiate the price increases they hoped would prove acceptable to government departments. Reference will again be made to this in Chapter 4.

The pressures were not, however, all in one direction. Following the 1964 White Paper the Registrar was pressing for modifications to the 1956 Act which would tighten it up, and a means of dealing with information agreements was high on the list. In the upshot the Act of 1968 represented a concession to both sides in that both requirements of the N.E.D.C. and the Registrar were embodied.

VI. THE 1968 RESTRICTIVE TRADE PRACTICES ACT

The Act contained two important features designed to strengthen competition. The first is that it made information agreements registrable. It embraced information arrangements relating to prices, terms, quantities supplied, processes applied, persons and areas supplied and costs. It was, however, left with the Department of Trade and Industry to decide what categories shall be placed upon the Register. In February 1970 information agreements relating to prices and terms and conditions were in fact called up.

The second related to penalties for failure to register. Some disquiet had been expressed about the provisions of the 1956 Act respecting the Registrar's power to uncover unregistered agreements and the machinery for inducing voluntary compliance with the registration requirements. Sections 14, 15, 16 and 18 of the 1956 Act were particularly relevant to these issues. Section 14 stated that if the Registrar has 'reasonable cause to believe' that a person was party to an unregistered agreement he could give notice to that person to notify whether he was in fact party to such an agreement. If the reply was in the affirmative the party in question was required to furnish particulars and Section 15 provided for him to be examined under oath before the High Court. (Section 16, amongst other things, provided penalties for giving false statements.) All this sounded quite impressive. However, as Valentine Korah has pointed out, it is doubtful whether the powers of the Registrar under Sections 14 and 15 adequately dealt with cases where he merely had cause for suspicion[68] and in many instances that may be all he can fairly say. But there was the further problem that if a party to an actual agreement decided to reply in the negative (to the Registrar's notice under Section 14) it was difficult to see how the Registrar could make any progress, particularly when there were no external symptoms to seize upon. (The latter would be so in the case of a well-managed cover-price system as opposed, for example, to a case of collective discrimination.) The obvious way to get round this problem is to allow the Registrar to descend unexpectedly and seize documents as is possible under U.S., Canadian and E.E.C. law. But the Registrar was not invested with this power.

The 1956 Act was also somewhat deficient in respect of the consequences of failing to register. According to Section 18, provided the failure to register was wilful, the Court could treat an unregistered agreement as if all the restrictions in it were contrary to the public interest. This suggests that parties to an unregistered agreement who considered it unlikely to be upheld might decide that it was just as well not to register. Even if it was subsequently uncovered, and even if failure to register was deemed to be wilful, the worst that could happen would be no worse than might be expected to happen anyway.

The 1968 Act did not provide for more powers of discovery. This was unfortunate. Rather it sought to tackle the general problem from the angle of the consequences of failure to register. Basically the Act said that if the parties to an agreement do not register it within the prescribed time limit, and it subsequently came to light, it was void and it was unlawful to give effect to it. Pleas of ignorance, and therefore lack of wilfulness, could cut no ice whatsoever. As a further inducement the Act imposed a statutory duty to register and this carried the possibility that anyone who is disadvantaged by an unregistered restriction could sue the parties to it for damages.

There were, however, a number of possibly retrogressive features. The Department of Industry and Trade could exempt from registration certain agreements of importance to the national economy. The conditions for exemption were as follows:

(a) that the agreement is calculated to promote the carrying out of an industrial or commercial project or scheme of substantial importance to the national economy;
(b) that its object or main object is to promote efficiency in a trade or industry or to create or improve productive capacity in an industry;
(c) that that object cannot be achieved or achieved within a reasonable time except by means of the agreement or of an agreement for similar purposes;
(d) that no relevant restrictions are accepted under the agreement other than such as are reasonably necessary to achieve that object; and
(e) that the agreement is on balance expedient in the national interest;

and in considering the national interest for the purposes of paragraph (e) of this subsection the Board shall take into account any effects which an agreement is likely to have on persons not parties thereto as purchasers, consumers or users of any relevant goods.

In Parliament Mr Edmund Dell for the Board of Trade stated that few exemptions would be granted. Interestingly he cited the Chemical Industry Association as an instance of the kind of agreement which might find favour.[69]

The Act also allowed government departments to exempt agreements, made at their request, relating to prices where the object is to prevent or restrict increases or secure decreases. This was clearly an adjunct to the then existing prices and incomes policy, with its early warning system and collective negotiation of proposed price increases.

One final feature of the Act was the inclusion of a new gateway. This stated,

(h) that the restriction does not directly or indirectly restrict or discourage competition to any material degree in any relevant trade or industry and is not likely to do so.

This was clearly designed to apply in the case of information agreements. They may prove to have no restrictive effect but would fall unless a gateway is satisfied. It could be argued that gateway (b) would be capable of accommodating any benefit which might accrue. However, the benefit may be too small to satisfy gateway (b)–hence the need for gateway (h). This gateway was not however tied solely to information agreement cases.[70]

REFERENCES

1 This phrase covers inter-connected bodies corporate.

2 Monopoly being defined as in the 1948 Act.

3 The emphasis here is presumably upon behaviour, particularly of an oligopolistic kind, which is not covered by the word 'agreement'. There does seem to be some evidence of an overlap between monopoly and restrictive practices legislation. Thus monopolies legislation clearly covers the practice of price leadership (as is exemplified in a 1971 reference), whilst price leadership could in certain cases enshrine the idea of an arrangement as defined in the *Basic Slag* case and after.

4 See Section 6.

5 See Section 21.

6 The specific wording of the 'tailpiece' is as follows: '. . . and is further satisfied that the restriction is not unreasonable having regard to the balance between these circumstances and any detriment to the public or to persons not party to the agreement (being purchasers, consumers and users of goods produced or sold by such parties, or persons engaged or seeking to become engaged in the trade or business of selling such goods or of producing or selling similar goods) resulting or likely to result from the operation of the restrictions'.

7 Thus passage through a gateway does not guarantee exemption.

8 Expert witnesses are allowed. These include economists. The Registrar was clearly very dependent upon economists since: (a) industry is not likely to supply evidence against agreements; (b) empirical evidence of what conditions will be like under competition may not be available if there is a long history of restriction, and therefore the predictive powers of the economist have to be called upon. The other main source of evidence for the Registrar came from the buying side of an industry.

9 The parties to an agreement which has been declared contrary to the public interest or abandoned give an undertaking to the Court that they will not operate the agreement either in its original or in some varied form–the latter being referred to as 'to the like effect' of the original agreement.

10 This would not, however, apply to agreements which were deemed to have 'no economic significance'. The Board of Trade could upon a representation from the Registrar have them removed from the register. See Section 12.

11 See Section 7 (3).

12 See Sections 8 (7) and 31. The relative immunity is common in anti-trust laws–see, for example, the provisions of the Webb–Pomerene Act in the United States and the West German Cartel Law.

13 The *Watertube Boilers* case arose out of such an agreement.

14 The wire rope industry followed this course of action–see the separately published case studies.

15 A. Hunter, *Competition and the Law* (London, 1966) pp. 158–9.

16 See C. Brock, *The Control of Restrictive Practices from 1956* (London, 1966) p. 51.

17 Gateway (a) has been used infrequently and always unsuccessfully.

18 Hunter, *op. cit.*, p. 159.

19 *Ibid.*

20 *Ibid.*, p. 116.

21 J. B. Heath, *Not Enough Competition?* (London, 1961) p. 35.

22 R. B. Stevens and B. S. Yamey, *The Restrictive Practices Court* (London, 1965) pp. 70–5.

23 Hunter, *op. cit.*, p. 151.

24 See separately published case studies.

25 This view is one we have formed from an investigation of transcripts of evidence and it has also been put to use by those who were witnesses.

26 For a sustained treatment see Stevens and Yamey, *op. cit.*, Ch. 3.

27 P. W. S. Andrews, 'The Registrar's Report', *The Lawyer*, Vol. 4, No. 2, p. 16.

28 See for example, *In re Watertube Boilermakers' Agreement*, L.R.1 R.P., pp. 285–345, particularly p. 329.

29 See account of *Wire Ropes* case in separately published case studies.

30 See *Wire Ropes* and *Transformers* cases in separately published case studies.

31 See V. Korah, *Monopolies and Restrictive Practices* (London, 1968) pp. 152–3.

32 *In re Yarn Spinners' Agreement*, L.R.1 R.P., pp. 118–99.

33 *In re Blanket Manufacturers' Agreement*, L.R.1 R.P., pp. 208–84.

34 The fact that the Registrar was able to choose the order in which he proceeded with agreements on the register may well have been a significant factor in the early successes in that he was able to select agreements where he had more than an ordinary chance of achieving his objective. Perhaps because of this fears expressed during the passage of the Act that the early agreements would pass too easily through the 'gateways' were not realised.

35 There is probably some truth in this but in addition it seems that as time passed Counsel for Respondents became more adept and discovered, sometimes almost by accident as in the first *Black Bolts and Nuts* case, arguments which found favour with the Court.

36 No attempt is made at this point to review the kind of arguments which found favour with, or failed to impress, the Court. However, the reader will find the most important successful arguments reviewed in the first chapter of the separately published case studies and in the second chapter thereof a number of cases which failed are discussed. (Cases upheld related to watertube boilers, black bolts and nuts, cement, permanent magnets, standard metal windows, books [Net Book Agreement], importation of sulphur, glazed floor and wall tiles, iron and steel scrap, and fish [Distant Water Vessels' Development Scheme].)

37 J. B. Heath, 'Restrictive Practices and After', *Manchester School of Economic and Social Studies*, Vol. 29, May 1961, pp. 173–202.

38 *Ibid.*, p. 176.
39 *Ibid.*, p. 180.
40 *Ibid.*, p. 184. Subsequently, in 1962, Lord Chandos, then chairman of A.E.I., achieved considerable publicity by advocating price leadership as a way of avoiding 'excessive' competition or over-rigid cartelisation–see *The Times*, 11 April 1962.
41 Heath, *op. cit.*, p. 184.
42 Heath, *op. cit.*, p. 186.
43 Registrar of Restrictive Trading Agreements, *Report for the Period 1 January 1960 to 30 June 1961*, Cmnd. 1603, p. 3.
44 Cmnd. 2299.
45 *Ibid.*, p. 6. See the discussion of the *Basic Slag* case below.
46 *Ibid.*, pp. 6–7. See the discussion of the second *Black Bolts and Nuts* case.
47 *In re British Basic Slag Ltd*, L.R.3 R.P., pp. 178–97; *In re British Basic Slag Ltd's Application*, L.R.4 R.P., pp. 116–56.
48 *In re Austin Motor Company Ltd's Agreement*, L.R.1 R.P., pp. 6–20.
49 L.R.3 R.P., p. 196.
50 L.R.4 R.P., pp. 154–5.
51 *In re Black Bolt and Nut Association's Agreement (No. 2)*, L.R.3 R.P., p. 43.
52 *In re Newspaper Proprietors' Agreement (1964)*, L.R.4 R.P., p. 398.
53 L.R.5 R.P., pp. 315–50.
54 That is to say, one in which, for example, list price changes are notified to competitors before the change is made operative or tender prices are disseminated before they have been lodged. This contrasts with a post-notification arrangement where, for example, a change in a list price would only be communicated after it had become operative.
55 L.R.6 R.P., pp. 49–114.
56 The Mileage Group of the Tyre Mileage Conference.
57 The silence of ministers was paralleled by a silence on the part of commentators–see Bow Group, *Monopolies and Mergers*, (London, 1963) and Conservative Political Centre, *Monopoly and the Public Interest* (London, 1963).
58 It eventually merged with the Federation of British Industries to form the present Confederation of British Industry.
59 N.A.B.M., *Monopolies and Restrictive Practices Legislation* (London, 1962).
60 This continued to be the basis of C.B.I. policy–see speech by Mr John Partridge, president of the C.B.I., reported in *The Times*, 27 May 1971.
61 An example of this was the standing of merger policy on its head following the creation of the Industrial Reorganisation Corp.
62 *British Industry*, 22 July 1966, p. 7.
63 *Hansard*, 28 February 1967, Cols 68–9.
64 N.E.D.C., *Rationalisation and the Restrictive Trade Practices Act* (London, 1967) p. 1.
65 J. Roeber, 'Time for new look at restrictive practices', *The Times*, 18 September 1967.
66 National Board for Prices and Incomes, *Prices of Bread and Flour*, Cmnd. 2760, p. 13.
67 National Board for Prices and Incomes, *Costs and Prices of Aluminium Semi-manufactures*, Cmnd. 3378, 1967.
68 The reader who wishes to pursue this matter further should see Korah, *op. cit.*, p. 144.

69 *Hansard*, 30 April 1968, Cols 1,009–21.
70 The 1964 White Paper envisaged this type of gateway and envisaged its use in the case of information agreements although again it did not see that as its sole function.

Chapter 3

THE THEORY OF COMPETITION POLICY

. . . quod . . . si monopolium appellari non potest . . . certe oligopolium est.

St Thomas More[1]

I. INTRODUCTION

This book investigates the operation of competition policy under the 1956 Act. It would then seem highly desirable that some view of the theory of competition policy should be presented. At first sight it may seem surprising that such a presentation should be necessary at all; surely the theory must be well established if it has reached the status of legal enactment? Yet in fact it does not take very long to discover that not only is there no theory of competition policy; there is not even a coherent theory of competition.[2] In what follows an attempt will be made to clarify the issues involved. Firstly, the various approaches formulated by particular schools of writers will be examined. This will be followed by an attempt to identify the welfare elements involved in policy; and finally the nature of oligopolistic competition will be examined to see how far it may be expected to allocate resources satisfactorily in the light of the preceding welfare analysis, and to see also to what policy implications its existence gives rise.

II. REVIEW OF EXISTING THEORY

(i) *Static Optimality*

The first (and in many cases the last) approach to competition adopted by economists in general is that derived from what was once known as 'the new welfare economics'. This approach seeks to evaluate situations by reference to the divergence from an optimum stated in terms of equality of marginal rates of substitution and transformation. For reasons which must be obscure in view of the limitations of the approach, it has acquired real normative significance for a number of writers.[3]

In brief the Paretian conditions require that, *within the specified limits of the analysis* (the most important of which from our point of view are fixed *and* completely known technology, with the possibility of universal attainment of the optimum conditions), it should not be possible to reallocate resources so as to make some people better off without making anyone worse off. The community must then be on its transformation frontier. It must be impossible to produce more output from the same resources, or a given output with fewer resources. The marginal physical productivity of inputs must be the same in different uses. (Intuitively it should be clear that this is necessary, for otherwise there would be scope for increasing output by transferring resources to those areas where marginal physical productivity was highest; given diminishing marginal physical productivity in different employments the transfer would then continue until equality had been achieved.) In addition (by the same intuitive reasoning) we can see that the marginal utility of different goods for different consumers must be equated; the ratio of the marginal utilities of goods for one consumer must be the same for all consumers or there is scope for increasing welfare by reallocating output between consumers. The ratio of marginal utilities is the marginal rate of substitution; and the final condition is that the marginal rate of substitution is equal to the marginal rate of transformation, depicted geometrically in a two-good case by tangency between a community indifference curve and a transformation (production possibility) curve.

This optimum is achieved as consumers adjust their ratios of marginal utilities of the goods they consume to relative prices, to maximise their satisfaction, and as entrepreneurs adjust the marginal productivities of their inputs to factor prices to maximise their profits. Under perfect competition price will be equal to marginal cost, and the ratio of marginal cost is the marginal rate of transformation. Thus there is equality of the marginal rate of transformation through production, of price (the marginal rate of transformation through the market), and of the marginal rate of substitution.

But it must be emphasised that to achieve this requires perfect knowledge, including perfect knowledge of production functions, and the achievement of marginal cost pricing throughout the economy, each firm being faced with a horizontal average revenue curve to which the firm's (long-run) average cost curve is tangent at the latter's lowest point, which is also the point at which average costs equal marginal cost, and all rents have been competed away.

At this stage in the development of economic theory it should hardly be necessary to emphasise the overwhelming limitations of this approach.

Firstly, it ignores the possibility of divergence between social and private costs–the well-known problem of externalities. Recognition of the problem pre-dates the new welfare economics, being most especially associated with the name of Pigou, but the problem itself is just as relevant to the new as to the old welfare economics.[4]

Secondly, there is the highly important problem of income distribution. Essentially the optimum located by tangency between the transformation curve and the community indifference curve is dependent on the proposition that the distribution resulting from factors being paid according to their marginal productivity is optimal–a proposition which a society committed to redistributing income received through the price system is unlikely to accept. More seriously from a theoretical point of view, the marginal productivity theory of income distribution is truly only a theory of demand for factors–and with various supply situations for factors, different income distributions result. These will then produce different community indifference curves. But the Paretian approach offers no criteria for choosing between situations where different community indifference curves are tangent to the same transformation curve.

Thirdly, there is the problem highlighted in the now famous article by R. G. Lipsey and K. Lancaster, 'The General Theory of the Second Best'.[5] This indicates that where it is not possible to achieve Paretian conditions for some part of the economy, welfare may actually be decreased by achieving them elsewhere in the system.

In addition there is the problem highlighted by G. B. Richardson[6] who has argued convincingly that perfect knowledge is an assumption totally incompatible with the other assumptions of perfect competition.

A number of other problems associated with this analysis arise because of its totally unreal view of the nature of economic decision-taking especially in relation to the firm: but since many of these apply also to the theory of imperfect competition, which does explicitly purport to contain a theory of the firm, there is no need to raise them at this stage.

But, in summary, 'The typical Lausanne situation of free competition, in which everyone faces fixed conditions, is merely a limiting case of not very great theoretical or practical importance'.[7]

Certainly the relevance of the analysis to the problems of competition policy can be gauged from the fact that the sort of active competition between firms which characterises observed economic activity is missing under perfect competition.[8]

The apparent inevitability of non-Paretian situations in particular sectors of the economy also led to the development of the theory of 'imperfect competition'. This sought to arrive at conclusions about the equilibria of firms faced with downward-sloping instead of horizontal average revenue curves. After an initial attempt to tackle oligopoly, which was then abandoned in face of criticism,[9] the theory contented itself with dealing with a (very) large number case in which firms were able to arrive at price output decisions independently of reactions from their competitors. The theory arrived at the well-known marginal cost and marginal revenue equation, and at the equally well-known conclusion that free entry into an imperfectly competitive industry would produce the so-called 'solution' of tangency between the downward-sloping average revenue curve and the U-shaped average cost curve.

This was held to demonstrate the necessity of suboptimal resource allocation in two main ways. Firstly, since tangency between the two curves just described must (geometrically) occur at an output smaller than that at which the average cost curve reaches its minimum, the analysis was held to demonstrate the necessary existence of excess capacity. Secondly, in such a tangency situation, average revenue must be greater than marginal cost: and this was contrasted with perfect competition where the resource use at the margin was equal to the satisfaction derived. If downward-sloping average revenue curves could somehow be eliminated there was scope for meeting the Paretian criterion of a welfare change by making some better and none worse off. Coupled with this was the charge, much emphasised by some economists,[10] that the divergence between price and marginal cost meant that factors were not receiving the value of their marginal products. There was the further charge that consumer choice was distorted by the different degrees of divergence between price and average revenue found for different commodities: since consumers equated their marginal rate of substitution with the marginal rate of transformation through the market which now diverged from the marginal rate of transformation through production, they were necessarily placed in a suboptimal position if they pursued rational (i.e. maximising) behaviour. A uniform degree of divergence of price from marginal cost would not however solve this problem as this still left a distortion in the choice between income and leisure, even if it was realisable in practice.[11]

In addition to all this, there was also, where there was not free entry and tangency was not achieved, a divergence between average cost and average revenue at the equilibrium output, giving rise to 'supernormal' profits. From this arose the habit of referring to the 'degree of monopoly'.[12]

This general approach has been subject to a sustained and well-directed attack.[13] Little of its credibility, most especially with respect to its welfare conclusions, can be said to have survived. But it is necessary to examine it, for it implies two things which, if true, would be of great importance for this study: firstly, that suboptimality is inherent in the system even without the introduction of restrictive practices; and secondly, following this, that competition policy is futile since it cannot remove these apparently unavoidable and important distortions.[14] It may be as well to summarise the main objections to the approach.

Firstly, the theory assumes U-shaped average cost curves in order to substantiate its basic proportions. Empirical work however suggests that, at the very least, average cost curves have significant horizontal sections, and may often be roughly L-shaped.[15] If this is correct, there is no unique optimum and no determinate amount of excess capacity. Moreover knowledge of the marginal curves associated with the particular average curves assumed is necessary: otherwise firms are likely, even if profit maximisers, to cost on the basis of the horizontal section of the average cost curve, and not to enter an industry (or in the long run stay in it) if they are not fairly certain of an output which will enable them to reach the horizontal section of the cost curve.

But the firm is assumed to have knowledge of such marginal curves. This itself raises a major criticism of the theory: that like its perfectly competitive counterpart it is gifted with costless omniscence at least internally. In fact the firm is very unlikely to have knowledge of such marginal curves; even though some writers have argued that accounting procedures in well-managed firms can produce this information,[16] the evidence is far from convincing, and in any case the cost of gaining the marginal knowledge for the majority of firms is likely to be too high. (Indeed some of the firms examined in the course of this study did not even know their *average* costs for certain products.)[17]

If firms base their pricing upon average rather than marginal costs and revenues, and have largely horizontal cost curves, a lot of the analysis simply ceases to have any relevance. But there is another dimension to the knowledge problem. Costless omni-science is assumed to provide the firms with knowledge of best techniques and organisation: remove this assumption, which if valid would render most of the organisational superstructure of any firm redundant, and it becomes possible that the large number (held to be a fault of imperfect competition as preventing the attainment of optimum scale) may be necessary in order to achieve discovery, through competition, of best techniques, and organisa-tion and products. Simply to assume away this kind of problem on the basis of costless omniscience cannot give rise to a legitimate theory of resource allocation.

The problem of knowledge of marginal curves is sometimes avoided by some writers who assert that if a firm seeks profit maximisation it must be equating marginal cost and marginal revenue.[18] This may rightly be regarded as a tautological solution to the problem since any action in any degree of ignorance taken by a firm which *wishes* to maximise profits must be regarded as *being* profit maximisation. This is not very helpful, however, since a firm in a state of ignorance adopting a full cost solution is more than likely to adopt a price/output policy different from that dictated by (non-existent) knowledge of marginal curves.

But in any case very serious problems arise over the motive force for the whole of the supply side of the analysis–profit maximisation.[19] Even a little casual empiricism is likely to raise doubts about this. Thus firms universally resort to output ration-ing rather than price fluctuation in the face of short-run demand increases. It may well be allowed that profit is *one* of the firm's motives: but it is hardly satisfactory to leap from this to the conclusion that profit maximisation determines a firm's price/ output policy. Two ways out are usually offered, both tautological. One is to treat virtually anything the firm does as profit maximisa-tion. The other, not always easily distinguishable from the first, is to treat all observable departures from profit maximisation as *long-run* profit maximisation–which since the length of the 'long run' is never defined is fairly clearly meaningless.

In fact firms have many motives, and these may well vary over time (in different phases of the cycle and in different stages of growth of the industry). This problem will be returned to in more detail below; but even at this stage it is necessary to stress that a multi-motive firm is a complicated social organism. The so-called theory of the firm presented in imperfect competition analysis has no theory of that kind of firm at all.

All these considerations indicate then that the price/output

G

decisions of monopolistic competition theory and the resource allocation implications of these may tell us nothing about actual price/output decisions and resource allocation. This likelihood is greatly strengthened by recognition of the fact that the reactionless world of the analysis is very nearly as unreal as the world of perfect competition. After the failure (noted above) of the initial attempt to grapple with the oligopoly problem, this difficulty has just been swept under the carpet. Fuller attention will be paid to oligopoly below: but even at this stage it may be noted that the fundamental characteristic of industrial competition is oligopoly under conditions of uncertainty. It is then doubtful how useful a theory which assumes away both these characteristics can ever be. The traditional theory of the firm is really a series of deductions from maximisation subject to constraint, stated, however, not in Lagrangean form but geometrically, a presentation which lends a spurious precision to it.[20] Moreover, the theory has, apart from all its other defects, nothing sensible to say about forms of competition other than price flexibility–which means that a whole sphere of decisions affecting resource allocation is beyond its purview.[21]

Even this does not exhaust the deficiencies of the analysis. With reference to the specifically negative inclination of the average revenue curve which, together with the shape of the cost curve, is a source of many of the conclusions of the analysis, very little justification for the steep fall is provided. Yet it has to be steep if the degree of excess capacity is to be significant. In this connection it is instructive to note that the analysis does not distinguish time periods in relation to the average revenue curve, although long-run average revenue is likely to be more elastic than short-run. It has also been convincingly argued[22] that the combination of a steeply falling average revenue curve with free entry is implausible so that the amount of excess capacity (accepting for the moment the rest of the analysis) is not likely to be significant. In any case an influx of new entrants is likely to increase the elasticity of the average revenue curves of the existing firms.

The analysis of the falling average revenue curve is also sometimes coupled with a welfare implication that consumers should not have preferences. Obviously this is a highly arbitrary judgement.[23] Since consumers reveal that they prefer choice this is a component of welfare as differently defined[24]–indeed it has been argued that a world of perfectly competitive uniformity would not be at all congenial.[25] The denigratory attitude to preferences is sometimes coupled with an attack on advertising (though ironically enough, in so far as this acts as a barrier to entry, it may enable producers to reach their minimum cost output, even if this does involve their earning supernormal profits). But, apart from the fact that many firms are not selling to 'gullible consumers' but to experts, so that in large parts of the economy the problem does not arise,[26] it has been pointed out[27] that the profit maximisation assumption would not lead one to expect that if there were significant unrealised economies of scale some firms would attempt to take advantage of this by offering a low-priced standardised article.

The critique has concentrated in particular on the conclusion of the analysis concerning excess capacity and the 'tangency solution'. Many of the criticisms offered above, however, notably those aimed at profit maximisation and the ignoring of oligopoly problems, also apply to the conclusion of the analysis which seeks to establish a widespread divergence between marginal cost and price. In particular if firms wish to avoid attracting new entrants they may avoid a profit maximising policy; in terms of the analysis itself they may equate price and marginal cost–at least it is no longer axiomatically true that they will not. (If they do prevent new entrants being attracted this will also mean that the 'tangency solution' itself will fail to be realised, and thence the necessary conclusion concerning the prevalence of excess capacity is removed.) The conclusion of the analysis concerning the relationship of marginal cost and price is arrived at by the same path as that concerning excess capacity and uses the same faulty apparatus. The criticisms of that apparatus are then relevant to the conclusion.[28] But in addition it should be noted that there are important income distribution problems arising if the analysis were thought (as it was by some) to lead to policy prescriptions as the *enforcement* of marginal cost pricing in an imperfectly competitive economy;[29] and for dealing with income distribution we have no criteria at all. In addition, if supernormal profits are used to finance R & D, and if this has *any* positive productivity, then a concentrated structure (and any structure where average revenue curves are falling is bound to be more concentrated than one where they are horizontal) is likely to have lower unit costs. The price may then be higher than marginal cost but lower than it would be under an atomistic situation where price was equal to higher marginal cost because of the absence of R & D. This is outside the terms of the analysis but it is a perfectly real possibility.

Apart from all these difficulties there is the further one that it is not entirely clear what significance can be assigned to this ultra-simple analysis in a world populated by multi-product firms which, moreover, do not equate the profitability of their different lines (and who may indeed find themselves forced to supply relatively unprofitable items in order to complete a range).[30]

In the light of all these shortcomings it is truly surprising not only that this analysis has proved so long-lasting but that it should have been couched in such loaded language.[31] For in truth it affords not only no incontestable conclusions but indeed hardly any likely ones.[32]

Discontent with one particular aspect of both perfect and imperfect competition theory–their static nature, and in particular the assumption of a fixed and given technology–has led some writers to lay considerable stress on dynamic factors in the competitive process. It is to this part of the existing theory that attention will now be turned.

(ii) *Dynamic Aspects of Resource Allocation*

A dynamic approach to the theory of resource allocation is mainly associated with the name of Schumpeter[33] although a number of writers have adopted a similar treatment. The core of the approach lies in its view of the capitalist process as essentially one of change.[34] This implies that the role of competition policy is irrelevant as encouraging only marginal adjustments (which have no clear welfare effects) between competing firms.[35] Price competition is largely irrelevant.[36] Competition arises through invention and innovation, the mainsprings of change. It is the large strong firm which produces change. Such an approach rejects of course the use of perfect and imperfect competition theories as providing any kind of normative analysis, since they deal with small weak firms, as well as resting on a fundamentally different base in assuming a fixed technology.

This is an approach which appears periodically in economic literature. A later version of the theory rejects normal price competition as futile and possibly destabilising short-run competition:[37] it is only the long-run competition based on significant changes in products or processes which is important. An extreme version of the theory is to be found in Galbraith's notion of countervailing power. This views price competition as something past, having been replaced by the exercise of power and countervailing power by large units whose strength lies in their technology and who are the sources of change.[38]

The emphasis on the dynamic nature of competition leads to stress on two particular aspects of change. The first, and that which receives greatest attention, is the mechanism of innovation. It is usually argued that large firms with a high level of R & D expenditure (and a high degree of market power) are the source of both invention and (more especially) of innovation. Invention and innovation are the core of the capitalistic development process, and should be the focus of any theory of competition and of policy towards it.

The second aspect of change which is stressed is that, given its universal pervasiveness, the equilibrium either of the firm or the industry is a doubtful concept. Discontent is of the essence of the capitalistic process.[39] If the competitive mechanism is working properly the strong should be superseding the weak. This has been called the 'transfer mechanism'[40] but since international trade theory has a prior claim to the use of this term in another context, the term 'selection mechanism' will be used here. The differences between the strong and the weak which lie behind the operation of this mechanism rest on two elements: the innovations already discussed, and the differences between the costs of different firms which arise from differing efficiencies with a given technology. These exist either because some firms are better organised (since firms are not assumed to know automatically the best, i.e. the lowest cost, organisation) or from differing efficiencies associated with differing scales of production.

Promising (and indeed refreshing) though this approach is, it encounters a number of difficulties. Firstly, it should be realised that it contains no unambiguous welfare propositions. There is no optimum, or even a set of incomparable optima. The contrast with perfect competition is then, in a sense, not quite legitimate.

The dynamic approach does not seek to provide alternative *optima*: rather it provides an alternative view of the *mechanism* of resource allocation. In fact the welfare implications of the dynamic effects are far from clear. There is something indeed in common with a teleological theology; change is of the nature of capitalism and it is therefore right that capitalism should be allowed, indeed encouraged, to fulfil its nature, as the very act of doing so will ensure progress towards an ideal state. Whatever the philosophical merits of the general approach, this is hardly likely to commend itself to economists as a theory of resource allocation. In conventional economic terms the approach seems to rest on the assumption that any innovation or selection that increases market power is increasing welfare–which is either definitional (as revealing the preferences of consumers) or disputable.

But whatever the welfare implications, one conclusion of some advocates of the theory would seem highly questionable. This is the conclusion that price competition through price flexibility with a given technology is (at best) irrelevant. For it is surely perfectly reasonable to argue that it is just the uncertainties and competitive pressures induced by at least the possibility of price flexibility which provide the spur to industry to discover both optimal organisation with a given technology, and new advances in the technology of products and processes.

Indeed one of the major weaknesses of this kind of theory is its lack of attention to motivation. The Schumpeterian view is that the motive to innovate is provided by the temporary monopoly rewards of innovation. Yet this, which is a version of profit maximisation, is as open to criticism as an excessively simple-minded view of the operation of a firm as it was in the imperfect competition analysis. If, for instance, a firm is heavily influenced by the desire for security, it may avoid disturbing the existing structure by innovating, unless it is under some pressure which threatens its security (or threatens the achievement of its profit constraint, or whatever motive or complex of motives we attribute to the firm).[41] The same comments apply also to the motives which cause the stronger to eliminate the weaker. Without fear of destabilising action by the weak, the strong may well prefer a quiet life.

Empirical testing of the ideas presented in this approach is a little difficult, although in providing verifiable predictions it offers great advantages over the static analysis. There does seem clear evidence that the sources of *invention* at least are *not* overwhelmingly the large firms.[42] Moreover, in so far as progress is founded upon basic research, this lies largely outside the purview of even large firms and is the province of government.[43] With regard to total inventions of all kinds patent data is inconclusive; on the one hand large firms may not patent in the interests of secrecy, and on the other, worthless things are patented.[44] But at least it seems quite probable that the patent data does not support the Schumpeterian thesis.[45] However, two points should be made immediately. Firstly, even in invention the small firm may encounter difficulty partly connected with its size.[46] Secondly, Schumpeter distinguishes clearly between invention and innovation;[47] and it does seem that innovation is more likely than invention to be associated with large strong firms.[48] Small firms do suffer the difficulties of finding capital for innovation[49] and this affects individuals even more.[50] Nevertheless there are empirical limitations to the support for size. For although *expenditure* on R & D (neglecting its productivity for a moment) increases to some extent with size, it does seem that after a certain stage of development this no longer holds[51]. This suggests again that the role of motive is important and that beyond a certain size a firm may not be sufficiently threatened by competitive pressures.

But for all its limitations the dynamic analysis is very important from two points of view. Firstly, it directs attention to a fundamental deficiency in the static analysis of the competitive process: and if it were necessary to choose either the static or dynamic approaches exclusively, there can be little doubt that the latter would be preferable. Secondly, it stresses that short-run optimisation may not be compatible with the fastest rate of progress.[52] Indeed, with respect to perfect competition, Schumpeter, Galbraith and J. M. Clark have all argued that it is incompatible with progress.[53] (The sterile response of the advocates of perfect competition is that firms operating within it will spend 'as much as is necessary to achieve progress' on R & D, and this expenditure will constitute a uniform part of the cost curves of all the firms!) But of course all this raises a further welfare difficulty; there is no way of judging which is preferable, short-run optimisation or the fastest rate of progress, particularly as the dynamic analysis associated with the latter as noted above, offers no welfare criteria. Nevertheless in recognising the problem of the conflict a good deal of progress beyond the 'degrees of monopoly' hallucination has been made.

(iii) *Workable Competition*
Dissatisfaction with the manifest inadequacies of static theory, together with a desire to produce some sensible criteria for policy and to incorporate into them the dynamic considerations dealt with in the previous section, all combined to produce the theory of 'workable' or 'effective' competition, most clearly associated with the name of J. M. Clark.[54]

At first sight the idea is most attractive. Here it seems is a system which combines static and dynamic criteria and recognises the 'second-best' nature of many competition policy problems. It has been taken at this face value by a number of writers and has resulted in an enormous literature, much of it suggesting new criteria of workability to be incorporated into the system, and much of it concerned with the economic operation of particular industries (from which the additional criteria are often derived).[55]

The basic methodological approach of the system has two parts. Firstly, it directs its attention to various aspects of economic activity where situations may arise that are, if not specifically suboptimal, at least undesirable in the sense that there is a *prima facie* case for believing that there is either static misallocation of resources or interference with the mechanism of economic change. The approach is interested not only in situations where there is direct interference with what is judged to be desirable resource allocation, but also in those where incentives to 'best possible performance' are somehow interfered with or muted. Secondly, the approach attempts to formulate 'norms' or standards of 'performance' which provide a guide to the sort of situation which should exist if there is to be workable competition. Typical norms relate to such things as profits, innovations, costs, and barriers to entry.

Now at this stage an important distinction, rarely apparent in the literature of workable competition, should be broached. It is that between absolute and relative versions of these norms. The absolute versions seem to imply that there are absolute standards of profitability, entry barriers and so on, and that an industry may be judged by these. It is particularly apparent when the approach is used as the basis for analysing a particular industry.

The relative version, which is more in evidence in generalised discussions of the approach,[56] is less ambitious. In this version the idea of 'norms' indeed fails to have any strong significance. Rather a list of norms is used as a kind of 'shopping list' to see, firstly, if the industry differs significantly from other ('similar') industries in respect of e.g. its profit level, and secondly, what alternatives are open to the competition authorities to improve the situation – this last depending in part on the legal and institutional framework which is usually (though not always) taken as given.

The distinction between the absolute and relative versions is important: yet the way in which writers on workable competition switch from absolute to relative versions and back again would suggest that they are hardly conscious of it.[57]

The relative version is essentially the approach adopted by those who are faced with the problems of actually operating competition policy. It has, like the absolute version, serious defects, and their existence helps to explain the unsatisfactory nature of the operation of (for instance) British competition policy in dealing with some of the industries examined in the course of this study. Partly the trouble lies in the fact that it is really little more than a 'shopping list'. It has enormous advantages in comprehensiveness compared with the static or dynamic approaches. Practically no aspect of an industry's 'performance', including the happiness of its workers

and its conservation of the environment, not to mention its contribution to national defence, is excluded.[58] But this has two
important implications. Firstly, it contains no *theory*. Indeed it is
highly doubtful whether any coherent theory taking account of
all the diverse criteria employed could ever be formulated. Any
theoretical considerations that it does contain are derived entirely
from a rough 'rule of thumb' approach to static optimisation, and
from the ideas generally accepted on dynamic grounds. Not only
does it fail to recognise, let alone solve, the problem of conflict
between static and dynamic optimisation: the approach essentially
lacks any answer to the vital question, 'what do we want competition to do'? Indeed quite a lot of writers in this tradition seem
unaware that the question exists to be answered.

The lack of theory helps to explain the second problem (or
rather set of problems) that arises. This is that the approach via
a 'shopping list' gives, firstly, no way of evaluating the weight to
be attached to various norms. Thus if an industry is found to have
high profits and an excellent record of innovation behind a high
entry barrier, it offers no way of judging the 'workability' of
competition within that industry, nor of knowing whether
'workability' (let alone resource allocation) will be improved or
worsened by removal or modification of the entry barrier. It gives,
secondly, no way of evaluating situations where there is a clear
conflict of norms. Thus if an industry has a high entry barrier
which is arguably necessary to provide security for investment in
innovation, the realisation of economies of scale, or the spending
of funds on conservation or defence research, there is no way of
judging whether welfare will be increased if entry is facilitated
while investment in innovation is reduced, the atmosphere polluted,
and the Russians invade! It gives, thirdly, no guidance in discovering whether norms *are* interdependent. A company with good
working conditions may or may not provide these because it
enjoys a privileged position in the market place and its executives
are more concerned about human values than economic
'performance'.

The relative version of workable competition also encounters
operational difficulties. For instance, comparisons, with regard to
their profit rates, of industries which are 'similar' is often an
exercise dangerously close to question-begging. Such are the
difficulties that the comparison used may end up as one between
industries which have a roughly (sometimes very roughly) similar
technology and similar profit rates already.

Connected with this is a subsidiary but still important problem of discovering the true facts concerning an industry. Competition policy enforcers are no more gifted with costless omniscience than are firms. Thus the profit figures for one product of a multi-product firm may be virtually impossible for an outsider to discover even if the firm itself knows them–which is not always the case.[59] Similarly there is a major problem if the passing on of cost reductions is a 'norm' of workability, in discovering what cost reductions there have actually been.

But the main difficulty that arises with respect to workable competition springs from the very nature of the norms themselves. They are classified by Sosnick,[60] certainly the best writer on workable competition, as falling into three categories: those relating to structure, conduct and performance, respectively. But in looking at, first of all, the structure norms listed by Sosnick, it is necessary to ask what way there is of knowing (either absolutely or by reference to a 'comparable' industry): (1) how many is a 'large' or 'appreciable' number of firms; (2) what are 'moderate' quality differentials and how do we measure them; (3) how are we certain whether handicaps on mobility are artificial or not; (4) what is 'adequate' access to information; (5) what is enough to be 'some' uncertainty about whether a price change will be met; (6) what meaning is to be assigned to a requirement for 'continual opening of fresh areas and types of competitive contact'?

Surely these are not 'norms' in any recognisable sense but a list of areas for inspection.[61] But when attention is turned to conduct norms, the same sort of problems arise. Thus (1) what is a sufficient degree of 'striving' in independent 'rivalry' (a word which occurs with monotonous regularity in the literature of competition policy but is hardly ever defined? Again (2) what are the criteria for judging the 'permanently inefficient', or (3) what practices are 'unfair'? How do we distinguish (4) profit maximising price discrimination from other forms and decide which should and should not occur? How is it possible to distinguish which sales promotion is badly misleading–since the proponents of this approach do not propose to ban advertising and *all* sales promotion is to some extent misleading, hence the distinction between sales promotion and *'Which?'* What meaning is to be attached to the statement that buyers should react 'fairly rapidly' to differential offerings?

Nevertheless, given that a 'shopping list' is not completely useless, the structure and conduct 'norms' do offer areas where enquiry may prove fruitful, although any *evaluation* will ultimately rest on some assessment of static or dynamic efficiency or potential efficiency–or on sheer assertion. But it is difficult to see whether even this degree of usefulness can be attributed to the 'performance norms'. By what standard (1) are we to judge if performance is 'efficient'? This will be particularly difficult where there is no clear technical optimum. There may well be no optimum at all. Even if there is, and it depends on managerial rather than technical diseconomies arising,[62] its identification is not merely a matter of engineering data, even assuming the latter were freely available. How are (2) 'excessive' promotional expenses to be judged? How is it to be established what is the level of profits which rewards investment and efficiency and induces innovation? (All that can be said is that if they are present–which itself requires a judgement since 'efficiency' is largely immeasurable and the other two encounter the social science problem of there being no 'control' sample to judge by–then the level of profits is sufficient. This may or may not be true, depending, firstly, on whether these things, in so far as they exist, depend on the profits earned, and, secondly, whether there is any means of distinguishing sufficiency from excess profitability.)[63] How is it possible to judge (4) that output is 'consistent' with good allocation of resources? Surely this is what the *whole* problem is about (if allocation is defined in both static and dynamic terms). What criteria are there for judging whether (5) prices intensify cyclical problems or whether (6) quality conforms to consumers' interests? It *is* true that it may be possible in principle to discover whether (7) 'opportunities for better products and techniques' have been neglected. But the word 'better' requires a judgement that we have no criteria for making; and the problems of discovery in practice are formidable. We have no criteria for discovering the appropriate degrees of conservation (8) or aiding national defence, nor for judging either 'excess' political power or employees' welfare–these are all purely political judgements. Nor is there any way of judging (9) that success has accrued to those who give buyers what they want–except by looking at the successful and seeing if, in our unsupported judgement, they do this. Finally, how can it be assessed that entry is 'as free as the nature of the industry permits'? This is purely relative and involves judgements about whether it is in the 'nature of the industry' that entrants should have inadequate access to capital, or licences. Moreover, what is the implication for resource allocation if the entry barriers *are* in 'the nature of the industry'?

Some writers have also directed attention to other factors. Thus product duplication is to be taken into account[64]–though to deny it would be to deny consumer choice. (Indeed other workable competition writers see choice as a component of welfare.)[65] Again, built-in depreciation is singled out[66]–yet this may be a condition of the ongoing process of capitalist development, as it arguably is in the motor industry.

But essentially the criteria, even as reformulated after criticism,[67] involve question-begging. Thus what is a *'needless* reduction of durability', '*incomplete* standardisation' (when allowance is made for consumer choice), '*needlessly* hazardous or uneven quality' (and what is a 'needful' hazard)?

Of course some of those who have written on workable competition are aware of these problems. In particular Sosnick has written of the performance norms that

> . . . it is often feasible to detect at best only extreme instances of good and bad performance. Cost performance can roughly be surmised from engineering, intra-industry, intertemporal, inter-industry, and international comparisons; but even such light as these provide passes only dimly through a cloud of difficulties–variations in demands, products, product mixes, input prices, input qualities, long-lived commitments, cost accounting, obsolescence problems, distribution costs, etc. Likewise, in appraising profit performance, only certain extra-ordinary profit or loss rates could fail to be rationalised by the many accounting problems and the justifications of risk bearing, innovation, cost performance, and resource allocation.[68]

Moreover, Sosnick is not alone in his recognition of the in-adequacies of the 'norms'.[69] But many other writers do not seem to be aware of the problems or at least prefer to ignore them. Moreover, although particular reference has been made here to the work of Sosnick, this is not intended to imply particular criticism of this writer. Less ambitious and articulated treatment of workable competition[70] simply offer a less comprehensive 'shopping list' while going no way towards solving the problems raised above.

Not only is the approach little more than categorisation: it is also capable of leading to the conclusion that an industry which on any normal understanding is highly competitive does not have workable competition, at least according to some of the suggested criteria. Thus the British cotton industry would almost certainly fail inspection of its technical progressiveness and investment, let alone of its working conditions. Because the workable competition approach contains no *theory* of competition, either with respect to its objectives or limitations, it is unable to resolve such a paradox.

The conclusion is unavoidable then that workable competition offers not so much empty economic boxes as a series of unrelated measuring rods of indeterminate length and with no units marked on them–a view which is reinforced by frequent homely references to 'benchmarks'. It is true that for very extreme cases such as that of American Tobacco[71] the approach is not powerless: but in such cases so blatant are the distortions it is doubtful whether such an extensive 'shopping list' is necessary, and in any case some other apparatus must still be drawn on implicitly to supply criteria or value judgements.

But having been highly critical of workable competition there are three important points to be made. Firstly, it provides a great advance on anything previously formulated; to those who have to operate policy and are not simply left, like academics, to the undisturbed enjoyment of their prejudices, it represents a significant step forwards. Secondly, it is important to note that it includes major dynamic considerations, hence it is *quite* wrong to identify fully workable competition with perfect competition.[72] Thirdly, its range in identifying problem areas in resource allocation offers major advances over the exceedingly narrow view given by conventional static allocation theory whether in perfectly or imperfectly competitive formulations. It is even capable of accommodating proper firms. Moreover, the very fact that it does not offer cut and dried solutions makes a welcome contrast to the spurious precision of marginalist theory. In the formulation of an approach to the theory of competition policy which follows it will be necessary to take account of all these points.

III. AN APPROACH TO A THEORY OF COMPETITION POLICY

It is apparent from the preceding discussion that there is much in the alternative approaches to a theory of competition policy currently available that is highly unsatisfactory. It is now time to attempt to formulate an approach which is free from as many as possible of the shortcomings noted.

(i) *The Welfare Presumption*
The first requirement for any theory of competition policy is that the welfare presumptions should be formulated clearly. As already noted, this was missing altogether from the dynamic and workable competition approaches.[73] The welfare presumptions were stated

more clearly in the static analysis; but the latter contained the implicit value judgement that maximum output from given resources with a fixed technology, maximised welfare. It should be emphasised that this *is* a judgement, and at the same time an example of the emotive phraseology which pervades the static analysis; it is identifying output, within a narrow framework, with welfare.

Essentially the approach advanced here will build upon the same proposition, while making quite explicit that the identification of output and welfare *is* a value judgement. If society wishes to substitute other value judgements, then it is perfectly free to do so. If such alternative welfare formulations are offered then they should be justified as preferable to the one offered here. This last statement is itself a value judgement: and it is made on the basis that the output-welfare identification, subject to certain constraints which will be examined below, is that which is implicit in the vast majority of writings on competition policy (which do not state their aims) and in policy as it is seen to be operated.

Of course a host of other welfare criteria make spasmodic appearances in the literature[74] and J. M. Clark has made the interesting suggestion that the medieval idea of the just price is to be found in competition policy.[75] Alternative formulations are certainly perfectly possible. Thus one author identifies welfare with certainty; any reduction in uncertainty increases welfare, ergo restrictive practices increase welfare.[76] It does not seem to be a formulation which would command very widespread support.[77] Some writers cast their net much wider, encompassing such matters as progress, stability, employment, justice, freedom and other democratic ideals.[78] This is not necessarily invalid: it is simply a different kind of approach, but one which does not appeal very strongly for formulating the welfare objectives of competition policy. It is noticeable indeed that where authors give a comprehensive list of aims of economic policy, the aims given for competition policy are a good deal less ambitious; but no serious attempt to explore the relationship of one set of aims to the other and to economic welfare is made. Thus the discrepancy between cost minimisation and social product maximisation where unemployment exists could mean that society would wish to impose a constraint on output maximisation via cost minimisation additional to the constraints imposed below. It is desirable, however, that the treatment of such problems should be explicit; and accordingly it will be assumed here that competition policy is operating in a full employment economy with the level of employment being determined exogenously by government policy. By identifying output with welfare some of the implicit clashes of welfare objectives inherent in the literature of workable competition are avoided. Nevertheless it will be necessary below to introduce some constraints on the welfare function.

However, even before that stage is reached a difficulty over the identification of output and welfare arises as soon as it is realised that the analysis is not being confined within the strict framework of normal static analysis. For there is the difficulty of choice between output (welfare) now and in the future. The present approach is not concerned with optimisation within a totally static framework; and thus the problem of less jam today and more tomorrow, when the allocation of resources conducive to most today is not the same as that conducive to most tomorrow, must be faced. In principle this is solvable through the application of a social rate of time preference; but this is not an operational proposition and it can therefore have no place in a theory of competition policy. It will be necessary to settle for a reformulation of the static judgements in a dynamic context and, specifically, to settle for the highest rate of growth over time. Society may well wish to impose constraints on this, and indeed the income distribution constraint introduced below may well act as a constraint on growth maximisation. But the judgement offered here is that priority will be given to dynamic optimisation where there is a clash; and that static allocation within this framework is concerned only with maximising output from given resources *to the extent that this does not interfere with or reduce the rate of growth of production*. This does not however mean that static allocation is unimportant; and separate treatment will be accorded to it below.

Of course the approach is sectional. That is to say, competition policy is micro-economic policy.[79] This raises second-best problems. A reorganisation increasing the output of one section of the economy while leaving unchanged others with a potential for reorganisation will alter relative prices and distort consumer choice between the products of the different sections. A further judgement is then required. The one adopted here is that such a reorganisation is still desirable, despite second best problems, because reorganisation through competition policy of any economic system *has* to proceed on a sectional basis. (*Per se* approaches have proved incomplete and not really workable even apart from the fact that competition policy is always likely to be sectional in its operation because of problems of enforcement.)

The process of reorganising the economy to produce the fastest rate of growth *necessitates* incurring problems of the second best kind; and the judgement is made here that the loss of welfare (as conventionally defined) involved in the introduction of disproportionalities is insignificant, thus enabling us to concentrate on the particular view of welfare offered here which, to reiterate, identifies it (subject to constraints to be introduced) with output. Apart from the fact that such an approach is consistent with the basic view of welfare introduced here, there is in any case in terms of conventional welfare theory no *a priori* reason for preferring a situation where all prices are *proportional* to resource use to one where some prices have been brought closer to resource use than others; overall proportionality involves a distortion of the choice between income and leisure which will be reduced by bringing some prices nearer to resource use and there is no *a priori* way of saying whether the partial removal of this distortion, which of itself introduces a new distortion between relative prices, actually increases or decreases total welfare (conventionally defined).

(ii) *The Constraints*
The identification of growth of output with welfare must however be subject to constraints introduced on the basis of widely accepted value judgements. Basically there are four such constraints. First there is a 'consumer choice' constraint. This is introduced to deal with the problem that output cannot be identified with welfare under conditions leading to stockpiling and shortages–the kind of problem encountered in planned economies. The form this constraint takes is that of requiring that increases in output shall be accepted by the market at cost-covering prices: in practice, however, this can only mean that there are no distortions in the market requiring consumers to accept one collection of goods rather than another which they would prefer, *unless* such distortions are introduced because of the other three constraints specified below. The 'consumer choice' constraint, like the output-welfare identification, is implicit in a very great deal of the literature of competition policy, and indeed is basic to the intuitive understanding of competition and competition policy in the minds of most economists.

The three other constraints are not of such general acceptance within this particular context, but as value judgements they command widespread support. The first of these is an income distribution constraint. Every welfare system requires such a constraint–the Paretian quite as much as the one offered here.[80]

The most widely accepted of such value judgements is that producers should not be allowed to earn significant positive rents. Hence the popular objection to 'profiteering'. However, it is desirable to go rather further than this; and accordingly it is judged desirable that neither significant positive nor *negative* rents should be earned, either by producers or by factor inputs, except in so far as these are inescapable, e.g. due to inelastic factor supply. Thus for instance this constraint would apply not only to the American Tobacco Company's historic behaviour, but also to the negative rents earned by exploited labour hired by a monopolist.

In treating income distribution as a constraint on output maximisation it should be emphasised that it may not always have a directly constraining effect. Thus for instance the removal of circumstances allowing monopolistic rents to be earned may act as a spur to increased efficiency on the part of those exposed for the first time to the cold wind of competition; or the elimination of sweated labour may cause a reappraisal of technology in an industry, following the change in the relative prices of labour and capital, and thus bring about an increase in the efficiency of resource utilisation. But in other cases the nature of the income distribution constraint may be clear enough. Thus for instance removal of producers' rents may result in capital being diverted to areas unaffected by competition policy;[81] or the removal of sweated labour may bring about the decline of an industry.

The nature of the next constraint is perhaps less unambiguous. This is the power constraint. The value judgement is implicit in much (especially American) competition policy writing that there should be a limit on the power of private organisations. This is most likely to be a constraint where there is a conflict between the need to achieve economies of scale in production, research, and other dimensions on the one hand, and the need to restrain private power on the other. It will be a constraint too where the desire to grow large provides a motive force for the firms in an industry where the result of imposing a limit on size will be to reduce, through the consequent interference with managerial incentives, managerial efficiency and technological progress.

Of course it is not universally and inevitably true that the power value judgement should conflict with the basic welfare aims. For instance, it is conceivable that mergers which achieve economies of scale may slow up technical progress, through the removal or reduction of competitive pressures, so that, ten years hence, costs of production in a concentrated industry are higher than they

H

would have been in an unconcentrated state.[82] But in general the power constraint is likely to be a true constraint.

The exact point at which this constraint is applied is partly a statistical problem (depending on which measure of concentration is used) but chiefly a political problem. But that there should be *some* such point is accepted here, though it is not necessary for the rest of the analysis that it should be accepted, and it is true that it would command much less general acceptance than the distributional constraint.

There is little doubt about the constraining nature of the final type of constraint. This may be labelled generally the 'conservation' constraint, although it may be taken to extend rather more widely than the term implies.[83] This kind of conflict–efficiency in micro-economic resource use versus, for instance, pollution–is clear enough. The exact application of the constraint is a political matter: the value judgement involved commands widespread (and fashionable) support. It is one which takes explicit account of the divergence between private and social costs noted earlier in dealing with neoclassical allocation theory; but *precisely because of* the non-quantifiability of many social costs, it has to rest on political decision. It is as well that this should be seen clearly, and that economists should not pretend competence where they have none.

Spelling out the value judgements and constraints in this way has a number of advantages, not least that they are not concealed in a cloak of emotive language as they were in the neoclassical formulation. It also enables us to face squarely the problem raised by writers concerning resource misallocation arising from mistakes resulting from decisions made under conditions of uncertainty. The *classical* economists were accustomed to regard such mistakes as the price of progress[84]–indeed they would probably have regarded the Paretian preoccupations of the neoclassicists with, at the very least, amazement. In this treatment the classical view is accepted as a valid first approach. That is to say resource misallocation through mistakes is *not* in general accepted as a valid constraint on growth maximisation.[85] It seems reasonable to argue that the more certain the framework in which a business operates, the less the incentive to modernise and to seek best possible methods. Some mistakes have to be accepted as the price of an environment insecure enough to produce progress. But it is necessary to keep a due sense of proportion: and with regard to those few industries where the prospects of progress are small and the costs of mistakes very large–this applies essentially to agriculture–it does seem reasonable to take the opposite view.

(iii) *Static Efficiency with Uniform Costs*

Attention can now be turned to the different aspects of output optimisation. Static optimisation will be treated first, always bearing in mind that when it conflicts with maximisation of growth of output the latter should prevail, according to the judgements made in the previous section, unless a constraint dictates otherwise.

Static efficiency has two main aspects. The first is the elimination through competition of rents on market position. Assume for the moment that cost curves are uniform and of the shape shown in Figure 3.1 which will be designated L-shaped.[86]

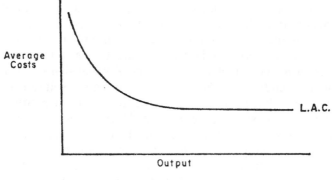

Fig. 3.1

The evidence for the existence of curves of this kind is fairly strong,[87] and is to some extent reinforced by the evidence gathered for the notion of 'vintage pricing', some of which we have also encountered in our study.[88] Of course central to the question of whether or not cost curves are this shape is the further one of the existence of a unique optimum, on which the neoclassical apparatus builds so heavily. Although the evidence is not completely conclusive it seems fairly clear that there is probably no unique optimum. The data assembled by Stigler in his classic article[89] shows constant costs over fairly large changes in output; and although for very capital intensive industries there may be continuing economies of scale,[90] these are likely to be offset by managerial diseconomies[91] and non-production (e.g. transport) costs[92] so that a flat long-run average cost curve is quite plausible.

This incidentally would help to explain the co-existence of large and small firms.[93]

Accepting the general existence of such cost curves then, statically efficient allocation is achieved when each firm is only earning normal profits (included in its cost curve) plus an allowance for a small barrier to entry in the form of goodwill–this being a concession to the problems of stability and avoidance of mistakes.[94] Price would then typically be at a level above the horizontal section of the cost curve by the amount of this allowance. For this to occur industry capacity must be sufficiently adjusted to demand that all the firms are on the horizontal sections of the cost curve. Consideration of the conditions for this to occur is deferred to the section below dealing with oligopolistic competition.

One of the major problems that this approach encounters is that of the multi-product firm. As has been pointed out elsewhere,[95] this means that there may be no unique costs for a particular product, as there may be (and usually will have to be) arbitrary assignment of overheads between products, e.g. on the basis of share of turnover–which raises the difficulty that share of turnover is not independent of price. There is no simple solution to this problem, as debates on real-life competition policy procedure over the validity of costings bear witness. Nevertheless there are two possible approaches to the problem. The first is to ensure that all obstacles, especially barriers to entry (above the minimum goodwill level), which could enable prices to diverge from the level suggested above, are removed. It then becomes possible that as great a degree of efficiency as the accounting techniques involved will allow, will be achieved. Intellectually this is hardly a satisfactory position; it may however be a policy-maker's only resort. Another possibility is that overheads are assigned on the basis of agreed accounting procedures which are common to the industry. While this may at least ensure that overheads affect the cost curves of the different firms by the same amount, it requires a degree of co-ordination which may not be compatible with the maintenance of competition; conversely, if competition within the industry remains strong, one firm may be able to gain an advantage over its rivals by departing from these agreed accounting procedures. There simply is no satisfactory solution to the problem of the multi-product firm, and it is necessary to accept an approximation to static efficiency. Nevertheless the problems posed by the multi-product firm for this analysis are significantly less than for neoclassical analysis.

(iv) X-Efficiency and Non-uniformity of Costs

Following the elimination of rents based on market position, the second main aspect of static optimisation is the achievement of Leibenstein's 'X-efficiency'.[96] In the previous section the argument proceeded as if cost curves were easily ascertainable and uniform. This is however not the case. Firms do not know all that there is to be known about optimal methods of organisation; and there may well be substantial cost savings to be achieved *even with a given technology*. Liebenstein is the author who has given most prominence to this idea and accordingly his term 'X-efficiency' will be used to mean what is, in the main, organisational efficiency.[97] It is held to be achieved by management stimulated by competition to seek the best forms of organisation within a given technological framework. Competition is then required to provide the stimulus to this as well as to compete away rents of market positions.

Differences in organisational efficiency may, according to Leibenstein, be very significant[98]–indeed the same author takes the view that the scope for improvement of resource allocation by improvement in X-efficiency is far greater than the scope for improvement through achieving static optimisation (conventionally defined).[99]

Closely related to the idea of X-efficiency is that of 'organisational slack' developed in the pioneering work of Cyert and March.[100] This phenomenon manifests itself during periods of prosperity for the firm: when the firm is under pressure, search procedures are instituted to cut costs by taking up the slack. It would seem clear that any policy which increases the degree of competition between firms should both increase X-efficiency and lead to taking up of slack.

If firms differ in organisational efficiency however, their costs will differ. It would seem in fact that they usually do differ.[101] The simple conclusion that we arrived at with respect to the price that we wished competition to achieve, now has to be modified to allow for different efficiencies. The requirement then becomes that price should be set at a level where it is equal to long-run average cost (including normal profits) plus the goodwill/stability barrier already introduced, plus an allowance sufficient to reward the efficient for being the most efficient (and no more). (This last looks dangerously tautological and inoperative: the point will be returned to in dealing with the *modus operandi* of competition policy.) Given any significant spread between the highest and lowest cost curves this should provide a price for the industry which is below the level satisfactory to the most inefficient, and thus cause the latter to reorganise or leave the industry–the presumption that such a price is desirable being subject to the power and other constraints.

The existence of differing costs associated with differing efficiencies with a given technology raises a difficulty for the analysis which should be faced squarely. If learning were to be associated with output this might imply a continuously downward-sloping long-run average cost curve rather than an L-shaped one as in Figure 3.1; and the empirical data providing L-shaped curves might owe its existence to extrapolation backwards from any given point on the learning/output curve. Without more empirical research there is no simple answer to this point; but the present evidence would lend more apparent support to the view that the typical cost curves are L-shaped with their horizontal sections at different levels for different firms; and this approach will be assumed here. (It is at least to the credit of the approach advanced here that it explicitly recognises this problem and that of the allocation of overheads: both are aspects of the problem within the firm which are completely ignored by conventional allocation theory.)

(v) *Dynamic Efficiency*
Conceptually distinguished from the achievement of static efficiency and X-efficiency is the achievement of technical change in order to lower costs. However, like the other two forms of efficiency, the competitive spur is held to be necessary to achieve this.

Casual inspection of the history of various industries suggests that major innovations in product or process are the important determinants of the course of their development and of the resource use involved in satisfying consumer wants. It is this which has led to the very valid stress on this particular aspect of allocation by Schumpeter and others, which has already been discussed. If the requirements of static efficiency and X-efficiency relate to the relationship of price to the cost curve, and the discovery of the minimum *position* of that cost curve in a given state of technical knowledge, the dynamic efficiency requirement is that there shall be no removable barrier to the introduction of changes in technology which will lower the level of the minimum attainable position of the cost curve and/or substitute new cost curves relating to products giving the consumer a combination of goods and services which he prefers to the one he previously had.

The conditions most favourable to the production of dynamic

efficiency would seem to be entrepeneurial motive and R & D. The first of these may be positive (the lure of extra profit as in the Schumpeterian case) or negative (fear of rivals in an oligopolistically competitive situation). The conditions required to produce these motives will be examined below in dealing with oligopolistic competition. The determinants of R & D have been dealt with to some extent already in examining the Schumpeterian view; but it should be noted at this stage that a lag enabling the innovator to attain an advantageous position is, at the very least, highly desirable. (It follows then that information agreements are likely to interfere with dynamic efficiency.) It is also important to note that it is highly doubtful whether it is legitimate to treat decisions about R & D expenditure purely in terms of maximising analysis, as some writers attempt to do, because, firstly, R & D expenditures do not automatically produce an outcome: inventive and innovatory returns will have to be weighted by the probability of their realisation and this makes any deterministic maximising analysis highly arbitrary in its outcome. Secondly, in addition to this, the producer has no certainty that what is *technically* an invention or innovation will become a *market* invention or innovation; since consumers usually do not know whether they would prefer a new product until they are actually presented with the choice, market research can provide no guide here.[102]

IV. OLIGOPOLISTIC COMPETITION

It now remains to consider, firstly, how far the market is likely to bring about each of the three different forms of efficiency distinguished, and secondly, what aid competition policy is required to give to bring about their achievement.

As a starting point it must be recognised that the form of competition which it is necessary to deal with, as that overwhelmingly prevalent in the real world, is oligopolistic competition. This is suggested by casual empiricism, in the light of the fundamental consideration that all that is required to produce oligopoly is not a particular number of firms in an industry, but simply that firms have to take account of the reactions of their rivals to their policy decisions.[103] Such interdependence is virtually all-pervasive.

In stating that interdependence exists, it is necessary, if the statement is to have much meaning, to explain within what the interdependence exists.[104] This raises the thorny problems associated with defining the market and the industry. There are various possibilities here but they reduce to two main ones. Firstly, there is the definition which relies on cross elasticities of demand,[105] and which derives various conceptually quite satisfactory cross-demand curves.[106] Among this family must be numbered the 'gap in the chain of substitutes' which every student is brought up on[107] but which is something easier to envisage than to identify. Although this general approach to defining an industry is conceptually satisfactory it is in general something that encounters difficulties of practical application. A second possibility is to use a techno-logical approach. This accords with common sense but has the difficulty that a multi-product firm may, on this basis, be deemed to be in several industries. Theoretically what is required is a concept of industry which will cover the firms included in the frame of reference of a particular firm taking a price/output or other competitive decision. To some extent in this study the problem has been side-stepped by looking at the industry largely as defined by a restrictive agreement. Thus attention has been primarily focused on *metal* windows although there is no doubt a significant cross-elasticity of demand between wood and metal windows. But the approach adopted does have one very significant advantage from a theoretical point of view: it is likely that any restrictive agreement, especially one which is deemed sufficiently successful to be worth spending time, trouble and money on defending in the Restrictive Practices Court, will contain by far the most significant firms included in any particular firm's frame of reference.[108] What is at least clear is that competition within a particular industry cannot be discussed without reference to what is included in that industry; and the way out taken here is no worse than any of the others suggested and may have important advantages.

Given that interdependence within the industry (however defined) is the prevalent characteristic of industrial life it is at first sight all the more surprising that conventional theory fails to provide us with any proper theory of oligopoly. The solutions adopted (apart from ignoring it altogether)[109] fall basically into three categories. Firstly, there are those building on the premise of known, reversible, single-valued reaction functions of the Cournot and Bertrand type.[110] It hardly needs stressing that these provide us with no answer at all. In effect they assume away the whole problem of the uncertainty created by interdependence. Secondly, there is the kinked demand curve associated with Hall and Hitch, and Sweezy.[111] This does explain price rigidities but it is a long step from this to providing a theory of oligopoly: in particular the theory does not provide any explanation of how the price at the kink was achieved.[112] Its empirical validity is open to question (but only question – it was derived empirically).[113] Perhaps most importantly it may have been over-generalised: thus Cohen and Cyert have argued that it is really only applicable to situations where the firms have not yet learnt the likely reactions of their competitors.[114] It would then only be suitable for an industry disturbed by new entrants (or a new industry). This introduction of learning brings a refreshing touch of realism to the analysis: but it cannot be pushed too far because if it were completely true the Cournot–Bertrand approach would become defensible.

Thirdly, there is the theory developed by Sylos-Labini on the basis of what has become known as the 'Sylos postulate'.[115] This involves the assumption that on the entry of a new firm other firms maintain their outputs constant and adjust their price so as to sell those outputs.[116] The theory developed on the basis of this and a number of other assumptions (the most drastic of which is perhaps similarity of costs for firms of similar size) is perfectly satisfactory as far as it goes; and it certainly represents an enormous advance on the other oligopoly formulations. Yet it loses its determinancy when the assumptions are altered – and there are plenty of other possible outcomes (as Bain, who has pursued similar lines of argument though in a less restricted form, has also emphasised).[117] In particular, existing firms in lowering their price may well, since they have no objective knowledge of their average revenue curves or of the demand curve facing the industry, lower price more than necessary and actually increase their sales. This will be particularly likely if the existing firms really fear the new entrance and/or feel that their position within the industry is already insecure. There is also the strong possibility that seeing a potential new entrant, firms will take action to deter it before any new entry move is made. In addition, both the Sylos postulate and those constructing oligopoly models on the basis of costs and entrants ignore the possibility of the demand curve for the product of the industry as a whole being shifted to the right by the new entrant's sales expenditure, or product innovation if the new entry is on that basis.

But perhaps most importantly, all this does not really amount to a theory of oligopoly, for, by concentrating on the problem of entry, it fails to provide any real guide to the behaviour of the already existing and interdependent firms within the industry.

For an answer to such a central problem the first instinct is perhaps to turn to games theory as epitomised in the classic work by Shubik.[118] This throws extremely valuable light on the non-predictability of oligopolistic situations, and it will be referred to further below. But it does seem clear that it provides insights rather than a theory which offers testable predictions. Without far more knowledge than we could have, it is not possible to say which strategy will be chosen; and a lot of the data which the approach normally assumes is known to the entrepreneur is not in fact freely available.

The theory of price determination originating in P. W. S. Andrews' *Manufacturing Business*[119] and fully articulated by H. R. Edwards,[120] takes oligopolistic analysis a very great deal further than many previous attempts in its approach to price determination, and its influence on the present treatment has already been acknowledged. But, of itself, it does not provide a theory of oligopoly. Firstly, where firms have different costs the price within the industry is indeterminate;[121] and, as already noted, there is no really satisfactory solution to this problem. Secondly (and this is probably tne greatest single defect of the theory) it offers no explanation of how market shares were either arrived at or maintained (or altered).

Of course it is true that the very complexity of oligopolistic competition makes it unlikely that there can be any one answer to this sort of problem. One of the major problems facing anyone attempting to analyse oligopoly is that oligopolistic competition takes so many forms.[122] Hence the futility of building everything upon a single postulate. The only characteristic common to all these forms of competition is that interdependence is assumed in making competitive moves.

Not only are there many different forms of competition, there are also many different types of competitive structure, including large and small number oligopoly, with and without price leadership, the latter being either 'dominant' or 'barometric'.[123] The actual strength and nature of the interdependence and of the competitive pressures within the group will vary from case to case; and this makes the outcome of any given situation, and the freedom of oligopolistic competitors to pursue different kinds of competition, highly variable and unpredictable. The primary aspects of interdependence are perhaps substitutability and the relationship of capacity to demand;[124] but attention has also to be paid to localisation, and there is also the important problem of the extent and timing of information available to the firms. This has already been discussed elsewhere;[125] the main point is that the greater the amount and speed of availability of information the greater the degree of interdependence, but that groups highly interdependent because of other factors are likely to require more information and thus to have resort to such devices as information agreements.

Important in assessing interdependence and stability is the degree of vulnerability of the firms. Shubik's valuable delineation of short-run and long-run market and financial vulnerability, and control vulnerability[126] is particularly informative here. In assessing the importance of these, and in judging the likely sources of competitive moves, it is important to note that, because of differences in vulnerability, small firms may have the greatest interest in stability since they are likely to fail first even if they are the most efficient.[127]

An important determinant of such stability may be the idea of a normal price. One author has argued that this provides a powerful stabilising force.[128] This seems persuasive; but the power of this one stabilising force will depend on a number of other factors affecting the interdependence and vulnerability of firms, and the same author recognises that such stability will be eroded in conditions of fundamental disequilibrium.[129] Other important factors must be the elasticity of demand for the whole industry, the ratio of fixed to variable costs, and the extent and direction of shifts to be expected in the demand curve facing the industry.[130]

All this makes generalisation about the nature of oligopolistic competition extremely difficult. But there are even further complications. Once we drop the simple profit maximisation assumption we have to recognise too that the motives of firms differ between industries (particularly with regard to the stage of maturity of the industry) and also between firms within the same industry.[131] In fact firms are no more single-motive than human beings–and a lot of human beings are involved in the decision-taking process of a firm.[132] This means that any single-motive treatment of a firm such as sales maximisation[133] or security of profit[134] is likely to be unsatisfactory. Moreover, the motives of a firm may well differ at different points of the cycle–empirical work on pricing in the cycle does not remove this possibility.[135]

At all events the psychological assumptions of traditional theory are extremely crude and restrictive.[136] The approach which would seem to have most to commend it is that of Cyert and March who identify five goals, arising to some extent from different levels of management. These are production, stocks, absolute sales, relative market sales (market share) and profits.[137]

Consideration of all these points make prediction of a firm's or group's behaviour in particular circumstances very difficult, now that we have left the world where firms with known and independent average revenue curves simply equated marginal cost and marginal revenue. But in fact the situation is more complicated still. In order to predict behaviour we need:

1. Knowledge of the *objectives* of the firm, and of how the various motives are compatible and how far some act as constraints on others (e.g. security versus profits). Games theory can help us here, but it will not solve the problem.
2. Knowledge of the *means* of the firm to adjust to whatever the flow of information suggests should be its course. This involves knowledge of business organisation, accounting methods, decision-taking procedures, and the lags involved. These will not only vary between firms according to differences in e.g. accounting methods, but also according to the size of firms, economic conditions, the maturity of the industry, and even the individuals involved.
3. Knowledge of the extent and timing of the information available to the firm, and of the subjective probabilities of accuracy which the firm assigns to the different elements of the knowledge it receives. Again games theory can help us to delineate the problem but it cannot supply us with the basic data involved.[138] Even if we had all the information listed above (not exactly likely in this world!)[139] this would still not be enough. We also need to know the frame of reference of the firm, which varies according to the problem being dealt with–and we need to know just how secure the firm feels in its environment, and how *hard* it is going to have to strive in order to achieve its aims.

Given the variability of all these elements, it becomes clear that constructing a general and universally valid theory of business behaviour is virtually impossible. It is possible to construct all sorts of mathematical models to give *a* solution (or to 'prove', given other circumstances, that no solution is possible). But this fails to provide us with a theory of managerial behaviour with clear implications for resource allocation.

V. A THEORY OF POLICY

If after all this it is to be possible to develop any kind of *theory of competition policy* it will have to be through selection of certain key aspects of the oligopolistic structure, which enable us to decide on desirable policy *without* knowing how enterprises and groups will react in every peculiar situation. What is essentially of interest from the point of view of a theory of policy, as distinct from a theory of oligopoly, is whether oligopolistic competition, whatever its unpredictability, provides enough incentives to achieve (as far as they possibly can be achieved) our three requirements of static efficiency, X-efficiency, and dynamic efficiency. We also want to know if there is anything inherent in the nature of oligopoly that will prevent the achievement of these three forms of efficiency, whatever the motive.

To begin with it may be possible to advance some tentative generalisations about price competition in oligopoly. A particular distinction has been advanced by G. B. Richardson between short-run and long-run price competition, only the latter being based upon innovation in process or product.[140] Although Richardson's deduction from this (that short-run price competition is irrelevant and undesirable) is not very strong because pressure on margins may be a necessary motivation to produce the innovations in which long-run competition is grounded (and in any case the absence of short-run price competition may fall foul of our distributive constraint) the idea is valuable as suggestive of the nature of oligopolistic competition. It is taken a stage further by Professors T. Wilson and C. V. Brown.[141] These authors are mainly concerned to establish that oligopolistic competition may be highly effective: and they distinguish between 'Type A' and 'Type B' price competition. The former involves 'an attempt on the part of a firm to expand its share of the market by offering to sell at a reduced published price'. (It will be clear that this could cover both the Richardson forms of price competition, but it is primarily intended to refer to the short-run version.) 'Type B' price competition 'means the operation of market pressures which will tend (i) to keep prices sufficiently low to prevent firms earning abnormally high long-term profits and (ii) to force down the level of costs'. Type B price competition is somewhat similar to the Andrews formulation noted above as it manifests itself at the stage of price formation: but whereas that concentrated on the level of prices, given certain data, this stresses also the existence and strength of pressures to alter the data. It is important because it implies that oligopolistic competition may be sufficiently strong to achieve the three efficiencies discussed above, and therefore be satisfactory from an allocative viewpoint.

Nevertheless Type A competition may be necessary to provide the degree of motivation to produce Type B–the same considera-tion as in the Richardson case. Indeed there is an important conclusion suggested here: that at least the potentiality of short-run or Type A price competition *is* necessary if Type B is to operate successfully. If this is correct it helps to provide an important rationale for competition policy; and it is important to recognise, as do Professors Wilson and Brown, that Type A competition is in fact prevalent in oligopolistic industries because although published prices may show little flexibility, competition is often active in discounts from these published prices. In addition, in important parts of economic activity, firms do not publish prices but operate on the basis of the tender system. The freedom of this form of competition to operate (the absence of restrictions), as well as its actual operation through discounts and tenders, will help to push prices towards a level accommodating the most efficient, thus aiding the achievement of the three forms of efficiency, both through improvements by firms and the operation of the 'selection' mechanism.[142]

The nature of oligopolistic price competition would seem *capable* of providing sufficient incentives for all three kinds of efficiency. But before deciding that it will *actually* do so, it is necessary to consider certain other strategic characteristics.

One of the most important of these is ease of entry. The analysis of this contains two parts: entry by new firms (which has been stressed in the pathbreaking work by Bain[143] and entry by firms already established elsewhere (chiefly associated with the important work of Andrews).[144] Entry by new firms depends, in the formal analysis of this aspect of competition, upon the relationship of the costs of the potential entrant to the prevailing price in the industry, and to the expected price after entry has added to total output. A barrier to entry then exists if the costs of the potential entrants are higher than those of the existing firms.[145] Such barriers may arise through access to patents, economies of scale, and so on. Other forms of barrier are those associated with advertising and goodwill (already accepted as a stabilising force).[146] Since a new entrant would have to spend heavily on sales promotion to overcome these, they can be regarded as imposing a cost disadvantage on prospective entrants. Barriers associated with difficulties of securing sufficient capital may or may not enter into costs, depending on whether the difficulty of obtaining capital is reflected in the prospective entrant having to pay a higher rate of interest (which will affect costs) or being subject to credit rationing (which will only directly affect costs if it limits scale of entry to a disadvantageous size). Barriers to entry associated directly with patents will be reflected in costs if the patent holders grant licences to new entrants, or if the existence of patents forces new entrants to find unsatisfactory ways round them.[147] Barriers to entry deriving from superior technology will clearly affect costs. Less tangible but not less important are the kinds of barrier to entry associated with the uncertainties of oligopolistic interdependence once entry has been made.[148]

Clearly the existence of barriers to entry has important implications for the realisation of the three required forms of efficiency. They are likely to reduce the impact of both types of oligopolistic price competition, and should, from the point of view of competition policy, be minimised.

Closely linked with this problem is that of the relationship of price to relative efficiency within an industry, and the question of whether price is set to accommodate the most efficient (as required for static efficiency) or the least efficient. The *a priori* reasons for thinking that price will be determined by the most efficient are not very convincing.[149] Apart from the social pressure on the most efficient to take a price which will accommodate the less efficient (and in an oligopolistic and highly localised industry this can be considerable), and the possibility of the most efficient becoming inefficient through lack of stimulus, there is the important point that the most efficient producer is not usually the one threatened by potential entry–and he may well have developed a technology which a new entrant would find it very hard to match.[150]

The empirical evidence on this is by no means conclusive.[151] In some instances the formula 'average cost of the most efficient (including normal profit) plus an efficiency premium' seems to be realised. However, even where this is achieved (and it is far from universal, especially where restrictive agreements are in operation) the size of the necessary premium is indeterminate, and there is scope for price to rise above this level in an industry with a wide spread of costs. Because of this indeterminancy it becomes necessary, in order to achieve all the different forms of efficiency, that entry barriers should be as low as possible in order to create circumstances the most conducive to price setting at the lower end of the range of indeterminancy. Where restrictive practices exist price will tend to the higher end unless the entry threat is very real and immediate; and because of this, and the lack of fear experienced by the marginal producer that price will go to the lower end of the range while restriction prevails, such restrictive practices tend to prolong excess capacity.

Some writers believe, on *a priori* grounds, that the firms which are most efficient will change over time.[152] If this is correct (and certainly the most efficient have a favourable environment for the development of organisational slack) then restrictions are apparently less harmful. However, two other considerations tend to discount this: firstly, the growth of organisational slack is more likely in a price agreement; secondly, the incentives to the inefficient to supplant the efficient are much reduced in such a context.

Another important factor, if oligopolistic competition is to achieve efficiency, is the degree of rivalry between firms. Now 'rivalry' is a word frequently used in the literature of competition policy, and the need for it is as frequently emphasised. Yet the word is hardly ever defined.[153] In the context of the present discussion it involves the deployment of all the forms of price and non-price competition in an effort by each firm not only to maintain its market share but also to secure it and, in the event of any short fall by competitors, to increase it. This requires effort and constant attention on the part of a firm to all possible ways of fortifying its position *vis-à-vis* its competitors. So long as resort is not permitted to restrictions (for security) this is productive of a high level of managerial incentive to seek all three kinds of efficiency. In the absence of restriction (or devices such as information agreements) this should ensure that the whole price–product mix of oligopolistic competition is brought into full play.[154]

The question that has to be answered, having examined these particular problems of oligopolistic price competition, barriers to entry, and rivalry, is whether oligopolistic competition is likely to achieve a sufficient degree of price competition and rivalry, and produce sufficiently low barriers to entry, to achieve static efficiency, X-efficiency and dynamic efficiency. In the light of what has already been said it seems likely that it will. Oligopolistic price competition can be highly effective, especially given a high degree of rivalry, and this should erode supernormal profits and produce static efficiency (always allowing for the small goodwill barrier and the efficiency premium). The same pressures which produce static efficiency should aid X-efficiency. With regard to dynamic efficiency the pressures inherent in rivalry and price competition should provide a sufficient incentive, while the barriers to entry, to some extent inherent in oligopoly, will provide sufficient means to finance the R & D for dynamic efficiency. This view is reinforced by the findings of empirical research that R & D increases up to a certain size but not beyond it, and that a four-firm concentration ratio of rather less than 50 per cent is probably required.[155] Moreover, since oligopolistic competition is essentially a price–product mix it will, if effective, provide a favourable climate for innovation.

The only real difficulty lies in the existence of the very barriers which finance R & D, the greater the barriers, the greater the scope for price to diverge from the level associated with static efficiency, and the more the reduction in managerial incentives. But in general oligopolistic competition manages to achieve a very good balance, and if it tends to lean on the side of dynamic efficiency where this conflicts with static efficiency, this is desirable if the welfare judgements made above are accepted.

On the whole it seems perfectly possible that oligopolistic competition is capable of meeting the three efficiency requirements. But this must be subject to one major qualification. Of its very nature, oligopolistic competition, partly because of the degree of uncertainty inherent in it (which, it has been argued above, has itself a beneficial effect on managerial motives) has a tendency to produce collusion and cartelisation. Of course instability is not the only motive for this; other motives might be the removal of pre-existent imperfections, the erection of tariffs,[156] recession leading to excess capacity or the rise of a predominant buyer (both of which may affect stability), obsolescence in product or process, or state interference.[157] But the main motive is usually a desire to increase stability and certainty, and to reduce rivalry.[158]

In terms of the analysis previously advanced, such collusion and cartelisation will have a number of very undesirable effects. It will interfere with the operation of the selection mechanism, which must otherwise be a powerful force in spreading throughout an industry all three kinds of efficiency. It increases the scope for arbitrary redistribution of income to producers and thus falls foul of our distributive constraint. It increases security thereby interfering with entrepreneurial incentives, diminishing rivalry and removing the need to operate search procedures. It impedes changes in the price–product mix; and it removes the stimulus to introduce such changes. This in turn raises the possibility that the price–product mix may not be the one the consumer wants, e.g. too much quality at too high a price (a familiar problem with cartels); thus it would fall foul of our consumer choice constraint. If the agreement is strong 'potential entry' on its own is unlikely to be strong enough to control these effects; and removal of all possibility of Type A price competition is likely both to interfere with Type B and with innovation. This last point arises because empirical evidence suggests that innovation is mainly undertaken by old firms;[159] and the removal of the possibility of any pressure on margins removes the most important innovatory incentive facing the most significant single group of old firms.

I

Of its very nature oligopolistic competition is also likely to produce mergers, and these may interfere with the achievement of the three kinds of efficiency, although this will not *necessarily* happen. Many of the motives to merge certainly raise the suspicion of such interference.[160] They include the desire for security (as do restrictive practices), evasion of competition policy, the purchase of goodwill, and control of scarce factor inputs. Fear of a third party (which is, since it is feared more than the prospective merger partner, likely to be more interested in efficiency) also plays a part, as does a desire to avoid competition in markets in which the firm taking over is already established, getting control of patents (which may however improve efficiency), and research economies (the problem of R & D tailing off with size has already been mentioned). Even those motives which seem conducive to efficiency may only be so in the short term; thus direct cost economies may be offset in the longer term by reduced innovatoriness in the more secure situation, and in the case of the multi-product firms may result in the creation of monopolies for a number of the products, often without any direct cost saving involved. The achievement of indirect cost economies, e.g. in advertising, may be even less unambiguously beneficial, reducing rivalry as well. The desire to secure increased funds for growth may seem a clear enough benefit: but it is perhaps arguable that in many cases these should be obtained through the capital market rather than at the cost of eliminating a competitor. Mergers involving vertical integration may achieve cost economies at the expense of closing sources or outlets to rivals. Conversely if this triggers off mergers elsewhere in order to keep productive capacity in operation,[161] there probably is some benefit in these mergers, *given* the earlier ones, but the benefit may be marginal since, through the mergers, commercial independence is removed and total rivalry reduced. Finally, mergers undertaken as an outlet for investment funds as a firm grows[162] have both advantages and disadvantages; they keep existent the threat of entry but the divergence of energies into a new sphere reduces rivalry in the old one although it increases it in the new one.

VI. CONCLUSIONS: REQUIREMENTS FOR COMPETITION POLICY

The preceding analysis of oligopolistic competition, and of those aspects which are strategic from the point of view of a theory of competition policy, suggests a number of conclusions about the form that such policy should take.

The main conclusion must clearly be that competition policy should seek to establish conditions which will, as far as possible, bring about the three forms of efficiency required: static efficiency, X-efficiency and dynamic efficiency. Because of the difficulties associated with the formulation of 'norms' however (these were raised above in the discussion of the workable competition approach) competition policy to achieve these efficiencies has to be directed towards the creation of conditions under which it may be expected that efficiency will be produced given the characteristics of oligopolistic competition already discussed. The alternative of trying to discover whether particular industries actually achieve the efficiencies, in terms of engineering and accounting data, is a fairly futile undertaking, in general terms. Rather, given the view developed earlier that oligopolistic competition can be highly efficient if unfettered, competition policy must look to the creation of suitable conditions for competition to work itself out, while assuring that the four desirable constraints specified above are met as far as possible.

There will however be two main exceptions to stopping short at this. The first is that in cases where, despite attempts to create the correct conditions, institutional and other constraints emerge which have the effect of producing unambiguous indications that the efficiency conditions are not being fulfilled, so that, whatever tests are applied, there is no doubt that some direct intervention is required.

The second main exception relates to the existence of restrictive practices. It should be clear from the foregoing views of oligopolistic competition that there is a presumption against the desirability of restrictive practices; and, conversely the *general* arguments offered in defence of restrictive practices are certainly insufficiently convincing to allow of a general permission of their operation.[163] (The same may be said of information agreements. Indeed the argument that secrecy and a lag before competitive imitation are necessary to produce innovation in product or process seems clear enough.)[164] But experience of *per se* rules suggests that they are, for practical purposes, inoperable in their strict form. In any case, given that it is *possible*, however unlikely the circumstances, that a particular restrictive practice meets the efficiency requirements, a *per se* approach is undesirable. Then what is essentially the procedure associated with the 1956 Act should be adopted, i.e. the onus is to be placed upon firms wishing to operate a restrictive agreement to show that, because of the agreement, they achieve the three forms of efficiency. This would depend on the exercise of a degree of judgement by the competition authority: but in principle there is no objection to this. The hardest of the efficiencies to establish would be X-efficiency; but there is nothing to stop firms being asked to show how their costs have been reduced through organisations not associated with changes in technology.

Since, as has been argued above, mergers also have considerable potential for interfering with the attainment of the efficiencies, it is clearly desirable that a similar procedure should be extended to them. The appropriate procedure[165] would be for firms contemplating a merger to have to present to the competition authority a general case in respect of the presumptive effect of the merger on all three forms of efficiency. It is not inconsistent with this to argue that, in the interests of competition policy to achieve efficient resource allocation, the selection mechanism should be encouraged, and all obstacles to its operation, especially pronounced barriers to entry and restrictive practices, removed as far as possible. Rather it is attempting to ensure that mergers *are* part of the selection mechanism, and not a device to block its operation.

The foregoing would seem to suggest two further important considerations in the framing of competition policy. Firstly, since the emphasis is to be on the *creation of conditions* in which oligopolistic competition is to be effective, the approach should be much wider than that of the present legislation. It should look in particular to entry barriers of all kinds, and at the existence and use made of market power from as many angles as possible. It is here that the 'shopping list' provided by workable competition may prove extremely valuable in suggesting areas for examination.

Secondly, in seeking to achieve conditions for the efficient operation of oligopolistic competition, consideration should be extended to a much wider range of alternatives than is customarily included. It is true that, at any moment in time, what are the relevant alternatives is to some extent a matter of the legal framework. But in the longer term this is not fixed. Consideration should be extended to tariff changes,[166] structure changes, divestiture, modifications to entry barriers (e.g. limitation of advertising in the detergent industry), and even, in exceptional circumstances, modification of patent rights. Consideration should be extended to all possible ways in which oligopoly can be made to work effectively, with particular attention being paid to the level of incentives to entrepreneurs.

Competition policy should then approach an industry with a view to detecting the existence of impediments to the operation of competition; and it should look at these impediments not with a view to evaluating their overall magnitude, nor to seeing how they compare with the impediments found in some similar industry, but rather with regard to what are the alternatives relevant to that industry. The primary impediment to the operation of competition is likely to be the existence of restrictive practices, although the firms operating these should be given the chance to demonstrate that these do in fact contribute to static efficiency, X-efficiency and dynamic efficiency. But the alternatives to (for instance) the existing level of barriers to entry (in the form of advertising, patent restrictions, access to capital, and so on) should all be considered; as should the alternatives to the existing pattern of ownership and control. It should be the constant aim of competition policy in this way to utilise the competitive potential of oligopoly and to achieve the three forms of efficiency required, while ensuring the operation of the required constraints.

REFERENCES

1 *Utopia* quoted in J. A. Schumpeter, *History of Economic Analysis* (London, 1954) p. 305.
2 For a survey of the literature see especially B. de G. Fortman, *Theory of Competition Policy* (Amsterdam, 1966); P. W. S. Andrews, *On Competition in Economic Theory* (London, 1966); T. Wilson, 'Restrictive Practices' and J. J. Spengler, 'Role of Competition and Monopoly in Economic Development', both in J. Miller (ed.), *Competition, Cartels and their Regulations* (Amsterdam, 1962).
3 See e.g. G. J. Stigler, 'Perfect Competition, Historically Contemplated', *Journal of Political Economy*, Vol. 55, 1957, pp. 1–17, 14.
4 A. C. Pigou also set the tone for the later welfare economists in his static approach to the problem of competition and resource allocation–see his *Economics of Welfare*, 2nd edn (London, 1924) especially p. 308.
5 *Review of Economic Studies*, Vol. 24, No. 63, 1956–1957, pp. 11–32.
6 'The Theory of Restrictive Trade Practices', *Oxford Economic Papers*, Vol. 17, 1965, pp. 432–49, 436.
7 O. Morganstern, foreword to M. Shubik, *Strategy and Market Structure* (New York, 1959) pp. viii–ix.
8 See P. Hennipman, 'Monopoly: Impediment or Stimulus to Economic Progress' in E. H. Chamberlin (ed.), *Monopoly, Competition and their Regulation* (London, 1954) p. 426.
9 R. Triffin, *Monopolistic Competition and General Equilibrium Theory*

(Harvard, 1940) reprinted 1962, pp. 44–6, 68–70; J. Robinson, 'Imperfect Competition Revisited' reprinted in *Collected Economic Papers* (Oxford, 1960) Vol. II, pp. 222–38, 228.

10 See A. P. Lerner, *The Economics of Control* (New York, 1944) *passim* especially Ch. 6.

11 *Ibid.*, Ch. 9.

12 See T. Wilson, 'The Inadequacy of the Theory of the Firm as a Branch of Welfare Economics', *Oxford Economic Papers*, Vol. 4, 1952, pp. 18–44, especially pp. 34–42 for a damaging critique of this. Chamberlin, it should be stressed in fairness, rejects such a view–*op. cit.*, pp. 258–9, 266.

13 See especially Wilson, *op. cit.* and I. M. D. Little, *A Critique of Welfare Economics*, 2nd edn. (Oxford, 1957).

14 A more recent line of argument has been that the 'tangency solution' is unstable and that it will lead to mergers, that competition policy may interfere with these mergers which are necessary to avoid excess capacity, ergo competition policy is harmful. See D. Dewey, *The Theory of Imperfect Competition, A Radical Reconstruction* (London, 1969) pp. 190, 199. Apart from other criticisms of the theory which will be made below, it should be noted that this conclusion depends on the assumption that costs are unique, known and fixed, that the unique cost curve has a unique optimum, and that mergers are always undertaken to reach that optimum (instead, for example, of being undertaken to prevent disturbance of a potentially unstable situation because each firm has a plant with excess capacity which it wishes to avoid rationalising, seeking security rather than profit maximisation).

15 See especially J. Johnston, 'Statistical Cost Functions in Electricity Supply', *Oxford Economic Papers*, Vol. 4, 1952, pp. 68–103, and references cited therein; A. L. Minkes, 'The Paint Industry in Great Britain', *Journal of Industrial Economics*, Vol. 3, 1954–1955, pp. 144–70; W. J. Eikman and G. E. Guthrie, 'The Shape of the Average Cost Curve', *American Economic Review*, Vol. 42, 1952, pp. 832–8; J. Johnston, *Statistical Cost Analysis* (London, 1960). See also R. S. Koot and D. A. Walker, 'Short-Run Cost Functions of a Multi-Product Firm', *Journal of Industrial Economics*, Vol. 18, 1970, pp. 118–28. Further references are cited below. In citing empirical studies the intention has been to establish a basis for statements rather than to exhaust all possible references.

16 J. S. Earley, 'Recent Developments in Cost Accounting and the Marginal Analysis', *Journal of Political Economy*, Vol. 63, 1955, pp. 227–42; 'Marginal Policies of "Excellently" Managed Companies', *American Economic Review*, Vol. 46, 1956, pp. 44–70.

17 These firms were operating under a restrictive agreement and simply accepted the price fixed, without any very clear reference to costs, by the cartel. Without the prop of the cartel they might go as far as average costing, or simply follow a price leader. Indeed in some circumstances there is much sense in P. W. S. Andrews' suggestion that pricing may depend on an estimate of *a competitors' costs*–see his *Manufacturing Business* (London, 1955) pp. 145–204 *passim*.

18 See R. G. Lipsey, *An Introduction to Positive Economics* (London, 1963) p. 258.

19 The problem of the firm's motivation will also be discussed below in the treatment of oligopoly.

20 See also R. M. Cyert and J. G. March, *A Behavioural Theory of the Firm*

(New Jersey, 1963) p. 8 for a summary of the items excluded from the conventional 'theory of the firm'.

21 Like that of perfect competition, this theory also affords no role to stocks, although these play an important part in the decisions of real firms.

22 See H. R. Edwards, *Competition and Monopoly in the British Soap Industry* (Oxford, 1962) pp. 103–4.

23 This of course does not deter some of our professional colleagues; indeed the claims made by economists in favour of the 'utility' standard after the Second World War are a striking illustration of this.

24 See A. Hunter, 'Product Differentiation and Welfare Economics', *Quarterly Journal of Economics*, Vol. 69, 1955, pp. 533–52.

25 J. M. Clark, 'Competition and the Objectives of Government Policy' in Chamberlin, *op. cit.*, p. 325.

26 E. A. G. Robinson, 'The Problems of Management and the Size of Firms', *Economic Journal*, Vol. 44, 1934, pp. 242–57, 247.

27 Wilson, 'Inadequacy of the Theory of the Firm', p. 25.

28 See Wilson, *op. cit.*, for further criticisms.

29 On this see the valuable survey by N. Ruggles, 'Recent Developments in the Theory of Marginal Cost Pricing', *Review of Economic Studies*, Vol. 17, 1949–1950, pp. 107–26.

30 Andrews, *On Competition in Economic Theory*, pp. 87–8.

31 This is identified and condemned in Wilson, 'Inadequacy of the Theory of the Firm'.

32 'Is there any other subject where the student is led so far astray in his undergraduate work on the implicit understanding that, if he carries on long enough, he may be put right later?' Wilson, 'Restrictive Practices', p. 119. See also Edwards, *op. cit.*, p. 10, n.1. Defence has now been reduced to the sort of level that this kind of theory *may* give good predictions even if it is theoretically and empirically inadequate. Of course so *might* a fruit machine. On the methodological issues involved see Cyert and March, *op. cit.*, pp. 298–311.

33 J. A. Schumpeter, *Theory of Economic Development* (Harvard, 1934) Ch. 6; *Business Cycles* (New York, 1939); *Capitalism, Socialism and Democracy*, 2nd edn (London, 1947) especially Chs 7, 8.

34 There is an ironic contrast between Schumpeter's own approach and his enthusiastic championing of Walras in his olympian *History of Economic Analysis*.

35 Schumpeter, *Capitalism, Socialism and Democracy*, pp. 83–5. Indeed Schumpeter goes on to argue (*op. cit.*, Ch. 8) that restrictive practices, like patents, are positively favourable to innovatory competition.

36 'This [dynamic] kind of competition is as much more effective than the other as a bombardment is in comparison with forcing a door', *ibid.*, p. 84.

37 G. B. Richardson, 'Price Notification Schemes', *Oxford Economic Papers*, Vol. 19, 1967, pp. 359–69.

38 See especially J. K. Galbraith, *American Capitalism: The Concept of Countervailing Power* (Boston, 1956) especially Ch. 9.

39 This is one of the main themes of the important study by J. Downie, *The Competitive Process* (London, 1958).

40 *Ibid.*, Ch. 6.

41 On the complex of motives of a firm see especially Cyert and March, *op. cit.*; H. A. Simon, 'Theories of Decision-Making in Economics and Behavioural Sciences', *American Economic Review*, Vol. 49, 1959,

pp. 253–83, 262–5; R. Marris, *The Economic Theory of 'Managerial' Capitalism* (London, 1964); and A. Berle, 'The Impact of the Corporation on Classical Economic Theory', *Quarterly Journal of Economics*, Vol. 79, 1965, pp. 25–40.

42 See especially J. Jewkes, D. Sawers and R. Stillerman, *The Sources of Invention* (London, 1958).

43 See C. I. Barnard, 'A National Science Policy', *Scientific American*, Vol. 197, No. 5, November 1957, pp. 46–9; R. R. Nelson, 'The Simple Economics of Basic Scientific Research', *Journal of Political Economy*, Vol. 67, 1959, pp. 297–306, 297, 302.

44 See S. Melman, 'The Impact of the Patent System on Research' cited in Spengler, *op. cit.*, p. 54; see also F. Machlup, 'An Economic Review of the Patent System', in *ibid.*, p. 44.

45 See F. M. Scherer, 'Firm Size, Market Structure, Opportunity, and the Output of Patented Inventions', *American Economic Review*, Vol. 55, 1965, pp. 1097–125.

46 See Nelson, *op. cit.*, pp. 302–4.

47 Schumpeter, *Business Cycles*, Vol. I, pp. 8–9, 84–192, especially pp. 84–6.

48 Nelson, *op. cit.*, pp. 302–3; W. R. Maclaurin, 'The Sequence from Invention to Innovation and its Relation to Economic Growth', *Quarterly Journal of Economics*, Vol. 67, 1953, pp. 97–111; 'The Process of Technological Innovation', *American Economic Review*, Vol. 40, 1950, pp. 90–112; 'Patents, Technological Progress–A Study of Television', *Journal of Political Economy*, Vol. 58, 1950, pp. 142–57.

49 This problem is familiar in Britain in connection with studies which have arisen out of the original concept of the 'Macmillan Gap'. See also C. F. Carter and B. R. Williams, *Industry and Technical Progress* (London, 1957) pp. 136–53.

50 *Ibid.*, pp. 72–5.

51 J. W. Markham, 'Market Structure, Business Conduct and Innovation', *American Economic Review*, Vol. 55, *Papers and Proceedings*, 1965, pp. 323–32, 328.

52 This point is made strongly by Schumpeter, *Capitalism, Socialism and Democracy*, p. 83.

53 *Ibid.*, pp. 104–5; Galbraith, *op. cit.*, pp. 86–8; J. M. Clark, 'Competition: Static Models and Dynamic Aspects', *American Economic Review*, Vol. 45, *Supplement*, 1955, pp. 450–62, 456–7.

54 J. M. Clark, 'Towards a Concept of Workable Competition', reprinted in A.E.A., *Readings in the Social Control of Industry* (Philadelphia, 1942) pp. 452–75.

55 See bibliographies appended to S. H. Sosnick, 'A Critique of Concepts of Workable Competition', *Quarterly Journal of Economics*, Vol. 72, 1958, pp. 380–423; and 'Towards a Concrete Concept of Effective Competition', *American Journal of Agricultural Economics*, Vol. 50, 1968, pp. 827–53.

56 A typical example of this is N. H. Leyland, 'Competition in the Court', *Oxford Economic Papers*, Vol. 17, 1965, pp. 461–7.

57 See e.g. Sosnick, 'A Critique', pp. 383, 387. However, the same author does quite clearly distinguish between the relative and absolute versions later in the article (pp. 402–3). See also the distinctions broached in C. Kaysen and D. F. Turner, *Antitrust Policy* (Harvard, 1959) pp. 81–2.

58 Sosnick, *op. cit.*, pp. 389–91.

59 This is strikingly apparent to anyone reading the transcripts of the *Permanent Magnets* case. See separately published case studies.

60 *Op. cit.*, pp. 386–91. Lest the discussion here should seem particularly critical of Sosnick it should be stressed that this writer is cited because he provides the best summary of the literature of workable competition. He himself is far from uncritical of the approach, as the title of his 1958 article and the quotation below (p. 108) indicate. Moreover, the treatment in his 1968 article ('Towards a Concrete Concept') is even more critical, although the criteria therein specified are still very vulnerable to the kind of criticisms offered here.

61 Some writers (see especially Kaysen and Turner, *op. cit.*) while recognising the difficulties of evaluating conduct and performance, and indeed stressing these, believe that the correct approach is to concentrate on market power–essentially on structure.

62 See O. E. Williamson, 'Hierarchical Control and Optimum Firm Size' reprinted in D. Needham (ed.), *Readings in the Economics of Industrial Organisation* (London, 1970) pp. 89–109.

63 On this see Wilson, 'Restrictive Practices', p. 118; and Kaysen and Turner, *op. cit.*, p. 62. In any case, when following the British procedure, it is quite impossible to establish accurately the profitability of one product of a multi-product firm especially when this is an insignificant part of turnover.

64 Thus the Prices and Incomes Board was critical of 'excessive variety' in bread. Cmnd. 2760, 1965, pp. 12–14.

65 Hunter, *loc. cit.*

66 S. Sosnick, 'Operational Criteria for Evaluating Market Performance' in P. Farris (ed.), *Market Structure Research* (Iowa, 1964) p. 98.

67 Sosnick, 'Towards a Concrete Concept', p. 842.

68 'A Critique', pp. 397–8.

69 See also M. S. Massel, *Competition and Monopoly, Legal and Economic Issues* (Washington, 1962) p. 221. See also Kaysen and Turner, *op. cit.*, pp. 54–5 who point out that it is not possible to evaluate 'performance' and 'progressiveness'. There are difficulties of finding a comparable industry and of being sure that it is not a poor performer, there is a lack of disinterested experts, and in any case economic analysis does not provide any framework for evaluating 'progressiveness'. In addition they ask how are relative weights to be assigned to 'progressiveness' and 'efficiency'. They also find (*op. cit.*, pp. 56–8) such concepts as 'fairness' even more nebulous.

70 See, for instance, The U.S.A. Attorney General's Committee on Anti-Trust Laws, 'Workable Competition' reprinted in A. Hunter (ed.) *Monopoly and Competition* (London, 1969) pp. 71–91.

71 See Edwards, *op. cit.*, p. 116 for details of this.

72 G. J. Stigler, 'Report on Antitrust Policy: Discussion', *American Economic Review*, Vol. 46, 1956, p. 504; see also A. Silberston, 'Price Behaviour of Firms', *Economic Journal*, Vol. 80, 1970, p. 524, who seems to imply a similar view.

73 It is hardly satisfactory to say that 'the maintenance of competition predominates as a policy objective on account of its presumptive efficiency' (A. Hunter, *Competition and the Law*, London, 1966, p. 23) and leave the matter at that. This is to jump the gun indeed. *If* we want efficiency (and this requires a judgement), *then* we have to ask ourselves whether competition achieves this.

74 See Spengler, *op. cit.*, pp. 8–17.
75 J. M. Clark, *Competition as a Dynamic Process* (Washington, 1961) p. 64.
76 Dewey, *op. cit.*, p. 198; Cyert and March, *op. cit.*, pp. 295–6.
77 It should be noted that this is a proposition distinct from that advanced by some writers (e.g. G. B. Richardson) that uncertainty leads to resource misallocation via waste.
78 See e.g. K. E. Boulding, *Principles of Economic Policy* (Englewood Cliffs, 1959) p. 19.
79 An alternative approach is to be found in C. E. Ferguson, *A Macro-economic Theory of Workable Competition* (Duke, 1964) which follows the targets/instruments approach of J. Tinbergen's *Economic Policy: Principles and Design* (Amsterdam, 1956). This takes into account such targets of economic policy as employment and price stability, which are largely ignored here, and which, if the British experience under the 1956 Act is anything to go by, a micro-economic approach cannot really accommodate. But the macro-economic approach advocated in Ferguson's interesting book is not more free from constraints than the micro-economic one adopted here (see Ferguson, *op. cit.*, especially pp. 63–5); it is innocent of any theory of competition at all, as the term is normally understood. Perhaps most seriously, the author seems to adopt the exceedingly *simpliste* view that investment automatically produces growth, whereas those adopting a micro-economic approach stress the nature of the competitive environment in which investment is made. (For criticism of the simple equation of investment and growth see in particular H. G. Johnson, 'A Catarrh of Economists?', *Encounter*, Vol. 30, No. 5, May 1968, pp. 50–4.)
80 It is perhaps worth emphasising that 'hypothetical compensation' is both theoretically unsatisfactory and non-operational. See Little, *op. cit.*, pp. 96–116, 122–5.
81 Even without this constraint such a problem would be covered by the value judgement above, that the sectional nature of its procedure should not act as a bar to competition policy.
82 This point has been made by G. C. Allen, *Monopoly and Restrictive Practices* (London, 1968) p. 33, and by T. Wilson.
83 See E. J. Mishan, *The Costs of Economic Growth* (London, 1967). Dr. Mishan would not of course accept the welfare judgements made throughout this chapter; but without accepting the sweeping assertions of this author it is still possible to recognise that 'conservation' may cover a wide field indeed.
84 See especially J. E. Cairnes, 'Our Financial Burthen', *Victoria Magazine*, Vol. 31, 1864, pp. 385–95, 392–4, for clear articulation of a view often implicit in classical economic writing.
85 However, a small entry barrier deriving from goodwill is judged desirable below, in order to produce a degree of stability.
86 The apparatus used here is essentially that developed in Edwards, *op. cit.*, Pt I, which itself may be seen as stemming from Andrews, *Manufacturing Business*.
87 See especially the references to the work of J. Johnston given above.
88 See Silberston, *op. cit.*, pp. 526–7. In fact it seems likely that the high price does not even adequately cover costs in the early stages of development—hence the industrial view that new products 'have to go with a basis of sausage-making'.

89 G. J. Stigler, 'The Economies of Scale' reprinted in Needham, *op. cit.*, pp. 110–28.
90 See J. Haldi and D. Whitcomb, 'Economies of Scale in Industrial Plants' in *ibid.*, pp. 74–88.
91 See Williamson, *op. cit.*
92 See Haldi and Whitcomb, *op. cit.*, p. 87.
93 Various other possible explanations are available, including obsolescence in big firms, economies relating to plant rather than firm, adaptability and ability to specialise of small firms. See Andrews, *Manufacturing Business*, pp. 274–85.
94 See Edwards, *op. cit.*, pp. 20–4, 25–32, 32–7, 78, 88–94.
95 D. P. O'Brien and D. Swann, *Information Agreements, Competition and Efficiency* (London, 1969) p. 112.
96 H. Leibenstein, 'Allocative Efficiency vs X-efficiency', *American Economic Review*, Vol. 56, 1966, pp. 392–415.
97 The essential point here is that differences in costs with a given technology are involved: thus X-efficiency can cover under its broad 'organisational' heading the combination of factors, the gathering and use of available technical knowledge, and a host of other elements.
98 *Ibid.*
99 The statistical material on which this contention is based is extremely dubious: but the qualitative judgement of those with experience of working in and studying industry would certainly confirm his view. Moreover, it is perhaps preferable to *attempt* some quantitative evaluations than to make bald assertions of the kind favoured by those taking the opposite view, e.g. R. F. Harrod, *Economic Essays* (London, 1952) p. 131.
100 Cyert and March, *op. cit.*, pp. 36–8 and *passim.*
101 See the summary of evidence collected by the Monopolies Commission in Edwards, *op. cit.*, p. 68.
102 See the instance of 'Babycham' sited in Marris, *op. cit.*, pp. 140–1.
103 See G. C. Archibald, ' "Large" and "Small" Numbers in the Theory of the Firm' reprinted in Needham, *op. cit.*, pp. 164–70. The idea is valid although forcing the argument into the terms of neoclassical price theory is not very useful.
104 Edwards, *op. cit.*, p. 25 points out that this is also necessary if the idea of market shares is to have any meaning.
105 A. G. Papandreou, 'Market Structure and Monopoly Power', *American Economic Review*, Vol. 39, 1949, pp. 883 97.
106 See A. G. Papandreou and J. T. Wheeler, *Competition and its Regulation* (Englewood Cliffs, 1960) pp. 22–30ff. See also N. Kaldor, *Essays on Value and Distribution* (London, 1960) Vol. I, p. 64; and R. L. Bishop, 'Elasticities, Cross-elasticities and Market Relationships', *American Economic Review*, Vol. 42, 1952, pp. 779–803.
107 J. Robinson, *Economics of Imperfect Competition*, reprinted (London, 1948) p. 17.
108 Nevertheless it is true that some agreements have not contained an important producer of the product or products which are the subject of the agreement. However, the important outsider is usually clearly identifiable either as an individual (Crittall in the *Metal Windows* case) or as a group (the small battery makers) since the proceedings and framework of the agreement constantly reflect the outside threat.

109 As in the later versions of imperfect competition analysis.

110 A. Cournot, *Researches into the Mathematical Principles of the Theory of Wealth*, trans. Bacon (New York, 1897); J. Bertrand, 'Théorie Mathematique de la Richesse Sociale', *Journal des Savants*, 1883.

111 R. L. Hall and C. J. Hitch, 'Price Theory and Business Behaviour' reprinted in T. Wilson and P. W. S. Andrews (ed.), *Oxford Studies in the Price Mechanism* (Oxford, 1951) pp. 107–38; P. M. Sweezy, 'Demand under Conditions of Oligopoly', *Journal of Political Economy*, Vol. 47, 1939, pp. 568–73.

112 See W. Fellner, *Competition Among the Few* (New York, 1949) pp. 181–3.

113 G. J. Stigler, 'The Kinky Oligopoly Demand Curve and Rigid Prices', *Journal of Political Economy*, Vol. 55, 1947, pp. 432–49 reprinted in A.E.A., *Readings in Price Theory* (London, 1953) pp. 410–39.

114 K. J. Cohen and R. M. Cyert, *Theory of the Firm: Resource Allocation in a Market Economy* (Englewood Cliffs, 1965) pp. 249–54.

115 F. Modigliani, 'New Developments on the Oligopoly Front' reprinted in Needham, *op. cit.*, pp. 194–213.

116 P. Sylos-Labini, *Oligopoly and Technical Progress* (Harvard, 1969). See also Silberston, *op. cit.*, pp. 521–2, and Edwards, *op. cit.*, pp. 82–3. As Modigliani (*op. cit.*, p. 196) has noted, H. R. Edwards anticipated many of the conclusions of Sylos-Labini and Bain in his article 'Price Formation in Manufacturing Industry and Excess Capacity', *Oxford Economic Papers*, Vol. 7, 1955, pp. 194–218, which in turn developed the analysis of Andrews' *Manufacturing Business*.

117 J. S. Bain, *Barriers to New Competition* (Cambridge, 1956).

118 M. Shubik, *Strategy and Market Structure* (New York, 1959).

119 London, 1949.

120 *Competition and Monopoly*.

121 See *ibid.*, Ch. 4 for an attempt to solve this problem.

122 See J. Robinson, *Collected Economic Papers*, Vol. II, p. 228.

123 Stigler, 'The Kinky Oligopoly Demand Curve', pp. 431–4.

124 On this see O'Brien and Swann, *op. cit.*, pp. 115–17.

125 *Ibid.*, pp. 120–3.

126 Shubik, *op. cit.*, pp. 293–6; see also O'Brien and Swann, *op. cit.*, p. 118.

127 Shubik, *op. cit.*, p. 308.

128 Downie, *op. cit.*, pp. 109–10.

129 *Ibid.*, p. 119. However, the same author's conclusion (*op. cit.*, p. 124) that price competition is undesirable under such circumstances is less persuasive as it may be an important means of righting the disequilibrium. Nevertheless, given disequilibrium and instability, the consideration, noted above, that the largest rather than the most efficient are the most likely to survive, is important.

130 Richardson, 'Restrictive Trade Practices', p. 444. Edwards (*op. cit.*, pp. 40–6) has also stressed the relative speed of demand transfer compared with investment realisation. Conventional theory has tended to concentrate on the equilibrium of the firm rather than the group–see Andrews, *On Competition*, p. 18.

131 It has already been argued that the profit maximisation assumption is neither realistic nor particularly useful (see above; see also O'Brien and Swann, *op. cit.*, p. 112). As Fortman has pointed out, 'Under perfect competition profit maximisation is the only thing producers can try to do. It is a condition of survival to them. But in other market structures they

have the possibility of employing an individual business strategy,' *op. cit.*, p. 68. See also Papandreou and Wheeler, *op. cit.*, p. 94.

132 'The goals of a business firm are a series of more or less independent constraints imposed on the organisation through a process of bargaining among potential coalition members and elaborated over time in response to short run pressures.' Cyert and March, *op. cit.*, p. 43.

133 See W. J. Baumol, *Business Behaviour and Growth* (New York, 1959).

134 This is particularly stressed in K. W. Rothschild, 'Price Theory and Oligopoly', *Economic Journal*, Vol. 57, 1947, pp. 299–320, although it would not be accurate to regard the treatment therein as of the single-motive variety.

135 See R. M. Cyert, 'Oligopoly, Price Behaviour and the Business Cycle', *Journal of Political Economy*, Vol. 63, 1955, pp. 41–51. Cyert's work does not remove this possibility because: (1) in large firms changes in *motives* may take a long time to be reflected in price, having a previous impact on other micro-economic variables; (2) *price* data · is highly misleading because oligopolistic 'price' competition most often breaks out in the form of *discounts*; (3) a certain amount of oligopolistic 'price' competition is in the form of tenders; (4) the existence of organisational slack, on which Cyert's work has laid such illuminating emphasis, means that motives can change without this being reflected in published prices.

136 See G. Katona, *Psychological Analysis of Economic Behaviour* (New York, 1951).

137 Cyert and March, *op. cit.*, pp. 40–3.

138 This explains why ingenious computer simulations of oligopoly situations (see e.g. Cyert and March, *op. cit.*, pp. 312–25; Cohen and Cyert, *op. cit.*, pp. 339–82) produce only the general conclusion that in any given situation a firm may respond in various ways.

139 On some of the difficulties involved see M. Shubik, 'Objective Functions and Models of Corporate Optimisation', *Quarterly Journal of Economics*, Vol. 75, 1961, pp. 345–75.

140 See Richardson, 'Price Notification Schemes'.

141 T. Wilson and C. V. Brown, 'Price Competition under Oligopoly' (unpublished).

142 The argument that Type A price competition will cause uncertainty and thence interfere with investment plans (Richardson, 'Restrictive Trade Practices', p. 445; see also N. Leyland, 'Growth and Competition', *Oxford Economic Papers*, Vol. 16, 1964, pp. 3–7) does not seem very strong *a priori*; it is just as possible to argue that uncertainty will improve resource allocation by making firms more exact in their calculations of costs and returns – or that artificially created certainty may bring about over-investment unless co-ordination is added to price-fixing.

143 J. S. Bain, 'A Note on Pricing in Monopoly and Oligopoly', *American Economic Review*, Vol. 39, 1949, pp. 448–64; 'Economies of scale, concentration, and the conditions of entry in twenty manufacturing industries', *American Economic Review*, Vol. 44, 1954, pp. 15–39; *Barriers to New Competition*; 'Conditions of Entry and the Emergence of Monopoly' in Chamberlin, *op. cit.*, pp. 215–41.

144 Andrews, *On Competition*, p. 16; the approach is, however, perhaps best formulated in Edwards, *op. cit.*, p. 68ff and in E. Brunner, 'A note on Potential Competition', *Journal of Industrial Economics*, Vol. 9, 1961, pp. 248–50. Andrews makes the interesting point that quite a small scale of

entry may be viable for firms already established elsewhere, through the spreading of overheads (*op. cit.*, p. 79). See also H. E. Hines, 'Effectiveness of Entry by Already Established Firms', *Quarterly Journal of Economics* Vol. 71, 1957, pp. 132–50.

145 See, however, the interesting possibility (though it is little more) suggested by Richardson ('Restrictive Trade Practices', pp. 446–7) that a newcomer may be able to enter through securing better capacity utilisation than existing firms. The difficulty obviously arises with this argument that, firstly, the existing firms are unlikely to allow the entrant to pursue a price policy which will achieve this, and, secondly, cost curves are unlikely to be of a shape which would make this a real possibility.

146 This has been stressed by Edwards (*op. cit.*, p. 18ff, especially pp. 27–31) who sees it as an important stabilising force.

147 Barriers to entry may also be associated indirectly with patents through the latter financing cost-reducing and product-improving research–see D. P. O'Brien, 'Patent Protection and Competition in Polyamide and Polyester Fibre Manufacture' *Journal of Industrial Economics*, Vol. 12, 1964, pp. 224–35.

148 See Hines, *op. cit.*, p. 149. Ironically enough then a successful competition policy, which has the effect of increasing uncertainty within an industry, *may* also reinforce barriers to entry; but, as Hines points out, the *potentiality* of entry remains and this is likely to affect the behaviour of firms within the industry. It may favourably affect all kinds of competition within the industry.

149 See especially Edwards, *op. cit.*, pp. 108–10.

150 Indeed conventional marginalist theory (see the diagram used by Edwards, *op. cit.*, pp. 108–9) seems to offer a more coherent reason for thinking that the most efficient will determine price–*except* that, since entrepreneurs do not have the kind of information on their cost structure posited by such theory, and market shares have yet to be determined (a difficulty shared by both 'average cost' and neoclassical theory), the behaviour which will seem most intuitively acceptable to the entrepreneur will be that of charging a higher price than the minimum acceptable to him.

151 See Wilson, 'Restrictive Practices', pp. 130–2. In the *Metal Windows* case it seems that price was not set to accommodate the most inefficient; and though the cement producers did not exclude extreme values, the price arrived was in relation to *all* costs. In both the *Carpets* and *Magnets* cases the marginal firms simply did not *know* the relationship of the general price to their particular costs; and in the *Tile* case the price seems (for long) to have been sufficient to accommodate all but the marginal producers of fireplace tiles.

152 Downie, *op. cit.*, pp. 91–2; Edwards, *op. cit.*, pp. 111–12.

153 See, however, Downie, *op. cit.*, pp. 12–14.

154 See also Rothschild, *op. cit.* reprinted in A.E.A., *Readings in Price Theory*, pp. 440–64, 453.

155 See especially F. M. Scherer, *op. cit.*, and 'Market Structure and the Employment of Scientists and Engineers', *American Economic Review*, Vol. 57, 1967, pp. 524–31; W. R. Maclaurin, *Innovation and Invention in the Radio Industry* (New York, 1949); Hennipman, *op. cit.*

156 Allen, *op. cit.*, p. 18.

157 As for instance in Britain in the 1930s. Historically the rise of trade unions may also have played a part.
158 Joint profit maximisation *could* follow this as a second stage–see Fellner, *op. cit.*, p. 33.
159 See especially N. R. Collins and L. E. Preston, 'The Size Structure of the Largest Industrial Firms', *American Economic Review*, Vol. 51, 1961, pp. 986–1011.
160 See D. Needham, *Economic Analysis and Industrial Structure* (London, 1969), Chs 8, 9; and G. D. Newbould, *Management and Merger Activity* (London, 1970).
161 Thus the takeover of Pressed-Steel by B.M.C. was arguably the main cause of the loss of independence of both Rover and Jaguar.
162 See E. Penrose, *The Theory of the Growth of the Firm* (Oxford, 1963) pp. 144–5; and M. Gort, *Diversification and Integration in American Industry* (Princeton, 1962) p. 85.
163 The reasons generally given include stability, quality of the product, finance of R & D, technical co-operation, employment, exports, counter-vailing power, prevention of excessive concentration, and economies of scale through standardisation. For a summary and damaging critique of these see Wilson, 'Restrictive Practices', pp. 142–61. A number of such reasons were advanced in connection with the restrictive practices examined in the course of this study: and examination of them on their merits is deferred until the appropriate sections below.
164 See also Clark in Chamberlin, *op. cit.*, pp. 327–8.
165 As implied in T. Wilson, 'A Review of Policies on Monopolies, Mergers and Restrictive Practices' in J. B. Heath (ed.), *Papers and Reports of International Conference on Monopolies, Mergers and Restrictive Practices at Cambridge, 1969* (London, 1971) pp. 68–9.
166 See Monopolies Commission, *Report on the Supply of Man-Made Cellulosic Fibres*, 1968, p. 79.

Chapter 4

THE IMPACT OF THE LEGISLATION

It is clearly not easy to oblige businessmen to compete if they object to doing so. Those brought up in an environment where restrictive practices were the rule are likely to be more actively concerned with circumventing the intentions of the law than in co-operating in its application. This is especially so when they remain unconvinced that free competition is in the public interest, just as they are sure that it is contrary to their own.

G. C. Allen, *Monopoly and Restrictive Practices* (London, 1968)

Read not to contradict and confute, nor to believe and take for granted, nor to find talk and discourse, but to weigh and consider.

Sir Francis Bacon, *Of Studies*, 1597

In 1969 the authors undertook a large-scale research project, the aim of which was to try to assess the effect of the 1956 Restrictive Trade Practices Act on British industry. As indicated in the Introduction this is a formidable task which would require an army of research workers and a very large fund of money. In practice what was accomplished was an intensive investigation of 18 industries together with a concurrent investigation at a less intensive level of 22 more. The 18 major case studies are listed below in Table 4.1 and against each is indicated whether the agreement was upheld by the Court, struck down by it or whether the parties thereto decided to abandon it.

Within the confines of this volume we have not been able to report the detailed studies of the major industries. These have, however, been published separately and are available from the Department of Economics, Loughborough University of Technology. What follows is an assessment of the impact of the legislation based in part on these eighteen studies and the lessons to be drawn from this assessment. The description of the individual industries is necessarily allusive and the interested (or sceptical) reader will find it necessary to consult the supplementary volume of case studies. In Table 4.2 we list the minor case study industries.[1] As indicated in our Introduction these have not been written up individually

TABLE 4.1 Major Case Study Industries

Cement	Upheld by the Court
Standard Metal Windows	,,
Permanent Magnets	,,
Glazed Tiles	,,
Transformers	Struck down by the Court
Carpets	,,
Glass Containers	,,
Wire Rope	,,
Tyre Distribution	,,
Bread	,,
Roadstone	Abandoned without contest before the Court
Sanitary Ware	,,
Electric Motors	,,
Surgical Dressings	,,
Electric Cables	,,
Baths	,,
Automotive Batteries	,,
Steel Drums	,,

and their main function was to broaden the compass of our study; the results we derived from them helped in framing the broad conclusions contained in this chapter.

Although forty case studies do not provide the basis for an infallible overall assessment, we believe the size of the sample, together with the diversity of the industries within it, gives grounds for confidence that the picture we now present is broadly indicative of what happened, at least up to 1971 when our study ended. The work of J. B. Heath has provided useful background data and, of course, the Registrar's Reports provide a statistical picture of legal events.

TABLE 4.2 Minor Case Study Industries

Pipes (sewage and drainage)	Polythene film
Galvanised tanks	Black bolts and nuts
Wire mesh	Silica and general firebricks
Leavers' lace	Tyre mileage
Switchgear (sold to Area Boards)	Metal bedsteads
Chocolates and sweets	Electric lamps (filament exceeding 28 volts, discharge and fluorescent)
Sand and gravel	Gas meters
Electric meters	Jute spinning and weaving
Hard fibre rope and twine	Paper bags
Aluminium castings	Steel arches and light rails (for mining)
Files and hacksaws	Watertube boilers

K

The purpose of this chapter is threefold. The first part attempts to summarise our impressions, based not only on the major but also the minor studies, of the general pattern of events flowing from the 1956 Act. The second part seeks to show with the aid of the major and minor studies what the effect has been on resource allocation–we are therefore carrying the reader back to the kind of considerations outlined in Chapter 3. The final section contains our conclusions and recommendations as to the adequacy of, and changes needed in, British anti-trust law. Also we shall comment on the impact of other branches of legislation upon the competitive process. Some suggestions will also be made about public and private purchasing policy.

I. BROAD PATTERN OF EVENTS FLOWING FROM THE ACT

(i) *The Nature of Agreements*
Before dealing with the actual pattern of events it is relevant to ask what kind of agreements did the Act encounter? Granted that agreements, often operated by trade associations, were well nigh ubiquitous, how inclusive were they? To what extent did the parties to them conform in respect of prices to be charged and the like? Were prices related to costs in some systematic way and in particular did prices reflect the costs of more efficient producers? Were agreements exploitative or protective in character?

(a) *Coverage.* It must be admitted that in only a few industries can it be said that all, or virtually all, producers were party to the relevant agreement. There are three clear cases out of forty–cement, wire rope and Leavers' lace. The latter involved Lace Productions (1948) Limited which effectively acted as a common selling agency. Producers of Leavers' lace sold their output to Lace Productions which determined selling prices. Profits were divided among the producers who were also shareholders.[2] There were also other partial cases. Thus in the case of the very largest transformers all the producers appear to have been members of the Transformer Manufacturers' Association although at the small end of the market (distribution transformers) there were many outsiders. Also in the case of electric cables there were no outside producers of supertension mains, telephone and submarine cable. These latter were products where technology and relatively large fixed and working capital requirements acted as barriers to entry, although the preference of public purchasers for the products of established firms may also have played a role.

(b) *Effectiveness*. Does this mean that agreements were a good deal less effective than has been thought? The answer seems to be in the negative. Although few industries were such that 100 per cent of the industry's domestic sales emanated from agreement members, it is also true to say that the overwhelming proportion did. The figure was often in the 80 per cent plus range–see Table 4.3.[3] An additional factor which undoubtedly limited the effectiveness of outside competition was the fact that rings tended to contain most, and often all, the largest and best-known firms; heavy electrical equipment is a case in point.[4] This almost certainly meant that they could command business by virtue of their name and reputation for quality and outsiders would not necessarily have an advantage if they cut prices.[5] It is also tempting to suggest that outsiders may not have presented much of a threat since they may either have followed the ring price or only cut marginally below it. In some cases this was true,[6] but it was not universally so. Thus in the case of the smaller sizes of electric motors and transformers outsiders undercut substantially (although their productive capacity was obviously limited). A case *par excellence* is Brook Motors which undercut small motor agreement prices by as much as 25 per cent and grew fat in the process. But such instances should not be overrated. Market segmentation was also important. In the case of sand and gravel supplies in Central Scotland the large firms tended to be members of associations and only they were capable of dealing with really large contracts. The outsiders who tended to be small were therefore not capable of undermining the price agreement in this segment of the market.[7]

If outside domestic competition was severely limited–and there were many exclusionary devices such as collective exclusive dealing and aggregated rebates designed to keep outsiders at bay–what about imports? On many occasions we have asked buyers about their attitude to imports at this period. Almost invariably their reply indicated that they did not resort to importation. The only two cases which spring to mind which contradict this rule are wire ropes (where shipping companies are in a good position in the normal course of business to buy foreign) and hard fibre ropes (where imports seem to have exerted a restraining influence on price increases).[8] If we ask why imports were so relatively unimportant the answers are many. One was sheer lethargy, although as we will point out the situation is changing and today there are many honourable exceptions. Another was 'buy national' attitudes. But the others are more excusable. Some products are not likely to be transported over long distances. This is true in the case of

TABLE 4.3 Market Shares of Agreement Firms

Products and Sub-Products	%	% Relates To	Year
Woven Carpets	75	U.K. output	1960
Wire Rope–Mining	100	U.K. output	1963
Engineering	100	U.K. output	1963
Locked coil	100	U.K. output	1963
Glass Containers	80	U.K. output	1959
Electric Cable–Submarine	100	U.K. output	1948
Telephone	100	U.K. output	1948
Mains up to 30kV	79	U.K. output	1948
Mains above 30kV	100	U.K. output	1948
Rubber and thermoplastic	76	U.K. output	1948
Cement	100 approx.	U.K. output	1959
Standard Metal Windows	90	U.K. output	1956
Permanent Magnets	75	U.K. output	1960
Leavers' Lace	100	U.K. output	1948
Hard Fibre Cordage	95	U.K. output	1956
Surgical Dressings	95‡	U.K. output	1956
Roadstone	90–100§	U.K. output	1957
Steel Drums	100 approx.	U.K. output	1956
Sanitary Ware	92	U.K. output	1956

Table 4.3 (*contd*)

Products and Sub-Products	%	% Relates To	Year
Black Bolts and Nuts	90	Sales in U.K.†	1959
Electric Lamps–Filament	80	Sales in U.K.	1950
Fluorescent	59	Sales in U.K.	1950
Tiles–Earthenware glazed	91	Sales in U.K.	1962
Enamel	83	Sales in U.K.	1962
Floor	80	Sales in U.K.	1962
Watertube Boilers	75	Sales in U.K.	1959
Electric Motors–Small	63	Home sales	1952
Large	88	Home sales	1952
Tyre Mileage	100	Home sales	1955
Transformers–Small	75	Home plus export sales*	1952
Large	95	Home plus export sales*	1952
Jute–Spinning	96	U.K. capacity	1962
Weaving	85	U.K. capacity	1962

* Home sales relates to sales by U.K. firms in the United Kingdom.
† Sales in the United Kingdom relates to sales, from all sources, in the United Kingdom.
‡ Estimated.
§ Typical range in regional markets.

roadstone. It is not correct to say that there is no foreign trade in roadstone but the high weight in relation to value severely limits trade possibilities. Bulk in relation to value is an obvious inhibitor of trade in products such as steel drums. Another factor is international cartels. Thus in the case of electric cable we have been informed that imports from North America were precluded on grounds of price but in the case of European supplies the activities of the International Cable Development Corporation (I.C.D.C.) were highly relevant. Other factors were tariffs and differing technical standards. There were also a whole series of special factors. Thus in the case of jute goods the Dundee industry enjoyed the protection of Jute Control–a branch of the Board of Trade and then D.T.I. In the case of bread the need for freshness was an inhibiting factor. In the case of cement quality differences, difficulties about ensuring reliability of supply together with the long runs of imports necessary to justify investment in transport equipment militated against resort to foreign supplies.

(c) *Enforcement*. Granted then that outside competition was muted, is it possible that signatories to agreements were themselves less than honourable when they came to operate them? We have on several occasions been invited to accept the notion that price agreements having been agreed, the ink was scarcely dry before the parties were undermining them.[9] We reject this view almost entirely. It stems in our estimation from an understandable but actually unwarranted suspicion of other people's intentions. The evidence clearly indicates that in the main agreements were operated honourably. In the case of roadstone we were able to check this by virtue of our analysis of prices tendered over many years. In the case of sanitary ware a similar view was advanced–the favourite description was that price lists were 'cut to ribbons'. There may indeed have been some backsliding but it has been exaggerated–how else is it possible to explain the steep price fall which occurred almost immediately after the agreement was abandoned? Other case studies confirm our conclusion. If we take two cases at random–surgical dressings and metal bedsteads–interviews with purchasing officers in the hospital service have indicated that the prices charged by the Surgical Dressings Manufacturers' Association and the Metal Bedstead Association were rigidly controlled to the last penny. Perhaps the only case which stands up under investigation is paper bags. Here there was an industry consisting of large numbers of small semi-artisanal entrepreneurs and certainly the abolition of the agreement led to no perceptible effect on the level of wholesale prices, although since this data ignores discounts the evidence is not as sound as would be desirable.

(d) *Price determination.* We now turn to the actual determination of prices. Were cartel prices based on costs–more to the point were they based on the costs of the more efficient producers? It is true that in some industries pricing on the basis of the costs of a few more efficient producers was practised.[10] This was true of some wire rope products. Here costs were submitted by a cross-section of the industry and the six lowest were selected and averaged. Any individual costing which was 10 per cent above the straight average was excluded. Then again in the case of small electric motors a weighted average of the six lowest costs was the point of departure for pricing. In the case of transformers a sample of eleven or more producers provided costings and at various times between three and five of the lowest costings were selected and averaged (on a straight basis)–again this was the point of departure for pricing. However, two points are relevant here. Firstly, it is important to stress that such *relatively* commendable systems were hardly the norm–more will be said about that later. Secondly, even the lower cost averaging system was far from perfect. Thus there is no evidence that the firms of accountants who were often appointed to process the costings ever checked to see whether the costings they handled were accurate; the temptation to put some 'water' in them must have been great. Then again even if costs were in the above sense genuine, and only the lowest costings were selected, the system was still open to one very damaging criticism–it did little to check the maintenance of excess capacity. It is possible to explain the likelihood of excess capacity under condition of cartelisation without resort to the kind of dubious argumentation of static allocation theory. It seems highly probable that under such conditions firms will be disposed to maintain excess capacity in order to be able to take advantage of any unexpected increase in demand. Little or no penalty attaches from keeping such capacity in existence provided (a) prices are set to cover the costs so incurred and (b) demand is relatively price inelastic as it often is (i.e. transformers and cement).

We can now return to the point made earlier to the effect that relatively commendable pricing systems were not the norm. A number of case studies have illustrated this. For example, and indeed surprisingly, a number of agreements which found favour with the Court were far from satisfactory. We have drawn attention to this in the case of cement which appears in the separately published case studies. In the case of permanent magnets the Association relied on costings supplied by one firm. In the case of tiles there was no very close relationship between prices and costs. In the case of black bolts and nuts eleven out of forty-four firms were supposed to return costs relating to one hundred products. In practice not all firms complied fully and as a result in some cases as few as two costings were received. Wide variations between costings existed but despite this a straight average was applied. In respect of hundreds of sizes and types no costings existed.

In addition to all this there were many industries where no system of relating prices to costs existed. In the case of carpets prices were arrived at in a mysterious way which did not relate to costings, partly apparently because the accounting systems of the firms were deficient. Then in the case of sand and gravel[11] and roadstone detailed costings do not seem to have entered the picture. The Federation of Wholesale and Multiple Bakers did not introduce a costing exercise until the necessity for justifying its agreement before the Court became apparent.[12] The paper bag industry appears to have been innocent of any costing system; the price list was from time to time revised but no periodic reassessments in the light of current costs of the more efficient appear to have occurred. Some systems quite clearly excluded such considerations from collective deliberations. Thus in the case of glass containers the cost structure of the industry was accepted and prices were set at a level which would generate a weighted profit margin of 10 per cent on costs. In the case of the Large Electric Machine Agreement (i.e. large electric motors) where tender sales were involved prices were determined first by averaging the lowest half of the proposed tenders and later by averaging all proposed tenders. The price agreement operated by the watertube boilermakers was also apparently not based on lowest costings. Rather the parties met to consider tenders and decided who was to be the preferred supplier. The tenders tabled were then opened and the preferred supplier was allowed to reduce his bid to that of the lowest tabled.[13]

(e) *Strategies.* If we ask what motivation lay behind agreements it is possible to distinguish between exploitative and protective strategies. Generally we have concluded that strategies were defensive in intent. Trade associations did not seek to extract the last penny of profit. Rather their *intent* was to secure a reasonable profit and to protect the industry from what they regarded as the deleterious effects of uncertainty and competitive rivalry. There is no doubt that, as a significant number of trade association secretaries have admitted, prices were in many instances set at a level which would protect the less or least efficient. As a result, however modest the *intent* in some cases, *actual resulting prices may have tended towards exploitative levels*. It is perhaps also worth mentioning that in discussions with businessmen we found little if any justification for the kind of agreements which existed in the 1950s. This view was particularly marked in the case of heavy electrical goods.

(ii) *The Initial Impact of the Act*

We can in fact distinguish two possible stages at which an initial impact was possible. The first relates to the period of time surrounding the passing of the Act. Did trade associations decide to abandon rather than register agreements? Did they decide to modify them? The second relates specifically to the period after registration. Did agreements show signs of instability even before the *Yarn Spinners* case?

(a) *Non-registration.* In respect of stage one the late P. W. S. Andrews expressed the view that in some industries trade associations and other bodies elected to abandon agreements rather than to register them. We decided to test this hypothesis by selecting at random sixty agreements existing before 1956. These agreements had not been the subject of an industrial, as opposed to a practice, reference to the Monopolies Commission.[14] We then investigated the Register to see if any of the agreements had not been placed upon it. We found eight cases (i.e. 13·3 per cent of the sample) of non-registration. This is a surprisingly high percentage and suggests that the Act was having an effect even during its inception. It does not follow that these agreements ceased to operate–the parties to them may have decided to go underground. However, at this relatively early stage, when the attitude of the Court was not known, this seems unlikely. Again it could be argued that the agreements which were dropped were those which were regarded as being of little effect; trade associations may have felt they were not worth proceeding with. This is a possibility but we doubt if it was a significant factor. Within our forty case studies we have identified two cases of abandonment before registration. One was in the case of the gas meter producers who decided to abandon the agreement of the Gas Meter Conference on the day the Act came into force. The other was the Electric Lamp Manufacturers'

Association (E.L.M.A.) which ostensibly abandoned the fixing of electric lamp prices in 1956. (We are referring here to price-fixing only and not supporting arrangements such as exclusive dealing. Were we to include the latter then we should, for example, have to take account of the dropping of exclusive dealing by the British Starter Battery Association.)

(b) *Modification.* It is also possible that industries decided to modify agreements in ways which would make them potentially more acceptable to the Court. It should be added at this point that our investigation of agreements on the Register clearly indicates that in 1957 particularly there was a great deal of activity in connection with the drafting and redrafting of agreements. It is well-known that many price agreements in the pre-1956 era were often buttressed by various exclusionary devices. These were obviously necessary since, if the agreements raised the return on capital above competitive levels, entry might thereby have been induced unless exclusionary devices could be deployed to ward off entrants. If we turn to our case studies we can confidently assert that in the case of batteries the exclusive dealing provision was removed although price-fixing remained. This was almost certainly due to the Act and of course it led to a transformation of the competitive situation in the industry as we have sought to show in our separately published case study. Another probable case is that of the hard fibre cord and twine manufacturers who according to the Collective Discrimination report of 1955 operated an aggregated rebate payable only to merchants who confined their purchases to British producers. However, in 1958 the aggregated rebate was dropped.[15] Here then was another sphere where the Act seems to have had an early impact on competition.

There were also other changes which might appear to be 'watering down' but on close inspection seem much more likely to be cases of 'whitewashing'. Thus the Federation of Wholesale and Multiple Bakers switched from a fixed to a recommended price. It gave rise to no practical change although no doubt it sounded better. Whilst on this subject we can also mention the case of the Tyre Trade Register. Although in evidence before the Court its object was said to be the safe fitting of tyres, it is interesting to note that before 1956 the stated objectives made no mention of this aspect. However, the redraft of 1957 did.

Another kind of change has already been referred to in Chapter 2. In a number of industries the home and export aspects of agreements were severed. This allowed the export aspect to be notified to the Board of Trade and for export price-fixing to continue. Perhaps more cynically it could be argued that it enabled the industries to continue to have a forum for the discussion of affairs of mutual interest. Wire ropes, sanitary ware, carpets, tiles and permanent magnets are case study examples (almost certainly they are not the only ones) of hiving off.[16] (The International Cable Development Corporation appears to have been a separate agree-ment–hiving off probably did not arise. Registration would presumably be required and of course it is likely to be a forum for British producers.)

Other changes at this time were really designed to buttress agreements. For example some were recast in the hope of making them more suitable for gateway pleading; this was the case in transformers. In other instances new elements were added such as provisions for the exchange of information. This was a far sighted move and is exemplified in the case of tiles.

Stage two relates specifically to the period after registration. During this period there is some evidence that the Act was already beginning to work in the sense that some agreements demonstrated either a degree, or indeed an increasing degree, of instability which was probably partly the result of an anticipation that a more competitive climate was an inevitability. As is shown by our separately published case studies an example is provided by the Surgical Dressings Manufacturers' Association. The registered agreement contains the rules as adopted on 23 January 1957. However, on 28 February the Association was severely shaken when Smith & Nephew resigned. On 30 December they were followed by Southalls. As a result what was described as a violent price war ensued. The Association had drastically to rethink its system of pricing in face of the fact that some 30 per cent of production was coming from companies outside the Association. In practice the latter was forced to adopt an outside competitor's price list as the basis for trading. The agreement was formally abandoned on 28 February 1959.[17] Another example is cable manufacture. It is quite obvious that various cable associations were losing their grip in the period between registration in 1957 and abandonment in 1959. Thus in 1957 Crompton Parkinson removed its subsidiary Derby Cables from the Cable Makers' Association and from then until the collapse of the agreement in May 1959 the air was increasingly thick with accusations of secret price cuts. Similar things were happening to other associations. From at least 1958 until abandonment in July 1959 the Mains Cable Manufacturers' Association was faced with increasing price instability. The other case which comes to mind is small electric motors. The agreement began to disintegrate in 1958 although it was not formally abandoned until September 1959. We have been led to believe that the agreement began to collapse when signatories began to retaliate against non-signatories.

(iii) *After Termination–The Shorter Run*

We have seen that some agreements were terminated before registration. However, it was really after 1959 (following the *Yarn Spinners* Judgement and in the light of the attitude of the Court during the Presidency of Lord Devlin) that the great bulk of terminations occurred. Strictly speaking some agreements were totally abandoned; others were filleted of all offending matter. What happened after? We should of course note that some agreements having been registered were defended before the Court and the decision to register and fight enabled the Respondents to continue to benefit from the operation of the agreement.[18] Thus the wire rope industry (other than the marine rope section) was able to continue its agreements until 1964. As we know in the majority of cases agreements so defended failed to find favour with the Court. Again we can ask–what happened then?

(a) *The extent of new competition.* In a number of cases the answer is that a competitive or partially competitive situation was established. In what proportion of the cases was this true? To answer this we have to begin by subtracting the six[19] which were upheld. That leaves thirty-four cases. How many of these were ones where the initial reaction after termination was a competitive or partially competitive one? Before we can make our calculations we have to note that batteries became partially competitive following the dropping of exclusive dealing. Also our separately published case studies show that surgical dressings, electric cables and electric motors were becoming competitive before the final abandonment of agreements. (In the case of electric motors and cables competition continued to intensify after abandonment.) Here then are four cases of competition. Looking at the rest of our sample it is, possible to identify perhaps another 17. That totals up to 21, or 61 per cent. This must be regarded as an optimistic figure. A pessimistic one would be 4 plus 14. That is 18, or 53 per cent. The truth probably lies somewhere between these two and towards the bottom end of the range.

Such competition evidenced itself overwhelmingly in the sphere of prices and discounts. There was also some product and service competition. Thus in the case of batteries there was a development of cheaper ranges largely if not totally as a result of new entrants who were often relatively small.

(b) *Price competition.* Price and discount competition was most evident in the case of wire ropes (other than marine), sanitary ware, drain and sewage pipes, electric cables, electric motors and electric meters. Wire rope prices tendered to four large buyers fell by varying amounts – 7 per cent, up to 8 per cent, 21 per cent and 25 per cent. Sanitary ware prices fell by 20 per cent. The price of sewage and drain-pipes fell by 25 per cent. During the period after termination cable prices continued to fall but if we take into account the reductions in the period before termination then the recorded fall was much greater. It was most dramatic in the case of rubber and plastic cable where the price fall was of the order of 25–30 per cent. The price fall in the case of small motors was of the order of 20–25 per cent – again some of this had occurred before abandonment. In the case of electric meters we encountered in the case of one larger buyer a fall of about 15 per cent.

The period from peak to trough varied. In the case of cables the fall was quite intense and much of it occurred in as little as six months. In sanitary ware it took about a year. Electric motors, wire ropes and pipes took about three years. Electric meters, however, was a long drawn out affair over six years. Given the existence of a basic inflationary trend these falls are quite impressive.

Not all industries exhibited this kind of intensive price competition. Thus carpets exhibited a more lively situation but there is no evidence of even a minor collapse in prices. In the case of the Steel Arch and Light Rail Association a dominoe effect was evident. The failure of the wire rope producers to find favour before the Court led to it abandoning its agreement and to the onset of more competitive conditions. In the case of Sheffield trades such as files and hacksaws the termination of agreements still left an identity of basic list prices but discounts were freely given and were flexible. Large buyers expressed themselves as being content with the degree of competition evident in respect of these latter products. In the case of switchgear sold to Area Boards prices before 1960 were said to be identical to the last penny. However, after that date competition was said to have emerged and interviews in 1970 testified to its continuance.

(c) *New entry.* In the short run the origin of competition and price falls was mainly the result of competition between established producers. In the longer term other factors became more important. One was new entrants. The latter were often associated with the introduction of new substitute products–a form of Schumpeterian competition. Another factor in the longer term was imports. Price falls in the short run stemmed from a number of factors. One was the paring down of unduly generous profit margins; for the efficient the protection of the relatively inefficient had been a source of handsome profit margins. Another factor was the search for increased X-efficiency, the latter being defined in the broadest terms. The third factor was probably the decision not to set prices at a level which would provide for the maintenance of excess capacity. Where the 'shake-out' of excess capacity was considerable, it seems likely that it bore particularly heavily on inefficient firms, some of which were squeezed out. In the case of wire rope the impression emerges that some relatively inefficient small firms, in a state of desperation, attempted to spread their overheads by undercutting. These cuts were matched and, given the inelasticity of total demand, they gained nothing in sales volume but experienced losses as prices fell below their relatively high costs. Sometimes the classical forces may have operated and firms may have left the market or totally ceased to trade. But sometimes, and wire rope seems to have exemplified this also, they were quickly bought out, possibly having offered themselves for takeover. British Ropes seems to have acted as public benefactor, the word public being here taken to refer to the producer interest. It is also necessary to note that sometimes the general state of demand at the time helped the price falls along. Some part of these price falls may have been due to short term instability arising out of a lack of experience in independent pricing strategy. As we have pointed out in our separately published case studies in many industries price policies had previously been determined collectively.

(d) *Resistance to competition–information agreements.* It is obvious that if we take the pessimistic figure of 53 per cent of the 34 cases as those exhibiting a competitive response, then it follows that anti-competitive devices were at work on a substantial scale. Undoubtedly the most important of these was the information agreement. Indeed in 17 out of 34 industries information agreements were introduced–i.e. 50 per cent. These are listed in Table 4.4. A number of points of explanation are needed. Firstly, there is no conflict between the point that 53 per cent of cases were competitive and the point that 50 per cent contained information

TABLE 4.4   Case Study Industries where Informational Arrangements followed the Termination of Formal Agreements*

Wire Rope–Marine variety
Transformers
Glass Containers
Roadstone–Area arrangements
Electric Cables–Three agreements
Electric Motors–Large and fractional horsepower varieties
Batteries–Vehicle
Galvanised Tanks
Tyre Mileage
Electric Lamps–Filament exceeding 28 volts
                        Discharge and fluorescent
Sand and Gravel–Area arrangements
Jute Spinning and Weaving
Firebricks–Silica and general varieties
Steel Drums
Surgical Dressings
Bread
Aluminium Castings

* Two other agreements could be added to this list. One relates to standard metal windows where, following the demise of the upheld agreement, apart from the circulation of price lists information is disseminated about sales and output of participants. Given the pattern of concentration it seems that the identity of the firms to which the data relates can be ascertained. In the case of sanitary ware information is circulated concerning market shares; exactly when this arrangement came into existence we could not ascertain.

agreements. Competitive includes partially competitive and some industries were substantially or significantly competitive even though an information agreement may have affected a part of the industry. A good example of this is afforded by wire ropes. Secondly, 50 per cent is a very significant figure, if paralleled in industry generally it suggests that the 1956 Act was subverted on a very considerable scale. Thirdly, the figure of 50 per cent is undoubtedly a minimum one since industry has not been too anxious to reveal the existence of such agreements even though they are overwhelmingly a thing of the past. It follows that we may not have located every case.[20] Moreover, the 50 per cent ignores the more informal kind of information agreement whereby the telephone is used to check phantom competition. We refer to this in our separately published study of carpets. Incidentally in a few cases there was a fairly quick switch from competition to information agreements. This was so in electric cables and surgical dressings and therefore they make an appearance in Table 4.4.

In some cases information agreements came into being more or less simultaneously with the abandonment of agreements but in others they pre-dated abandonment. This was, for example, the case in galvanised tanks, tyre mileage and apparently large electric motors. A most interesting feature arises in connection with their coverage. In some cases this seems to have been greater than in the case of the previous formal price fixing arrangements. This was so in the case of transformers. It was also true in the case of electric lamps. Thus the Monopolies Commission has pointed out that although E.L.M.A. was a tight ring, there were in 1950 important producers outside it who supplied 20 per cent of filament lamps and 41 per cent of fluorescent lamps. But in 1966 the proportion supplied by firms who were not members of the successor body (the Electric Lamp Industry Council Limited–E.L.I.C.) or were not controlled by E.L.I.C. members, was only 3 per cent.[21] Large electric motors seems a further possible case; thus Laurence, Scott and Electromotors, an important producer, were outside the Large Electric Machine Agreement but joined the subsequent Large Electric Motor Conference. If we ask why this happened we do not have to look far for an answer. Whilst there was a firmly based price-fixing agreement some firms could profit by under-cutting it. Indeed the agreement indicated to outsiders just how much they needed to quote down to just undercut ring producers. When the agreement was dissolved outsiders were faced with the disappearance of this convenience and indeed the prospect of instability. Their response therefore was to rush in and prop the industry price level up.

Agreements were largely concerned with price in its broadest sense. That is to say they often involved the reporting by individual firms to a bureau, and the subsequent dissemination by the bureau to the industry, of price lists and discounts, together with changes therein. This was the case in galvanised tanks. Prices also included tender bids (these were notified in the case of tyre mileage). Where selling involved the possibility of making quotations at other than normal terms, such special quotations were often notifiable. This was the case in jute spinning and weaving. The information bureau was notified of, and circulated, current price lists but where a party wished to depart from his list a procedure known as the 'special bargain' came into operation. This involved the filing of details of the offer-quality, quantity and price but not the name of the customer, although it was not difficult to guess who this was. These details were immediately circulated together with the name of the firm making the offer. Alternatively this information was available by telephone or telex. Arrangements of the various kinds discussed above were common. Less common were informational systems which related purely to discounts. One such case was starter batteries. Another was provided by the activities of the North-Western Area of the Federation of Wholesale and Multiple Bakers. From 1960 an informal understanding existed between plant bakers that none would grant quantity discounts or other special discounts in respect of supplies of bread, except to those whose names were kept on a list maintained by the secretaries of the North-Western Area,[22] without submitting a proposal to a meeting of constituent companies 'and considering the views expressed thereon at such meeting'.[23] An information bureau was established, apparently in 1964, and a list of discounts at that time agreed to was prepared and circulated. The list showed the names of shops to which bread was delivered by members and the discounts off the wholesale or retail price which were granted. From time to time additions, deletions and alterations to the basic list were circulated.[24] In other cases more generalised data was circulated. Thus in the case of aluminium castings the Light Metal Founders' Association circulated quarterly returns of average selling prices per 1 lb of sand, gravity die and pressure die castings. Also disseminated was advice to members of typical effects of changes in wage levels or materials prices on selling prices.[25]

In the main, and at this stage, information agreements were pre-notification affairs. Thus in the case of galvanised tanks, although the agreement stipulated that parties should notify the trade association secretaries within two days of changes in list prices and terms, in practice notification, and dissemination to the industry, took place before changes. The tyre mileage arrangements involved a pre- or post-notification option but in practice tenders were circulated amongst the tyre producers before they were lodged with local authorities. In the roadstone industry, following the abandonments of 1959 to 1961, a chain of pre-notification bureaus was established.

The object of these agreements was obvious. They enabled industries to maintain a common front in respect of list prices and terms. In the case of tenders they facilitated level tendering. In the case of arrangements such as the 'special bargain' two possibilities arose. Those making offers which were thought to be 'rocking the boat' could be pressurised and in addition the information disseminated provided a means of checking phantom competition.

In the main[26] the impression which emerges is that they were

L

remarkably successful. The success of the tyre mileage arrangement is almost legendary. The effect was to produce virtually total uniformity of rates quoted. During the period October 1961 to July 1965 there were 18 instances of tenders in respect of new contracts (or re-tenders where there had been old contracts). In 14 of the 18 all quotations were identical. In the case of 4 of the tenders where differences occurred, the divergencies were at the top end of the quotations; there was a common view among the lower quotations, which were in any case the only ones likely to be significant. As regards rate reviews, there were 294 quotations during the period and in only two cases were quotations not fully identical, and in one of these cases the differences were minimal.[27] In interviews with steel drum producers we were assured that they had been highly satisfied with their arrangement. In the case of lamps we have already noted that in 1956 the E.L.M.A. price-fixing agreement was dropped and in 1959 the recommended non-mandatory discount structure (of 1957) was also dropped. But price uniformity was maintained by two devices. Firstly, and outside the ambit of the trade association, companies notified each other of proposed changes in basic list prices.[28] This was a means by which companies obtained trial reactions–in addition there were discussions. Secondly, in respect of the discount structure to be applied to the basic lists there was an information agreement operated through E.L.I.C. As a result the Monopolies Commission observed

> We found by comparison of the price lists of the E.L.I.C. manufacturers that, with insignificant exceptions, the list prices of main brand lamps were identical, type for type, whichever manufacturer supplied them. (Main brand lamps, include all mercury and discharge lamps, most fluorescent lamps, and a substantial part of the filament lamps supplied by the members of E.L.I.C.) We also found that, until March 1968, the discount schedules operated by the members of E.L.I.C. were identical; each classified their wholesaler and user customers for discount purposes in the same way, and the net prices which they charged to such customers were therefore also identical, type for type. A similar uniformity of prices appeared also in sales of main brand lamps to the general public. On the face of it, therefore, the evidence suggested that despite the ending of collective price-fixing in 1956 and of resale price maintenance in 1967 there had been no appreciable increase in price competition.[29]

In the case of transformers the effectiveness of the arrangement was such that Sir Christopher Hinton, chairman of the C.E.G.B., was able to describe the situation as one in which

> ... the prices which we got were indistinguishable from, and as identical as, before the ring was dissolved.[30]

The effectiveness of information agreements as vehicles for the control of competition has to be supplemented by two other points. One was that they could be forums for collusion. Any doubts on that matter can be set at rest by reference to the *Galvanised Tanks* case. The other is that they could be cloaks for collusion. Thus in one section of an industry supplying building materials, following abandonment it was decided to form an information agreement. In practice prices were agreed. One firm would lead off (and notify the others) and the others would follow on a staggered basis. During the transition to a new price level it was agreed that customers would not be poached on the basis of price differences. The information system was a means of explaining the price uniformity which was actually the product of collusion. This practice was not unique to this particular industry.

In some industries, notably glass container manufacture, our study shows a rapid collapse of the agreement. But this was rare. However, given that substitute agreements did not have the underpinning of the previous formal price-fixing systems (which also operated in a period when the law was much less hostile), they did tend to collapse when subjected to excessive strain. Thus, fundamental changes in the demand for heavy electrical equipment by about the mid-1960s were undoubtedly the cause of the demise of arrangements in the field of transformers and heavy electric motors.

But many information agreements sailed on and it was only in the choppy waters of the *Galvanised Tanks* and *Tyre Mileage* era that they were either abandoned or changed into somewhat more innocuous post-notification affairs. The 1968 Act seems to have delivered the final *coup de grace*; by this time it seems evident that generally industry had decided to drop what remained rather than register. Two points need to be emphasised here. Firstly, it is a great mistake to see the abandonments of the post-1959 period as marking the general onset of competition. In a significant number of cases that did not come until ten years after the 1956 Act had been passed. Secondly, the *Galvanised Tanks* and *Tyre Mileage* cases stand comparison with the *Yarn Spinners* case as key decisions in postwar U.K. restrictive practices policy.

(e) *Price leadership.* There were other reasons than the use of information agreements for the failure of competition to emerge. One was price leadership. In the full account of electric cables it is shown that it was B.I.C.C. which led the industry out of the price war of 1959. Thereafter the evidence suggests that B.I.C.C. continued to be the effective leaders. The B.I.C.C. lead exercised a strong grip on the industry. This can be contrasted with the experience of the paper bag industry where, given that even in agreement days the Paper Bag Federation had failed to have much of an impact, it was doubtful whether a leader, or leaders, would make much impression. Nevertheless it is interesting that, when the industry agreement was abandoned in 1965, two large firms apparently stepped quickly into the breach and issued their own lists in place of those provided by the Federation. Thus there was no hiatus when the industry was without some kind of lead. One list related to sales to wholesalers, the other dealt with the direct-to-retailer trade. But the main role of these lists was that they acted as a guide–it could not be put any higher than that.

(f) *Agreement with a buyer.* Another way of avoiding competition was to have a supply agreement with a large buyer such as the C.E.G.B. There were examples of this in the manufacture of cable, particularly the supertension mains variety, and heavy switchgear. In the latter case the price agreement[31] was not terminated until 1965. Prior to that prices for equipment of 132 kV were agreed by the Associated Switchgear Manufacturers. In 1962 the C.E.G.B. had managed to induce the producers to accept competition in respect of 10 per cent of 132 kV equipment but this does not appear to have spread to 275 kV and 400 kV equipment.[32] However, in 1966 following the 1965 termination the C.E.G.B. entered into a purchasing agreement. Later the C.E.G.B. was joined by the two Scottish Boards–the producer parties being G.E.C. and Reyrolle Parsons.[33]

(iv) *After Termination–the Longer Run*
In some industries the experience in the longer term paralleled that in the shorter term–that is to say competition continued. This was so in the case of the carpet industry in which some loosening of restrictions was evident. This partly manifested itself in distribution (where, as will be apparent from our detailed case study, no real harm and quite a bit of benefit appear to have occurred). The tyre industry undoubtedly became more competitive, and this competition was intensified at a later stage as a result of excess

capacity in the manufacturing of tyres. The latter arose as a result of over-anticipation of demand levels following the tyre legislation of 1968. An increase in the level of discounts to distributors stemmed in part from the need to achieve high levels of utilisation of capacity and in part from the impact of imports. The discounts received by distributors have, since the ending of the Tyre Trade Register (which is discussed in detail in the full study), been partially passed on to the customers; and thus the discounting to the final consumer, which in our view the Tyre Trade Register was designed to prevent, has manifested itself. This discounting sprang in part from new entrants into the trade, and in part from existing members of it; and the manufacturers showed willingness to supply such outlets. Under such pressures resale price maintenance simply had to collapse. At the same time none of the deleterious effects of the ending of the Tyre Trade Register which the manu-facturers forecast have come about.

In investigating the replacement vehicle battery industry, we found that the smaller producers ('gyps' as they are contemptuously termed by the larger manufacturers) had succeeded in attaining a market share of about 60 per cent. It was their competition which exerted a restraining influence on the upward movement of prices and led to a change in the industry's marketing strategy with the progressive introduction of a range of batteries below the top price and quality category. In other industries the competitive conditions which emerged initially continued, as for example in surgical dressings; interviews with one hospital board in 1971 indicated that 'vicious competition' existed. In the case of metal bedsteads the same could not be said although some signs of rivalry were evident in tender prices. The position of the purchaser in respect of steel arches, light rails, files and hacksaws continued to be satisfactory.

(a) *Price wars.* Generally speaking, where price wars developed they were temporary after which the industry settled down and the members found some *modus vivendi*. But iron bath manufacture was an exception. The agreement of the British Bath Manufac-turers' Association was cancelled in March 1960. It was evident that even then conditions were becoming more competitive. There ensued throughout much of the 1960s a protracted price war. The origins are not easy to disentangle, not least because the major participant refused to discuss the matter with us. Excess capacity was probably a cause in certain sections of the trade but it is difficult to resist the conclusion that Allied Ironfounders was seeking a position of market dominance. Prices were pushed down and some companies decided to retreat from the trade. Others were acquired by Allied Ironfounders. However, there were some companies who were also intending to stay in the business (Carron and Ideal Boilers and Radiators) and they matched the cuts. As a result from 1965 to 1969 alone prices fell by upwards of 30 per cent. Eventually Ideal retired from the fray. The consumer has undoubtedly benefited, in the short run, but it is doubtful if this kind of competition is of any long-run benefit to him since it leaves the iron bath trade as a duopoly. Fortunately there are independent producers of steel-based baths, and plastic is likely to play an increasingly important role.

(b) *Ending of information agreements.* In the longer run we could also expect a number of industries to join the competitive category –i.e. those which had initially resorted after 1956 to information agreements. Competition would in such instances be emerging half a decade or more later than had been the case where industries had adopted a competitive posture immediately after abandonment of formal price-fixing. In the case of galvanised tanks the ending of the Galvanised Tank Manufacturers' Association (G.T.M.A.) information agreement did lead to competition. Tenders to a large buyer showed a lack of uniformity and a fall in price levels.[34] In the case of tyre mileage a similar break in uniformity was evident[35] and recent investigations (1971) confirm the persistence of this behaviour. In the case of steel drums the termination of the information agreement was followed, but not immediately, by a price war in 1967/68. The price level fell by up to 10 per cent, that is to say discounts of 10 per cent off-list were given by some firms. Interestingly, the industry managed to hold (more or less) the basic list level which was an advantage to it given that it is easier to cancel discounts than to raise basic list levels, particularly in a period of prices and incomes policy. In other cases agreements had collapsed before the *Galvanised Tanks* and *Tyre Mileage* cases. Thus glass containers soon manifested signs of competition with prices noticeably flexible downwards when there was a check to the growth of, or a slump in, demand. Perhaps the most dramatic aftermath occurred in the case of transformers. Prices fell by as much as 25 per cent in the case of the largest sizes and as much as 25 per cent to 41 per cent in the case of system and distribution transformers. These various instances are indicative of what seems to have happened in many (if not all) cases when information agreements departed from the scene or were watered down.

(c) *Effects of price competition–capacity.* The general effects of this price competition are several and we can illustrate them by a selective rather than exhaustive review of cases. One was to slim capacity down. In the case of transformers it was evident that in the light of future demands the industry was too large. The price fall had two effects. The fall in profitability had the result of forcing some firms to relinquish the production of transformers. But it should be added that these were generally the smaller producers. The other effect was to enforce a rationalisation of the industry. This could have taken the form of firms being literally driven to the wall but by and large it did not. Rather it took the form of mergers. G.E.C. for example, stepped in and acquired capacity and closed it down. Had price agreements existed there is a possibility that the fall in the volume of orders might have been compensated for by a rise in prices. At least the industry might have been tempted to avoid the consequences of the short-fall of demand by embarking on such a policy. This would have involved a wholesale misuse of resources. Fortunately competition broke through, prices fell and the industry had to pursue a more radical slimming down policy. In the case of steel drums there was some excess capacity which the information agreement had preserved. The price war had the effect of forcing some of this capacity out of production and to this extent was beneficial.

(d) *Cost consciousness.* Competition had other beneficial effects. On several occasions we have been assured that the more competitive climate of the 1960s made firms more cost conscious. The blithe attitude towards such matters which characterised the era of price-fixing has had to go. We show in our detailed case study of the transformer industry how the firms in the industry had to search for economies–the paring down of over-generous design standards was one example cited. Galvanised tanks was another example where competition led to the pruning of an unduly wide product range and to a paring down of over-generous design standards. Competition had another kind of beneficial effect–it had a stimulatory effect on innovation with the existing industry. This is always a difficult matter to prove but the full study of glass containers is interesting in this connection, and the view that such effect occurred is one which people involved with the industry, producers and consumers, did not gainsay. Another such case is batteries.

(e) *Competition and innovation.* In describing the more competitive climate which the 1956 Act established–sooner or later–it is of course difficult to disentangle two sets of forces. On the one hand the pre-existing agreements restricted rivalry within the group, and kept out new entrants and imports. The ending of these agreements helped to unleash such competitive forces. We do not of course underrate either the degree to which businessmen do not like competing or their ability to find ways (sometimes by moving from stratagem to stratagem as legal loopholes are plugged) of avoiding competition. The other major force is innovation. It can be argued that this is an independent factor and the degree to which in several industries, the competitive situation both became and remained lively was largely due to this rather than the 1956 Act. Several industries in which innovation played an important part are listed in Table 4.5. Nevertheless though innovation can

TABLE 4.5   Industries in which Innovation or Potential Innovation has Stimulated Competition

Case Industry	Innovatory Product
Woven Carpets	Tufted carpets
Glass Containers	Plastic containers
Paper Bags	Polythene bags
Steel Drums (Small)	Plastic drums
Galvanised Tanks	Polyethylene, glass fibre and asbestos tanks
Iron and Steel Based Baths	Perspex baths
Leavers' Lace	Raschel lace
Tiles (Ceramic)	Plastic and do-it-yourself tiles
Standard Galvanised Metal Windows	Aluminium windows
Rubber Cable	Plastic cable
Jute Cloth for sacking, bagging and carpet backing	Synthetic based sacks, bags and carpet backing
Salt glazed and vitrified pipes	Pitch fibre, concrete and plastic pipes
Sanitary Ware (Vitreous China)	Sanitary ware (plastic)

be an important independent source of competition we draw the readers' attention to two factors. Firstly, the record of trade associations in the field of innovation is not always a happy one. We would illustrate this by reference to the attitude of the British Metal Window Manufacturers' Association to the introduction of galvanised windows, and the Rubber Cable Manufacturers' Association to the introduction of plastic cable. Secondly, although it is not a universal rule, there is a clear tendency for firms in an established industry not to pioneer new products which are basically revolutionary substitutes for existing ones.[36] The rise of tufted carpets (discussed in the carpet study) is a good case and it is interesting to note that where woven producers entered this section of the industry they did in some cases do so gingerly at first on a consortium basis, while pursuing a joint advertising campaign to distinguish clearly woven carpets from tufteds. A somewhat similar reluctance was manifested by the galvanised tank producers when faced with new substitute products[37] and methods for producing tanks. Bath manufacture is another example of outsiders innovating in the use of plastics, and so is the bag industry in the use of polythene. Another example is the use of aluminium in windows. The list could be lengthened. The important point here is that in so far as innovation is heavily dependent on outsiders it is important to maintain and preserve freedom of entry. We have in fact pointed out that pre-1956 exclusionary devices were widespread. Given that the 1956 Act has helped to clear them away it can be argued that it has helped to foster innovation. The stress of the Monopolies Commission on the need for an attack on entry forestalling devices was well-founded.

A word of caution is now called for. We have painted a picture of competition breaking through, sooner or later, as the Court progressively interpreted the law. But it would be incorrect to present a picture of a movement uniquely in one direction—indeed we have indicated that even in the shorter run there were other tendencies at work. We have now as it were to present the other side of the coin.

(f) *Avoidance of competition—collusion.* The most obvious way of evading competition is to collude and our studies have indicated the existence of such behaviour on a not inconsiderable scale. It would indeed be wrong to imagine that, following the terminations of 1959 and after, and 1965/66 and after, competition continued to reign permanently and unalloyed. On several occasions it has been put to us that specific industries have resorted to clandestine discussions on prices. The very informality of discussions over gins is bound to make the enforcement task of the Registrar all that much harder. Detecting collusion is difficult.[38] In our Introduction we have cited the case of one industry which consistently led us to believe that in respect of raising prices it encountered the difficulty that firms were reluctant to lead off because of the possibility of being isolated. Such a problem may have been real enough at one stage in the period following abandonment. However, it was our impression that one particular episode led to an industry-wide re-appraisal of policy. The nature of that re-appraisal was made obvious when one extrovert revealed all by pointing out that some of the firms in the industry had just had a useful discussion at a seaside resort–a favoured spot for collusion.[39]

In some industries, following the termination of formal price agreements, prices fell–sometimes steeply. Such price falls undoubtedly had serious implications for profit margins although they had a beneficial side effect in that they tended to get rid of excess capacity and/or high cost firms. Where an overshoot occurred the problem which then faced the industry was one of restoring prices and profitability to more acceptable levels. In the longer term prices had to rise as the inflation of costs occurred. Here a price leader was called for and sometimes he emerged (e.g. British Insulated Callendar's Cables) and sometimes he did not. If he did not the answer was collusion. In one such case we are told of the institution of a monthly luncheon club at which the host made proposals about possible price increases. If there was a lack of unanimity the matter was left over until a later occasion. Once, however, there was complete agreement the price increase was implemented. Collapses of prices also occurred after the termination of information agreements. In one such case, where a steep price fall occurred and where a managed contraction of capacity followed, prices eventually turned upwards. The upswing of prices was almost certainly in part caused by an overshooting in the contraction of capacity but the upward movement was triggered off by collusion. In this case also our evidence is the admissions of a participant.

(g) *Government*. It is also important to emphasise that the government has itself been an important force in encouraging collusion. We referred earlier to the prices and incomes policy of 1966 and after which required firms to secure official approval for price increases. Clearly it was not likely that firms would be encouraged to make separate and possibly divergent requests. Rather, as we have been assured on more than one occasion, government departments required industries to go away and collectively deliberate on the increase to be asked for. This particular policy development is of considerable importance when it is recalled that in some industries information agreements survived until 1965 and 1966. It is not too fanciful to say that as one door to collusion closed, another was opened up.

(h) *Cost surveys*. Industry has in some instances shown a remarkable capacity for devising stratagems to evade competition. In one industry we were assured that the abandonment of an information agreement had been followed by the institution of a cost survey. Within the ambit of the trade associations, meetings were held to consider data on costs and profitability in the industry as a whole. Although explicit agreements about price increases did not occur, it was common for rather academic sounding propositions of the following kind to be put and discussed: 'If it is desirable that profitability be restored to the level of the previous year, an increase in prices of the order of x per cent will be needed.' Out of such discussions a meeting of minds could ensue even though no actual pricing decision was explicitly arrived at during the meeting. In this connection it is important to stress that the demise of formal price–fixing agreements was not always accompanied by the demise of associations.[40] The latter therefore remained as possible vehicles for other kinds of 'collusive' activity.

(i) *Price leadership*. Another vehicle for achieving stabilisation was price leadership–like collusion we have already discussed this as being a phenomenon of the shorter term. Again, like collusion, it became more evident in the longer term. Whether dominant or barometric in origin its effective coverage is variable. In the full study of wire ropes we have indicated that leadership may relate to list prices[41] with some flexibility remaining in respect of discounts. On the other hand it may be more rigid in that the leader is followed on both counts. In the case of wire rope it seemed evident that after the adverse Judgement of 1964, British Ropes was often the initiator of changes in list levels but that there was some limited flexibility in respect of discounts.[42] On the other hand steel drum manufacture was an industry in which, following the price war of 1967/68 (which in turn followed the ending of an information agreement), price leadership emerged and in this case there was reported widespread uniformity[43] not only of list prices but also of discounts. Other industries in which price leadership became evident in the due course of time are pipes and electric meters. In the former case The Hepworth Iron Company embarked upon a series of takeovers which by 1971 had led it to a market share of 70–80 per cent. This was plainly a case of dominant price leadership and perhaps, but with less certainty, the same could be said of British Ropes although it could not claim so large a share of the market. One other industry in which it is possible to identify a price leader is standard metal windows. Here, as we show in our full study, an upheld agreement eventually fell apart. There was also substantial merger activity; and as a result there was by 1968 a virtual duopoly, in the shape of Crittall–Hope and Ideal–Williams. The former is generally identified as the price leader although any power this might imply has got to be qualified by the fact that substantial competition exists in the shape of wood and aluminium windows.

One final point about price leadership relates to its limitations. Apart from competition from substitutes there are other possibly limiting factors, and it should not necessarily be equated in terms of control of the market with the formal price agreement of an earlier era. That is to say it lacks the moral commitment of an agreement and also the system of carpeting backsliders. The possibility that discounts may vary around a uniform list price has already been mentioned,[44] and the stabilising influence of price leadership in times of stress should not be exaggerated. Thus in the case of supertension mains cable prices fell by 30 per cent between 1968 and 1969; in the case of other mains cable some discounting was evident in 1970. Added to all this is the fact that the power of a price leader to raise prices much above a competitive level will be non-existent if conditions of free entry exist.

(j) *Agreement with buyer and other devices.* Other devices for the avoidance of competition are supply arrangements with nationalised industries (we instance an example in our full study of transformers). Some restraint on competitive forces has been achieved by companies coming together to form common sales agencies (i.e. steel drums) or consortia (i.e. transformers). Some stabilisation of market shares has been achieved by vertical integration (i.e. tyre distribution). It is also worth noting that in the case of electric meters the price fall discussed earlier was reversed after 1966 and by 1970 prices were about 25 per cent above the level of the early 1960s. This, according to a case before the Court in 1970, was due to the operation of an information agreement.

(v) *Mergers*
Although these have been referred to only incidentally in this concluding account, they were in fact an important phenomenon in many case studies. One of the most noticeable features of many of the industries studied in detail has been the decline in the number of firms producing particular products.[45] Not all of this decline was due to mergers (other forces were at work such as the dropping of lines of production and total cessation of trading) but mergers were undeniably a major factor. It must be added that

where the Schumpeterian factor of innovatory competition has been at work the decline in the number of firms producing the product in question may have been offset in some degree by the entry of firms producing a new substitute product (e.g. new kinds of baths) but this is by no means either inevitable or universal (as the case of transformer manufacture indicates).[46]

The basic question is simple–what has been the relationship between the 1956 Act and mergers? Did the Act give rise to them and in particular were they a means of circumventing it? Trying to find out why mergers occurred is a difficult process. Businessmen are surprisingly reluctant to say a great deal on the matter. It may be that recollection is difficult because even at the time the reasons were confused.

(a) *Economies of scale.* If we seek to explain mergers then we can say that the motives may be several. Firstly, mergers may be undertaken because the enlarged enterprise which will result will gain from the economies of large-scale production and distribution and because it will be more effective in the R & D field. This kind of justification can arise in two ways. It can be deployed as the rationalisation of, or ostensible reason for, a merger. It can also be the true reason. Given the great amount of discussion in 1966 and after which gave mergers and the large firm a favourable image it would be surprising if this kind of argumentation had not been encountered in the process of our research. However, it should be added that it has not been as frequently encountered as might thus have been expected. This is perhaps not so surprising if account is taken of the findings of Newbould who showed that in his sample the size and efficiency motive was encountered much less frequently than official and conventional wisdom would seem to have predicted. Indeed given that, as Newbould shows,[47] takeovers are often planned and executed in a few weeks, it is difficult to see how a proper investigation of the nature and significance of such economic benefits can be mounted. This is quite apart from a consideration of the problems of organisation and integration that inevitably follow in the train of a merger. It could be argued that the short time period is irrelevant because industry has contingency plans. Given the pressures on business, with its tendency to work from hand to mouth, we doubt whether the contingency plan argument has much to commend it in the case of small and even medium sized firms at least.

(b) *Scale and vulnerability.* Sometimes the economies of scale explanation shades into a kind of vulnerability argument. We encountered this in the case of sanitary ware where it was felt that in the future the industry would move from a labour intensive to a more mechanised capital intensive basis. If this happened only large firms would be viable. If one firm took over a competitor others therefore matched this in order to maintain parity of size. The suspicion arises that such merger matching is often largely grounded in fear and uncertainty.

Basically we would conclude from our study that although the economies of scale argument had been deployed, it has not been deployed as often as the conventional wisdom of the late 1960s might have led us to expect. In some cases we doubt whether it was the real reason. Clearly the 1956 Act does not by definition explain the core of genuine cases. Nevertheless there is the well-known trade-off between more concentration and a possibly less competitive structure.

(c) *Elimination of high cost producers.* A second explanation for mergers arises in connection with the undoubted differential efficiency which existed under, and was indeed protected by, agreements. Once price competition emerged, particularly if excess capacity existed, the inefficient were in a very vulnerable position. In such situations inefficient firms were sometimes disposed to offer themselves for takeover. There was some evidence of this in the case of glass containers and wire rope. Why, it may be asked, did not the more efficient, or the more liquid, firms allow the social Darwinian forces of competitive selection to operate? The answer seems to be that the less efficient might be forced to indulge in a bout of desperate price cutting and might as King Charles II remarked of himself, be 'an unconscionable time dying'. The larger (sometimes dominant) and more liquid firms therefore tended to accept such invitations if only to close the firms down and dispose of any realisable assets. There was of course some sales goodwill to be acquired. Clearly the firms so taken over were often only too well aware that it was the agreement which kept them in business and that once it went things were bound to change. It was also no doubt evident that the sale price would be better if the deal could be accomplished before competition reacted adversely on the balance sheet position. In some instances it seems possible, particularly in the case of small firms, that the decision to sell up was dictated not by how relatively efficient a firm was but how relatively efficient it felt it was. Smallness no doubt gave rise to feelings of vulnerability, particularly when the prospect was one of being launched for the first time into a situation where pricing strategy was a matter for independent formulation. Small firms typically have less cash and credit reserves if it comes to a real fight. Where there was a prospect of a lack of managerial succession, or a need to provide cash for death duties and so forth, the pressure to get out was intensified. One thing is clear–the theory of takeover raiding is inadequate as a total explanation of such acquisitions. The firm doing the taking over may have seen the move as a means of preserving stability. Alternatively it may have seen it as part of a continuing strategy for securing a firm grip on the industry; an exploitative motive may therefore have been present.

(d) *Eliminating excess capacity.* One situation where the 1956 Act undoubtedly triggered off mergers was that in which excess capacity existed. This brings us to our third motive. The excess capacity could have built up during the period of a price agreement; alternatively it could have been the result of a short-fall of demand which was regarded as being likely to persist at least in the medium term. The latter situation has been particularly important in a number of the cases we studied–e.g. in some sections of the cable and transformer industries and attention will be focussed on this aspect of the problem. Again it is possible to argue that the classical forces of competition could have been left totally in charge of engineering the contraction. Again in practice this does not seem to have happened. Rather once it was recognised that a reasonably long drawn out short-fall of demand was in prospect, firms often preferred to organise the contraction by merger followed by closure. This also had the added attraction that not only were the names of the old companies sometimes preserved in the new overall title, but the once separate companies still remained as identifiable entities in the new group. There was then a prospect of continued existence for both parties whilst, *ceteris paribus*, there was at least a fifty/fifty chance of demise in a primeval battle to the bitter end.

Such mergers could of course be said to be anti-competitive in the sense that they took the edge off competition. However, given that competition was in such circumstances likely to be highly deleterious to the firms involved in terms of its effects on profitability and investment, the mergers were arguably justified. The only danger was that the contraction of capacity could go too far and lead to an excessive return on capital. However, this could be subsequently corrected if free entry existed, or if the overshoot was accidental and the firms remaining in the industry later decided to add to capacity. The situation would, however, be dangerous if free entry did not exist or if there was a conspiracy deliberately to restrict investment.

An argument which can be adduced in favour of such mergers, as opposed to contraction through competition, is that it is by no means inevitable that under the latter system the most efficient will survive. Rather the survivors may be those who are most liquid or those who are able to subsidise their losses. By contrast after a merger the new company can make an objective appraisal of which plant needs to be closed. An extremely interesting study could be made of the degree to which, following mergers, there has been a real attempt at rationalisation. Were objective assessments made of the plant to be closed or did the victim bear the brunt? Were the companies truly integrated? Certainly we have encountered some cases where the latter has not occurred.

(e) *Dominance and control.* A fourth motive for mergers is that where it is no longer possible to restrict competition by agreement, the same end is sought by the takeover of competitors and the reduction in the number of competitors so as to produce a more 'manageable' structure. Here the underlying motives could again be twofold: defensive, in terms of a desire to reduce the uncertainties of competition, and/or exploitative. A desire to reduce competition has certainly lain behind some of the mergers covered by this study. We would also draw attention to the conclusions of Newbould who indicated that, according to his sample, a desire to reduce uncertainty and to exert greater control over the economic environment were very important factors in explaining mergers.[48] One example of mergers in which an anti-competitive motive seemed to be at work is mentioned in our study of iron baths. Ultimately it is difficult to see the price war and takeovers that occurred in any other light than a desire to dominate. Equally as we have seen in the case of pipe manufacture a series of takeovers has facilitated the emergence of dominant price leadership. The case of the cable industry is more difficult to interpret. On the one hand mergers were taking place before abandonment; but on the other it can be argued that the industry realised that in all probability the agreements would have to go and that some degree of oligopolisation would provide a sounder basis for control. In the event B.I.C.C. had acquired by 1959 a position which enabled it to take on that role. We have also witnessed a number of takeovers, of firms such as Pyrotenax and Reliance Clifton, which seem hard to justify on economies of scale grounds but can more easily be seen as the actions of a firm which wishes to exert as tight a control as possible over its environment. If the reader consults the study of roadstone he will find at the outset the quotation of J. B. F. Earle (himself for long active in the industry) very illuminating. According to this authoritative source the industry used information agreements as a temporary respite to 'organise the industry on a satisfactory but fundamentally different basis'.[49] Also, 'The giants respect one another's abilities–and with modern management, are continually looking for a respectable return on capital. They are not likely therefore, arbitrarily or short-sightedly to cut prices.'[50] All this suggests a deliberate policy of oligopolisation with the aim of producing a more 'manageable' structure. Such a view has been independently put to us by some who have had a long and deep experience of the industry.

(f) *Mergers and the growth of firms.* It would of course be naïve to assume that all the mergers have sprung from the effects of the 1956 Act. Here we come to another form of motivation which can be put as a series of propositions. Under normal conditions most firms are making profits–some of which are paid away as dividends but the balance is put to reserve. What will the latter be used for? Normally a firm will prefer to expand its productive assets within the field of its existing technological experience. Its ability to do so will depend on the rate of growth of the demand for its product. If the latter is slow either because the industry is at a point on its growth curve where expansion is slowing down, or if the economy generally is growing slowly, or both, then a problem arises. In this situation the firm is accumulating reserves at a rate which outpaces the ability of extra demand to absorb them; two possibilities then open up. One is to indulge in aggressive price (and other) competition. If it pitches its prices below that of its rivals, and they do not retaliate, it can enjoy a faster rate of growth of demand and profits put to reserve can be absorbed. However, such a policy is uncomfortable from a profits point of view. In any case it is by no means likely that rivals will remain passive–they will, under oligopolistic conditions, probably match cuts. The only condition under which a price cutting strategy may not be uncomfortable, and may not be matched, is if the firm has a decisive cost advantage. Given that the firm does not have such an advantage how does it employ its reserves short of becoming a conglomerate or paying out more generous dividends? The answer is simple–it takes over a rival.[51] Here we have to admit that the theory of the

M

firm tends to concentrate attention on competition as a process whereby price is employed to increase the market share of a firm at its rivals' expense. In the real world entrepreneurs are likely to treat price competition as being a weapon which must be deployed with restraint if oligopoly balance is to be preserved. If it alone is inadequate then the merger may prove to be an additional weapon of growth which obviates destabilisation. There is of course a bonus. The process leads to a more oligopolistic and 'manageable' structure. Surely one of the lessons of oligopoly is that it involves interdependence and therefore provokes the emergence of a live and let live philosophy. We are back to Mr Earle: 'They are not likely therefore, arbitrarily or short-sightedly to cut prices.' We are not saying that the 1956 Act is a farce because businessmen will not compete on price. All we are saying is that there is a limit to how far we can expect price to be used as a weapon of growth in a dynamic enterprise.[52]

(vi) *Other Aspects*
(a) *Buyer awareness.* We have already referred to the attitudes of buyers; in some degree the power of cartels in the pre-1956 period was due to their lethargy. Such lethargy expressed itself in a willingness to share work among groups of level tenderers, which was just what the participants in rings desired. It was more sensible to refuse to accommodate cartels and to place large orders with a single or at most a few firms. The juicy plums which could be won were likely to induce a competitive response. This is what happened in the case of a large transport authority which enjoyed competition in respect of tyre mileage and traction electric motors at a time when rings were rampant.[53] We have also pointed out that particularly in the 1930s, county surveyors adopted a benevolent attitude to the rings which began to emerge in the roadstone industry. Fortunately the situation has changed. In the case of roadstone we have observed the deployment of newer methods of buying such as spot tendering. We have also noted that the 1956 Act has had something to do with the keener methods of buying which now exist generally. We believe this keenness was encouraged by the chinks and indeed gaps in a once solid front which the Act opened up—these openings encouraged buyers to press for yet better terms.

(b) *Buyer concentration.* One observable tendency has been a greater concentration of buying power through centralisation. This has arisen in at least three ways. Firstly, established nationalised and public bodies have centralised their buying. This has, for example, been the case in the N.C.B. in respect of wire rope and the case of Regional Hospital Boards (as opposed to individual areas) in products such as surgical dressings. Secondly, some industries have been nationalised and centralised buying has resulted—an obvious example is the British Steel Corporation buying wire rope. The latter has sought to reduce the variety of ropes bought, to concentrate sales and give some promise of a continuity of demand as a basis for better terms. Thirdly, independent bodies have come together to form buying consortia; good examples are the activity of Area Electricity Boards in buying transformers and local authorities in purchasing metal windows.

One impression stands out in our survey of buying and that is that public bodies, particularly local authorities, are extremely keen buyers. The picture of the public sector as an area of lethargy does not square with our experience. Indeed it was in the private sector that we heard laments about the problems caused by discounts and longings for the days of uniform terms!

(c) *Upheld agreements and stability*. We have in our case studies considered industries where agreements have been upheld. Two impressions stand out in connection therewith. One is that the upholding of an agreement has not been synonymous with stability of either the industry or the agreement itself. In the case of standard metal windows the agreement collapsed, as we describe. In the case of black bolts and nuts it has shown signs of instability. In the case of tiles we found that there has been a wholesale buying up and closing down; one case is not a basis for generalisation but it does indicate that mergers can be quite common even when competition is largely ruled out. The other impression is that agreements have shown little sign of self-reformation. Thus the debatable system of pricing in the case of cement persists.

(d) *Terminated agreements and stability*. One of the by-products of the case studies has been the opportunity it presented to compare prognostications of what would happen when competition emerged with what actually happened. Almost without exception dire predictions have not been fulfilled. Often it was expected that exports would be adversely affected—there is no evidence for this. It was anticipated that R & D expenditure would be retrenched. Again we saw little evidence for this although admittedly in the case of transformers some paring down of spending in the phase of the acute price fall was reported. But this case was a very exceptional one. Perhaps the most interesting prediction was that goods would be debased. Thus in the case of carpets a kind of Gresham's Law was propounded: bad carpets would drive out good. Given that consumers are relatively ill-equipped with information as buyers of carpets this was a most likely place for debasement to occur – but there has been no sign of it. In the case of tyre distribution not only did the industry make dire predictions in the Court about the effects on safety of the ending of the Tyre Trade Register, but it issued material to this effect to the press. No such effects have emerged. In the case of industrial goods it was always improbable; industry is well equipped to spot quality deterioration and British Standards also play a blocking role. In case after case we have found the debasement prediction to be totally ill-founded.

II. RESOURCE ALLOCATION: THE MAJOR AND MINOR CASES

(i) *Basic Analysis*

(a) *Assumptions.* In considering the resource allocation effects of the 1956 Act we apply the apparatus of Chapter 3. The *level* of employment is taken to be determined exogenously by government and the *direction* of employment is taken as determined by regional policy. In addition we are accepting as valid a micro-economic, step-by-step approach, thus ignoring second best problems. On this basis it is possible to concentrate upon efficient allocation of resources in the terms of Chapter 3.

In Chapter 3 efficiency was divided into three forms. Firstly, there was static efficiency. This required that each firm should be on the horizontal section of its long-run average cost curve with normal profits included in costs and with the price above cost by an amount which reflected a small goodwill entry barrier. Apart from this requirement concerning the relationship of price to resource cost, the main policy implication here is that an industry should not suffer from excess capacity to an extent which prevents existing firms reaching the horizontal section of their cost curve, and, perhaps more importantly, that there should be no barriers to the elimination of such excess capacity and to the operation of the selection mechanism. In addition there should not be removable barriers to entry which would prevent new firms entering the industry from attaining a scale of production which would take them on to the horizontal section of the cost curve.

Secondly, there was X-efficiency. The main policy requirement here is that there should be a continuous search within firms in the industry for ways of taking up organisational slack and of reducing differences in the levels of the horizontal sections of the long-run average cost curves of firms with the same technology.

Thirdly, there was dynamic efficiency. This implies two main policy requirements. The first is that firms should seek to eliminate differences between them in the level of the horizontal sections of their long-run average cost curves which *do* arise from differing technologies. In other words there should be efforts by the less efficient to secure better technology thus helping the diffusion of the best *existing* technology throughout the industry; and the selection mechanism should operate so that there is a tendency for those who are not technologically successful to be supplanted. The second is that all firms, including the most efficient, should seek to *advance* their technology both of production and of product.

(b) *Method of procedure.* We then have to ask ourselves three questions in relation to the industries we have studied. Firstly, we have to ask ourselves how far each of these three kinds of efficiency appears to be manifested in these industries. Secondly, we have to ask ourselves if any of the four constraints specified in Chapter 3 (consumer choice, income distribution, power and conservation) are offended in the industries. Finally, and perhaps more importantly in terms of the apparatus advanced in Chapter 3, we have to ask whether the conditions of oligopolistic competition prevailing within the particular industry, are satisfactory for the achievement of these efficiencies. This latter question is perhaps the more important since judgement of the existence of these non-quantifiable efficiencies must (though made as a result of studying the industry in some detail) be incomplete on its own as an appraisal of an industry.

(c) *Oligopolistic conditions.* The main conditions for satisfactory oligopolistic competition which were outlined in Chapter 3 can be summarised as follows. Firstly, it is normally necessary that there should be both Type A *and* Type B price competition in existence. Secondly, there should be a price–product competitive mix where it is appropriate. Thirdly, there should be low barriers to entry. Fourthly, there should exist 'rivalry' as defined in Chapter 3.

If the conditions of oligopolistic competition within the industry are not satisfactory for the achievement of our efficiencies it is necessary to ask wherein lies the impediment or impediments to efficient resource allocation. Do these arise from mergers, cartelisation via collusion, cartelisation via an information agreement, or even from the Act itself?

(ii) *Particular Cases*

(a) *Upheld agreements*. It will be convenient to take each of the major case studies in the order in which it occurs in our separate collection of case studies. Looking first at the *cement industry* we found that the Act had not improved resource allocation. The requirement of static efficiency had been departed from significantly. Prices diverged from costs vary considerably in the basic nature of the particular agreement which was upheld. In addition to this the Court introduced a further element of divergency by abolishing an aggregated rebate (which the agreement firms gave prior to the case) without ensuring that its abolition was reflected in prices. (In handing back the aggregated rebate the Court arguably also offended against the income distribution constraint.) But in any case the process which was used by the industry of arriving at prices through the averaging of the costs of all works, and the existence of a transport subsidy element in the agreement, ensured the divergence of prices from costs. In addition the superimposition of the 1964 Act on the working of the upheld agreement has further worsened resource allocation when we define the industry to include distribution. Prices as related to distribution now bear even less relationship to distributive costs than they did before because of price cutting by builders' merchants which has diverted custom from direct sales by manufacturers even when this is economical. Moreover, it seems clear that, except during the activities of the Prices and Incomes Board, the common prices have covered the costs of old and inefficient works and there has been no incentive to either X-efficiency or dynamic efficiency. There has been no significant emergence of rivalry in the industry and there are in any case inherent barriers to entry which impede the working of oligopolistic competition within this industry. In fact it is true that the industry has *not* been static in technological terms; but for this the 1956 Act can take no credit at all. Not only was the Court's handling of such issues as the crucial ones of profit levels, and the role of the Independent Cost Committee within the industry, a good deal less than satisfactory, but the Section 22 provision (allowing the Registrar to ask the Court to reconsider an agreement) has proved entirely inadequate. Moreover, in shoring up a position of extreme market power the Court might be regarded as offending the power constraint.

In the *permanent magnets industry* it seems clear that the Act failed to improve what was essentially an old-style British engineering industry with a 'jobbing' approach to business combined with collusion. In terms of static efficiency it was apparent that prices diverged from costs; that their continued divergence from costs was ensured by the Court's upholding of the agreement; that there is nothing in an undertaking given by the firms, in relation to Section 22 of the 1956 Act, to supply the Registrar with details of costs and prices, which will remedy this; and that, in the short run such divergence was worsened by the Court's handing back to the industry of the aggregated rebate, as occurred also in the case of the cement industry. The preservation of an alliance of small firms, ensuring suboptimality and excess capacity, is likely to produce neither static nor X-efficiency. In relation to dynamic efficiency, we found that though the Court disapproved of the withholding of new magnetic materials from the market, it did nothing about it. Although the case was founded upon dynamic efficiency, as will be clear from our full study, the significance of lower costs from technical co-operation when prices are not related to costs is hardly unambiguous. In addition the relationship of technical progress, and in particular of a patent pool of which the industry made much, to the agreement was dubious. In sum, technical progress had continued, but the Act could not take the credit for this. Again, this is an industry where the Act cannot be said to have improved resource allocation.

When we looked at the *metal windows industry* we found that prices certainly bore a closer relationship to costs than they did before the onset of competition policy, but that this was due, to a considerable extent, to factors other than the Act. On the one hand, there was the reaction of the industry to investigation by the Monopolies Commission; and on the other, there were events in the industry which occurred after, and in spite of, the decision of the Court. The latter failed to take account of significant over-capacity in the industry and failed also to accord due weight to the divergence of prices from costs implied in the method of price formation used in the industry which we detail in our full study. It thus failed to advance static efficiency. At the same time, it is clear from our study that the agreement was *not* necessary to technical progress which continued as fast outside the Association as within it, so that the Court in upholding the agreement failed to make any contribution to dynamic efficiency. However, the Act itself did make *some* contribution in that the largest and most important producer left the agreement and declined to be involved in defending it before the Court. Nevertheless the subsequent decision of the Court itself (in upholding the agreement) could have had no improving effect on resource allocation. At the same time all three forms of efficiency have been greatly increased by events in the industry involving the break-up of the agreement approved by the Court, the merger of Crittall with Hope, and the acquisition of the latter by the Slater Walker group which has been followed by significant rationalisation. The Act, in summary, did little harm in the case of this industry, but this is largely because the Judgement of the Court was overtaken by events.

In the *glazed tiles industry* the Act produced a benefit in terms of efficiency, at least nominally, before the agreement came to Court. For the successive reformulations of the agreement (with an eye to reference to the Court) offended less and less, at least on the surface, against the efficiency requirements. But the Court upheld the agreement in the industry and did not accept non-equation of price with costs as a detriment. It also authorised the continuance of an alliance of firms implying muted rivalry, excess capacity, and little or no motive to X-efficiency. However, because of separate forces within the industry, rationalisation has in fact proceeded in the years after the case. The selection mechanism has operated successfully. The Court by approving the agreement, seems to have provided a level of prices which has financed the rationalisation of the industry. However, this itself arguably offended the income distribution constraint; and the mergers financed in this industry may well be regarded as offending the power constraint. Nevertheless it may be argued that efficiency has been improved, as a result of the Act, although in a way in which the Court never foresaw. But it is still the case that prices do not relate to costs, so that the benefits of standardisation are not passed on. Nor is there any incentive to X-efficiency in the interchange of costings which has proved ineffective. In short the Act has improved resource allocation within this industry but largely by accident; and the continuance of the agreement upheld by the Court may well constitute a barrier to further improvements in resource allocation in this industry.

(b) *Struck down agreements.* The *transformer industry* has a long history of barriers to efficient resource allocation and of the departure of prices from costs. Ease of entry as a check on all this is limited to manufacture of small sizes of transformers. The failure of the industry's agreement before the Court was followed by a period of regulation through an information agreement but competition broke out in the years 1964–1966. This was only partly because of the Act, however, because there had also been a sharp increase in excess capacity. However, this price war in our judgement increased efficiency by eliminating excess capacity and has thus aided the achievement of static efficiency and stimulated X-efficiency. It has also, through improved designs, increased dynamic efficiency. (Details are to be found in our full study of the industry.) To that extent the Act, in so far as it was responsible for the price competition, may be said to have improved the allocation of resources quite clearly. At the same time its effect has not been unambiguously beneficial; for there is some evidence that contraction has proceeded too far and that there may have been some adverse effect on dynamic efficiency through cutting back expenditure on R & D.

Resource allocation in relation to the *carpet industry* also seems to have been improved by the Act although it is difficult to be sure how much of the improvement is due to the Act itself. The situation before the industry's agreement was struck down by the Court was (as we show in our account of the industry) not as bad (in some ways at least) as it appeared; however, in other ways it was worse, especially with regard to its coverage of the range of carpets. Nevertheless the Act, through the decision of the Court, was responsible for the ending of a comprehensive fixed price and exclusive dealing arrangement. The fixed price interfered with static efficiency since it did not relate in any recognisable way to costings. Low cost manufacturers were unable to increase their share of the market; there was thus an obvious barrier to X-efficiency, to the increasing of dynamic efficiency and to the operation of the selection mechanism. This was also true of the distributional system for carpets. The ending of the agreement allowed prices to approach costs, although the equation, at the time of our investigation, was very far from complete. It produced, however, a great improvement in resource allocation in distribution and there had been a certain amount of elimination of excess capacity in manufacture through mergers, although these were only partially due to the Act, and they have been followed by only a limited degree of rationalisation and integration. As we show in our study a major stimulus to improvement in efficiency has been the rise of tufted carpets and the use of synthetic fibres in traditional carpets. The Act has then only had a limited role in what occurred but it has probably speeded these last two important developments considerably.

In the case of the *glass container industry*, which had a long history of regulation, the success of the Act in improving efficiency does not seem to be in doubt. At the time the industry's agreement came to Court, there were wide differences in costs, allowing significant departures from static efficiency. A price war followed the ending of the agreement (an attempt to interfere with this through post-notification failed) and this stimulated all three kinds of efficiency. Price competition (both Type A and Type B) have helped to achieve both static efficiency and X-efficiency, and it is notable from our study that technical progress improved significantly with the ending of the agreement. The only doubt that arises from a resource allocation point of view is in relation to some of the mergers which have taken place for these (which are detected in our study) have had somewhat ambiguous implications for resource allocation. While static efficiency was improved through the elimination of excess capacity, and there was genuine operation of the selection mechanism, the muting of competition achieved by the mergers allowed greater scope for prices to depart from costs.

In the *wire rope industry* prices were fixed by the averaging of the lowest costs which limited (though it did not eliminate) departures of prices from costs. The interference of the agreement with static efficiency was then to some extent not too serious but the motives to the achievement of X-efficiency and dynamic efficiency were at the same time largely removed. After the failure of the agreement in the Court this situation was stabilised by price leadership. Nevertheless after the ending of the agreement Type B price competition came strongly into evidence and there was also some Type A as well. Static efficiency improved and this was probably also true of X-efficiency. At the same time mergers, which improved static efficiency through the elimination of excess capacity, have proved a double-edged weapon in our view, through their effect in reducing the pressure of rivalry; and there is also some evidence of a reduction in technical co-operation. But as a judgement it seems fair to say that, on balance, the Act has improved resource allocation in this industry.

In the case of *tyre distribution* the Act worked well, and it is instructive to note that the Court procedure proved significantly more effective in dealing with it than did the procedure of a Monopolies Commission investigation followed (theoretically) by administrative action. Indeed the Act had achieved some freeing-up in tyre distribution before the case as a number of restrictions which interfered with all three kinds of efficiency were abandoned before the agreement was presented to the Court. In fact the ending of the agreement proved largely successful (as our full study shows) in improving resource allocation. In particular the selection mechanism has worked well. There was an improvement in the quality of service thus meeting our consumer choice restraint (consumers now pay only for as much service as they want) and improvements also in productivity and in the relationship of prices (of distributors' services) to costs. Of course the scope for the industry to substitute a different kind of agreement was much more limited in this case than in one where what was involved was a simple price agreement between producers. Where the Act does seem to have been unsuccessful in this industry is in relation to the growth of manufacturers' owned outlets. These muted rivalry and thus interfered with the stimuli to efficiency. The Act was simply not equipped to deal with this problem.

However, the case of the *bread industry* is a good deal less satisfactory. It is true that the industry's agreement was improved, at least to the extent of the reintroduction of costings, after it had been referred to the Court but before it actually appeared in the Court. But the ending of the agreement had very little effect on competition in the industry. Until relatively recently there were no signs of a search for X-efficiency and indeed resource allocation was worsened by forward integration with old plant. The Act was then largely ineffective, and intervention by other governmental agencies such as the National Board for Prices and Incomes did not really transform the situation. There were mergers in the industry, and although these may have eliminated some excess capacity they have also had the effect of blunting whatever rivalry existed. The Act has thus been virtually without beneficial effect upon resource allocation within this industry and the agreement on prices which it was necessary for the firms in the industry to reach in making common submissions under the prices and incomes legislation can be regarded as setting the seal upon the industry's immunity to the beneficial effects of competition policy.

The *roadstone industry* was subject to a highly effective system of regulation and it is to the credit of the Act that this was abandoned as a result of the legislation. Type A price competition emerged, stimulated by new entry. Yet it was by no means universal, and information agreements forestalled competition until 1968 in some areas. However, their ending, coupled with the emergence of excess capacity, encouraged both price competition and the search for efficiency. The extension by firms of their selling areas beyond those to which they confined themselves in the days of cartelisation may be regarded as symptomatic of this. However, mergers also occurred and although these eliminated excess capacity thus aiding static efficiency they not only muted rivalry, hence interfering with the motives to all three kinds of efficiency, but they also produced units which some consider to be greater than the managerial optimum for this industry. The deleterious effects of the mergers would certainly seem (in our opinion, which is based on the detailed study of this industry) to have been greater than their benefits. Nevertheless the Act seems on balance to have improved resource allocation in this industry which became distinctly more competitive, with prices, particularly for spot purchases, approaching much more closely to resource costs, and with local authorities in a much stronger position to exercise their buying power to improve resource allocation.

In the *sanitary ware industry* the Act produced the abandonment of an agreement in 1957. A recession in the industry, producing excess capacity, followed, and prices were now free to fall in response to this, which they did. Elimination of excess capacity continued through the 1960s. Though mergers had their usual double-edged effect and although also there was price leadership, it seems clear that prices came to approach resource costs more closely than they had done in the days of the agreement and that the selection mechanism did work. It is also clear from our study that there emerged a considerable stimulus to X-efficiency in the new competitive state of the industry, as, despite price leadership, ample evidence of Type B price competition manifested itself, and technical progress proved entirely satisfactory.

The same general conclusion would seem to apply in the case of the *electric motors industry*. Despite a long history of collusion, the agreements for all three categories of motor were abandoned as a result of the 1956 Act, and although information agreements were substituted in the case of fractional horse power and large motors, these did not prevent a significant improvement in all three forms of efficiency, particularly dynamic efficiency. As our investigation showed, the selection mechanism worked well, even though some of the mergers do not seem to have been primarily inspired by a search for efficiency.

It is also satisfactory to be able to take the same view of developments in the *surgical dressings industry*. As our full study shows, a fairly comprehensive price agreement was broken very largely as a result of the impact of the 1956 Act on an oligopolistic situation. Abandonment of the agreement in the face of the Act was in some ways a formality after the agreement had already fallen in a large measure; but it had almost certainly fallen because of the enactment of the Act. Various devices with a strong information content were adopted in order to stem the flood of competition; but these in turn had to be abandoned because of the legislation, and strong price competition emerged. Its emergence was assisted by the introduction of a much greater degree of centralisation of purchasing by hospitals, which encouraged full development of competitive tendencies initiated by the legislation.

There was every sign of a closer approach to static efficiency following the ending of the agreement, the motives for X-efficiency were strong, and there was evidence of dynamic efficiency. At the same time there was no *prima facie* evidence of infringement of any of the constraints. Only two doubtful developments need to be mentioned. On the one hand it was not clear how far the mergers which had taken place had been the result of the operation of the selection mechanism; and on the other there was the slightly disturbing development that retail sales seemed increasingly to be carrying hospital sales through cross subsidisation. While sales to hospital boards involved selling to experts and thus offered little scope for product differentiation (or quantity impairment: see Chapter 3, section II (i)) the same was not true of retail sales. This was, however, a 'second-best' problem: the strength of competitive pressures (and thus presumptively the efficiencies) had been increased in one market only. Following the judgements in Chapter 3 this should not be regarded as an argument against the improvements that had taken place even though there was little more that could obviously be done in relation to the retail market.

Collusion in the *cable industry* is, as we indicate, as old as the industry itself. When the Monopolies Commission investigated the industry it found considerable cost variations behind a common price structure. As a result of its investigation market sharing schemes, exclusive dealing arrangements, and rebate schemes were terminated in 1954. These were important barriers to X-efficiency and dynamic efficiency, as well as offending the consumer choice and, to some extent, the income distribution constraints, so that significant steps to improvements in resource allocation predate the 1956 Act. However, it was following that Act, in 1959, that the significant barrier to static efficiency, the common price agreement, was abandoned. This was no doubt due in a large measure to the Act, although technical changes and excess capacity also played their part. However the Act gave these factors freedom to have their effects. Elimination of excess capacity followed but a marked improvement in resource allocation was impeded to a significant extent (as our account of the industry shows) by mergers designed to reduce rivalry, by information agreements, by the intervention of the Industrial Reorganisation Corporation, and (allegedly) by various 'predatory practices'. Nevertheless, unsatisfactory though the situation is, and still was at the time of our investigation, there seems no doubt that it was better than it would have been without any 1956 Act. The industry may be regarded as one of the Act's partial successes, even though it can be regarded as no more than this.

In the case of the *metal bath industry* there is, on the whole, a happier story. There had been agreement on prices in this industry since the 1930s but after the 1956 Act was passed there was a long period of keen price competition of both types, as our study shows. It is true that the agreement was under pressure even before it was cancelled in 1960, because of over-expansion of capacity in the 1950s. But industries free to operate a price agreement have shown themselves capable of withstanding such pressures, and of preventing the elimination of excess capacity and the approach of prices to costs to achieve static efficiency. However, mergers in this industry had their usual ambiguous effect and the elimination of excess capacity proceeded so far that, as we show, a virtual duopoly resulted. This is not so serious as it might seem however, because, of the rise of plastic baths; and it seems fair to conclude that resource allocation in the traditional sector of bath manufacture, viewed in terms of all three efficiencies, was improved even if there were offsetting factors to consider.

Like so many of the industries we have studied the *automotive battery industry* has a long history of price agreements. It is, therefore, at first sight gratifying to observe that exclusive dealing was abandoned in 1956 so that small makers were no longer prevented from supplying the market with cheap batteries and were thus able to emerge as competitors. The Act in this way helped to meet the consumer choice constraint. In addition the agreement between Lucas and Chloride on original equipment was apparently abandoned in 1956, and in the same year the agreement between Chloride, Crompton Parkinson and Oldham covering traction batteries was also abandoned. All of this was apparently conducive to greater efficiency in all three forms. However, we investigated this industry in some detail, and closer examination reveals a rather less satisfactory story. On the one hand there was still very great cohesion between the major manufacturers. On the other an information agreement was substituted for the abandoned B.S.B.A. agreement. The Monopolies Commission found that as a result of the latter, retail prices and discounts were still uniform in 1963. Thus there was still divergence from static efficiency and (presumptively) from the other two forms of efficiency. The information agreement was abandoned in 1964 and thereafter there emerged strong price competition with the general price level falling in real terms. There were indeed clear signs of improvement in all three forms of efficiency after that date. It is true that there remained a degree of cohesiveness between the big manufacturers which mitigated against efficiency, and it is true also that there was a growth of manufacturer-owned outlets – as in tyre distribution. Nevertheless we found clear evidence of rationalisation, good technical progress, and an entirely satisfactory level of R & D. Thus all three efficiencies, and resource allocation in general, seem to have improved after 1956. But in relating this to the 1956 Act two caveats must be entered here straight away. Firstly, the 1956 Act is only partially responsible for all this; the Monopolies Commission's role in investigating the industry proved to be of central importance. Secondly, the Act is not equipped to deal with vertical integration by manufacturers which may be subversive of efficiency.

Finally, of the main studies, we have the *steel drum industry*. Here was an industry, typical of small-scale engineering, with a common price and discount agreement protecting many small-scale inefficient producers with old plant. The agreement was abandoned as a result of the 1956 Act but the effect of this abandonment on resource allocation was virtually non-existent for a long time because of the substitution of an information agreement which was as effective as the old agreement. It was, however, abandoned after the *Galvanised Tanks* case, and strong net price competition followed. This was productive of rationalisation and mergers. To some extent this increase in efficiency was transitory; although there remained, at the time of our study, continuing signs of the search for X-efficiency and dynamic efficiency, the achievement of static efficiency was more questionable. For, although there were some signs of flexibility, it is by and large true that price and discount uniformity had returned. Nevertheless the Act can be credited with achieving an improvement in resource allocation in this industry.

Turning now to the twenty-two industries of which we made a less intensive study, we found, in attempting to evaluate the effect of the Act on resource allocation, that there were roughly three categories of industry. In the first category came those industries in which there would seem to have been a significant improvement in resource allocation. These included, for example: galvanised tanks, switchgear (sold to Area Boards), gas meters and pipes (drainage and sewage). Thus in the case of galvanised tanks, particularly after the case in 1965, we found significant improvement in all three types of efficiency, no removable barriers to entry or offence of our constraints and both Type A and Type B price competition in operation. In the case of switchgear we found competition emerging strongly following the collapse of the price agreement in 1960, technical change in both product and process and rationalisation. In the case of pipes and gas meters the pressure of competition seemed to have improved all three forms of efficiency. In both cases we would particularly stress the improvement in resource use accompanying rationalisation.

In the second category were those industries in which the Act may be judged partially to have improved resource allocation but in which there were still significant lacunae evident in this connection. In this group were, for example: confectionery, tyre mileage, electric meters, hard fibre rope and twine, and electric lamps. In the case of confectionery it seemed that an agreement covering both price and quality changes which clearly infringed the consumer choice constraint was abandoned as was, ultimately, an agreement on margins, although consideration was given to defending the latter in the Court. Cohesiveness as between manufacturers was still evident although prices were freer to align with costs than previously and inducements to X-efficiency and dynamic efficiency were stronger. Nevertheless the freeing-up of this industry was still incomplete. In the case of tyre mileage, a degree of competition was only achieved after the historic case concerning the industry's information agreement, and even then it was uncertain how much rationalisation, or true freedom of prices to align with costs, had been achieved. The producers of electric meters did abandon an agreement as a result of the 1956 Act, and there was a period of price competition which resulted in the elimination of some capacity, though very little else. But even this instrument of efficiency was largely eliminated in the second half of the 1960s. In the case of hard fibre rope and twine the evidence suggested that in the first half of the 1960s competition was muted and therefore there was for a period some possibility for price to diverge from resource use and for the stimuli to X-efficiency and dynamic efficiency to be inhibited. The Act may claim some improvement in efficiency through the elimination of excess capacity particularly on the rope side. Competition in electric lamp manufacture did increase as a result of the 1956 Act, and there was a degree of evidence of improvement in X-efficiency and dynamic efficiency. But this came about only very slowly and more as a result of a second investigation into the industry by the Monopolies Commission. The achievement of the Act on its own here was very limited indeed.

The industries in this category can then only be regarded as partial successes of the 1956 Act. But at least the Act achieved *something* in relation to resource allocation there. This is frankly more than can be said for it in its effects on the industries in category three. Examples in this category are such industries as: lace, black bolts and nuts, watertube boilers and paper bags. The lace industry's use of resources seems to have been entirely immune to the operation of the Act although the 1968 Act may have had some impact here. In the case of black bolts and nuts and watertube boilers an alliance of firms was sanctioned by the Court and in the light of our experience we must question the value of such an arrangement in terms of its effect on resource allocation. Particularly in the case of black bolts and nuts we would point out that it is open to doubt whether the relationship of prices and costs was improved. In the case of paper bags the effect of the Act may have been minimal largely because there were signs that the agreement was significantly undermined before the 1956 Act came along.

(iii) *Conclusions Concerning Resource Allocation*
Taking both major and minor case studies together it seems clear that the 1956 Act has had a significant effect on resource allocation, and that this effect has been almost entirely for the better. In the cases of only very few industries, mainly with those with agreement upheld by the Court, can it be said that the Act has been far outweighed by the achievements in relation to all three kinds of efficiency, the achievement of conformity with our constraints, the removal of barriers to entry, and the stimulation of rivalry and competition in other industries.

(a) *Objections–profit impairment.* However, it is desirable at this point that we should take note of two major criticisms of the operation of the Act which are sometimes levelled against it by those in industry. Firstly, there is the argument that the Act has severely affected the profitability of industry and altered the macroeconomic distribution of income in favour of labour. This it is argued has harmful effects on investment. *A priori* there does seem to be some substance in this argument. The 1956 Act and the prices and incomes policy of the latter part of the 1960s (which largely affected prices and not incomes) can both be said to have tilted the balance of power strongly in favour of labour, which was unaffected by both policies. The power of labour to raise wages was almost entirely unimpaired: the power of industry to recoup

N

these increases by raising prices to maintain profit margins was seriously impaired. Two aspects of monetary policy assisted this. Firstly, credit rationing further increased the difficulties of firms wishing to recoup wage increases: put crudely, who was going to lead off with a price increase when the bank would not carry him if his competitors did not follow? Secondly, interest rates did not adjust to the going rate of inflation. Prime rate bank credit often cost zero or less. This meant that an incentive to protect profit margins had been removed. But there are four points which should be made about this argument. Firstly, although there is macro-economic data which would support this argument, we have found little evidence for *harmful* paring of profit margins in the industries we have studied--though we have found some. If our sample is at all representative then the *a priori* argument and the macro-economic data overstate the problem considerably. Secondly, the 1960s prices and incomes legislation lapsed; and one has only to look at the experience of the cement industry, of which details are given in our study, to see that industry hastened to make up any deficiencies in earnings which occurred as a result of that legislation. Thirdly, the subsequent changes in monetary policy and especially the freeing of the commercial banks' lending rate from bank rate has meant that interest rates have been free to rise to a level where they become positive net of inflation. Fourthly, the macro-economic data gives no indication of the extent to which the course followed, for example, by A.P.C.M. (Blue Circle Cement), namely revaluation of assets, has been responsible for the apparent fall in the share of capital; but it can be said with some confidence that such revaluation is an obvious course in a period of prices and incomes legislation, quite apart from the fact that there is evidence that the creation of conglomerates based on a shrewd appraisal of the extent of undervaluation of assets, has stimulated a number of firms who wished to avoid being taken over and 'realised' to revalue their assets. We must conclude then that the general argument is doubtful.

(b) *Export impairment.* The second criticism levelled at the Act by some in industry is that it has interfered with cross-subsidisation of exports through reducing home market profitability. We have already seen reason to doubt the significance and extent of such a reduction in profitability. However, allowing that it did occur to some very limited extent, let us examine the export argument on its merits. Let it be said, firstly, that the macro-economic data that is available, while it is hardly unambiguous, would not seem to support this contention; nor, perhaps more importantly, would the micro-experience of the industries we have studied. But in any case subsidisation of exports, though certainly indulged in by firms with protected home market positions, would seem to involve a misallocation of resources in anything but the shortest run. To this (which might be described as the *simpliste* position) the reply might be made that if other countries do this (that is, if they encourage subsidisation by lax competition policies) then we face relative depreciation of our exchange rate, which is likely to turn the terms of trade against us thereby reducing our international purchasing power, if we do not do the same. It does not, however, follow from this that the way to correct such a state of affairs is ourselves to adopt a lax competition policy since the price to be paid for this in terms of lost growth may be too severe if, as our study would seem to indicate, competition policy has positive productivity. Rather the remedy should be sought in tax or tariff policies – the latter being directed against the export subsidisers. Broadly based anti-dumping powers should be used here.

The Act can then be judged to have improved resource allocation, however incompletely, and to have done very little real harm. At the same time it must be clear that although the Act has gone *some* way along the path of improving resource allocation in most of the industries we have studied, a very great deal indeed remains to be done. But for the Act to do this will depend in some considerable degree upon amending the legislative framework in order to strengthen it. It is to this that we now turn.

III. THE LEGISLATIVE FRAMEWORK

It is now necessary to turn, in this final section of our conclusion, to consider the legislative framework of competition policy in the United Kingdom. We will discuss a number of apparent defects in the present provisions and procedure and we will then make our suggestions for remedying these defects. Suggestions will also be made about purchasing policy in the public and private sectors.

(i) *Main Defects*
(a) *Mergers*. It will be apparent from the preceding discussion that, in our view, mergers may well offend resource allocation requirements. They are often of a non-rationalising nature and completed with a view to stifling competitive pressure which otherwise would lead to greater efficiency in the allocation of resources. This is most obviously true in the case of horizontal mergers. But

it is also true that forward integration can be used to replace exclusive dealing (as in tyre distribution and battery manufacture cases) and the resulting structure may prove extremely rigid and restrictive. The apparatus for investigation of mergers which existed at the time of our study giving, as it did, arbitrary powers to the Department of Trade and Industry to do absolutely nothing was highly unsatisfactory. In addition the criteria then laid down for Monopolies Commission investigations (one-third of total production or assets of £5 million) was quite unnecessarily limiting in this field. Moreover, the 1965 Act which enables the Commission to investigate mergers if so requested by the D.T.I. leaves vertical mergers largely untouched.

This situation contrasts very sharply with that prevailing in the United States where, since the early 1960s, Section 7 of the Clayton Act has been effectively operated against mergers. It has been used to prevent the acquisition by leading firms of their competitors and has even been applied where the lessening of competition was still in its infancy. It is applied to both horizontal and vertical mergers and the likelihood of other mergers being triggered off is also taken into account as is the existence of a *trend* towards concentration (whatever its absolute level) in the relevant market. The attitude taken is indeed extremely severe. Joint ventures which do not establish that neither firm would have entered a market on its own have been held to violate the law as diminishing potential competition.

All this may seem somewhat draconian and even possibly harmful. It is undeniable that some mergers do improve efficiency. They can be an important manifestation of the selection mechanism. Indeed some of them, in industries we have studied, seem to have produced a degree of rationalisation quite unforeseen by their original sponsors. It is true also that if firms are granted legal immunity from being taken over this itself could mitigate against efficiency. But such arguments are hardly conclusive. Thus if a takeover is allowed to proceed this will increase the security of the firm making the takeover. Moreover, when all allowance has been made for the undeniable potential benefits of mergers the fact remains that our case studies are replete with examples of dubious mergers. Glass containers, baths, carpets, wire ropes, bread, sanitary ware and electric cables, are just a few of the industries which could be cited.

The British treatment of mergers has so far really involved little more than tentatively nibbling the edges of the problem. The role of the D.T.I. under the pre-1973 legislation was that of managing to combine a startling degree of inactivity throughout most of the field with a marked disinclination to refer even the most obvious candidates for investigation to the Monopolies Commission when pressed to do so.[54] The Commission, for its part (and really through no fault of its own) proceeded very slowly in dealing with merger proposals. Clearly some remedy for this situation was required, for competition policy as it existed at the time, with no effectively operable provision for mergers was very unbalanced.

(b) *Tariffs*. It was apparent to us in our investigations of particular industries, and it will be clear to the reader who consults our full case studies, that the growth of tariffs in the 1920s and especially in the 1930s made the operation of price rings very much easier. Conversely it should be apparent that conditions of extreme market power can be modified significantly by the removal of tariffs. This can be of assistance not only in the case of single-firm monopolies and very small number oligopolies (e.g. as in the case of rayon) but also where there is collusion by firms, the existence of which is known, but concerning which there is insufficient evidence for proceedings in the Court. Yet government has shown extraordinary reluctance to use this weapon of competition policy to improve domestic resource allocation. Partly this is for reasons of international politics; for it is certainly true that unilateral tariff reductions are one way of stripping oneself of bargaining counters. It is also partly due to the misleading application of arguments about external balance to competition policy–the new mercantilism which characterised the 1960s. The first of these involves political judgement, but it is somewhat doubtful judgement in the light of the policy of successive governments in G.A.T.T. and E.E.C. negotiations. The second, as should be clear from what was said above in section II of this chapter concerning exports, is largely fallacious. In view of this the refusal to use tariff changes as a weapon of competition policy can be regarded as the wilful abandonment by government of a potentially powerful weapon.

(c) *Legal loopholes*. The years since the passing of the 1956 Act have seen the closing of loophole after loophole which legal advisers found or thought they had found in that Act. Due to the diligence of the Registrar and his staff a series of cases, of which *Basic Slag*, *Galvanised Tanks* and *Tyre Mileage* are undoubtedly the most significant, have succeeded in strengthening the law and closing the major loopholes; and the 1968 Act, despite its undoubted defects in a number of respects (these will be returned to below) set the seal upon the Registrar's efforts. However, apart from mergers, which have already been discussed and which may quite legally be substituted for collusion, we found four other loopholes in the Act. The first of these related to trade association recommendations. Trade associations may issue circulars to their members making what are in effect recommendations about policy. Thus for instance we came across one case where a trade association had advised its members not to accept Barclay cards. This conduct brought a warning from the Registrar and a request for the withdrawal of the recommendation. This was complied with; but the members of the trade association adhered to the original recommendation. It will probably not have escaped the reader's notice that there are in fact a number of distinct categories of shops none of which accept such credit cards.

A second defect, which almost amounts to a legal loophole in the legislation relates to export agreements. These are usually agreements virtually identical in provisions to an agreement which covered both the home and the export market prior to 1956 but which now cover only the export market. There seems little doubt that, to put it mildly, the collective conduct at which firms arrive in export agreements may exert some influence upon their conduct in the domestic market.

The third legal loophole relates to the creation of joint marketing companies. Two firms may effectively share a market collusively simply by setting up a joint marketing company in which one of them has a majority shareholding. This was the device employed by Schweppes and by Kia-Ora (J. Lyons). It was not until June of 1971 that registration of this agreement was ordered by Lord Justice Stamp, following lengthy legal processes. The companies had previously argued that their device did not come within the ambit of the 1956 Act as Lyons were merely acting as a supplier to a subsidiary of Schweppes. The agreement is now registered but at the time of writing no proceeding with respect to it has been taken and the position of such devices is not clear.

Price leadership appears to prove another legal loophole. In practice it is not easy to separate price leadership from informational arrangements in general. It is, however, noteworthy that the 1968 Act relates explicitly to information agreements; it does not deliberately and explicitly set out to bring price leadership within the ambit of the 1956 legislation. It is also interesting to see that in 1971 price leadership was referred to the Monopolies Commission; again this suggests that the practice may be viewed as being outside the Registrar's purview. It is on the other hand easy to see how even though a price increase may be announced to customers before rivals yet the latter may in effect come to follow such increases and an 'arrangement' may in fact arise.

These are the main legal loopholes. However, there is another device which, although not involving a loophole in the Act itself, does involve the creation of conditions under which the policies of independent companies may be co-ordinated. This is the device of interlocking directorates. In the United States these are prohibited by Section 8 of the Clayton Act. Moreover, by this legislation, interlocking can be disentangled after it has taken place. There is no provision whatever in the United Kingdom for dealing with such directorates despite the fact that they supply an open invitation to the muting of competition.

(d) *Illegal evasion.* One thing which emerges very clearly from our study, even though we have not always been able to cite the industries concerned for fear of bringing repercussions down upon the people who have helped us, is that the present legislative framework for the operation of competition policy is significantly inadequate to deal with evasion of the law. There seems, it is clear, to be a fair amount of unregistered collusion. In some industries there are periodic attempts at organising rings, especially where contracts are involved; and 'gentlemen's agreements' not to make products which will be sold in the market of other producers really come into the same category. The report of the Registrar for the years 1966 to 1969 does indeed hint at awareness of substantial secret collusion.[55] It is true that, under Section 6 of the 1968 Act, agreements have to be registered *before* they take effect; and that, under Section 7, affected parties may sue for damage caused by an unregistered agreement being in operation. It is also true that if the Registrar detects an unregistered agreement he may apply to the Court for an order against that agreement, breach of which would be contempt of Court. But these are muted sanctions indeed; there is a good deal of evidence to suggest that they are a good deal too muted. Moreover, the decision of Justice Cross, and the Court of Appeal in the case of the *Registrar of Restrictive Trading Agreements* v. *W. H. Smith & Son Limited and Others*[56] means that the Registrar's powers of investigation are severely limited–by an interpretation of the Act which seems to defy common sense.

Of course it is true that secret collusion is much less watertight than an open legal collusion. Thus it was put to us by one firm which had tried such collusion that 'Apart from M.P.s there are no more unscrupulous people than businessmen.' What our interviewees meant was that secret collusion does not work because of non-adherence by some parties to the agreement. In so far as this is true the Act can be credited with achieving greater flexibility than existed before. But there is enough evidence to suggest that secret collusion is still capable of substantially muting the forces which make for efficiency.

There is also the problem of unregistered information agreements. There seems little doubt that a great many of the agreements which were ostensibly abandoned to avoid registration under the 1968 Act have simply gone underground. They are capable of producing a high degree of cohesion and a very low intensity of competition with a correspondingly low degree of efficiency in the allocation of resources. But the Registrar's chances of detecting them seem to be, if anything, even slimmer than his chances of detecting secret but explicit collusion.

(e) *Government intervention.* Readers of the detailed case studies, published separately, will note that, in industry after industry, the Second (and First) World War was of crucial importance in establishing a price ring as the controlling force in an industry because of the co-operation with, and indeed elevation of, that ring by the Board of Trade. It seems equally clear that government intervention in industries in the latter part of the 1960s had similar undesirable effects. In particular the prices and incomes legislation was responsible for the preparation of common submissions by such industries as bread and sanitary ware. These obviously and necessarily involved collusion on price increases. That same legislation spawned Section 2 of the 1968 Act which empowers various government departments to approve agreements made to restrict increases in prices; an agreement thus approved is exempt from registration while the order is in force. It requires little imagination to see the potentiality of this. No less than ninety agreements were approved under this section.

Thirdly, ministries sometimes sanctioned increases in prices beyond those recommended under the prices and incomes legislation and in industries where pressure for a better allocation of resources was patently required. (The cement industry, which was able to find succour in the Ministry of Public Buildings, is a case in point.) Fourthly, government action taken under the aegis of the now defunct National Plan and in the various Little Neddies weakened competition policy. Not only was it responsible for Section 1 of the 1968 Act—which empowered the D.T.I. to approve agreements judged to be in the 'national interest' and exempt them from the proceedings of the 1956 Act–but the Little Neddy meetings seem to have proved suitable forums for agitation for reversal of Court decisions. Thus for instance we learnt that in the case of tyre distribution that there had been attempts, meeting with official encouragement, to re-introduce the Tyre Trade Register by this means.

There seems little doubt that government was insufficiently aware of the dangers of a number of courses of action which it pursued, particularly in the late 1960s, when viewed in the context of competition policy. Effectively it acted as a referee who changed the rules when it seemed a convenient moment. Samuel Brittan has argued powerfully against such 'pragmatism' on the grounds that this reflects 'the fashion or political pressures of the moment'.[57] This is an important consideration particularly as the motivation for such action, usually not spelled out, may be fallacious. The same author's suggestion that Section 1 of the 1968 Act was in fact based in a large measure on the failure of the export gateway in the 1956 Act, and that exemption of agreements was provided for with this in mind, and his further suggestion that much of the activity of the I.R.C. was influenced by the same kind of 'mercantilism', is extremely important in this respect.[58]

(f) *Incomplete coverage.* The legislative framework for competition policy at the time of our study was also incomplete in two important respects. First of all, although the Monopolies Commission was empowered to investigate services, the legislation under the 1956 Act in relation to restrictive practices does not cover services. There did not seem to be any economic reason whatever why services should be afforded this privileged position. Secondly, the nationalised industries were exempt from the purview of either the Restrictive Practices Court or of the Monopolies Commission. We cannot see any *economic* as distinct from political reason why nationalised industries should be excluded from surveillance. Nationalised firms have shown themselves capable of engaging in restrictive practices–as in the *Galvanised Tanks* case which involved Richard Thomas and Baldwin–and although they are covered by the existing law when they act collusively with private firms there is nothing whatever to control their operation of predatory practices. Nor has the Monopolies Commission any power to investigate the single firm monopoly position of nationalised industries. The problem of the nationalised industries may not be a serious one, but there is no clear reason why they should be granted total immunity from competition policy. It should be added that the immunity of the nationalised industries strengthens the belief of private industry in the case of laxness in competition policy.

(g) *Unsatisfactory nature of the gateways.* A number of criticisms of the gateways in Section 21 (1) (b) of the 1956 Act were advanced in Chapter 2 of this book and these stand. Gateway (a) is clearly redundant. Where public safety is involved legislation specifically directed towards that end is required. In any case the plea of public safety usually amounts to little if anything more than window dressing. Gateway (b) clearly has to stand. It may be that a reformulation specifically in terms of efficiency would be desirable–a point considered in Chapter 2. Similarly although gateway (c) may be considered redundant it has done no harm that we have been able to discover in the course of this study and it is probably best left there, as there is no point in making restrictive practices legislation seem unfair, even though the gateway itself is vulnerable to criticism as we have already seen. Again, gateway (d) is vulnerable to criticism; but the situation which it envisages certainly does exist and it is only because the legislation has been evaded in various ways that few industries have had to rely on this gateway. Gateway (g) is necessary because, together with gateway (b), it underlies the whole approach of the 1956 Act. But having said that, it is quite clear that gateways (e), (f) and (h) are entirely unsatisfactory. The employment gateway (e) is a strange anomaly. Employment policy is not the same as competition policy. Employment problems should be dealt with by the normal combination of national macro-economic policies and special regional economic policies. The Court has obviously taken the same view from the *Yarn Spinners* Judgement onwards and has thus forced government to accept this view–hence the Cotton Industry Reorganisation Act. Gateway (f) is both redundant and, in its underlying thinking, fallacious. The export argument has already been dealt with to some extent in section II above on resource allocation; and indeed much of the export argument in fact implies the idea of cross-subsidisation dealt with there. But it is perhaps worth stressing, in addition to these criticisms and those made in Chapter 2, that distortion of the allocation of resources and muting of the pressures towards efficiency in that allocation in the interests of short-term gain to the balance of payments is not a policy which has much to commend it on economic grounds. Gateway (h), which was added under the 1968 Act, and allows a firm to plead that its agreement simply does no harm, has already been criticised by two of the authors of this book[59] and the criticism still stands. Such are the dangers of even ostensibly innocuous agreements to exchange information that positive gains should be established under Section 21 (1) (b) if the agreement is to be approved.

(h) *Defects of Court procedure.* Although, as will be seen below, we believe that the judicial treatment of restrictive practices is desirable and that this characteristic of the legislative framework should be retained, it is still true that there are defects in the procedure of hearing agreements in the Court. There are three defects which seem to us to be worth mentioning in the light of our studies in this book. Firstly, although precedent is said to be an advantage of Court procedure, and it undoubtedly is, its scope seems to be somewhat limited. Thus if the Court had been consistent between the *Cement* case on the one hand and the *Permanent Magnets* and *Glazed Tiles* cases on the other it would have required price reductions in the latter two cases in order that profits in those industries should be lowered to a level which accorded with the security of a price agreement. Secondly, the picture which the Court receives of an industry may be very far from complete. This was, we found, particularly true in the case of carpets; and it is doubtful, had the Monopolies Commission not already made the discovery, whether the Court would have been able to learn of Dunlop's secret ownership of subsidiaries in tyre distribution. Thirdly, we cannot help but be unfavourably impressed by the freedom given to Counsel in the Court. In one case in particular an expert witness was subjected to questions about his career and qualifications which had absolutely no relevance whatever to the case. This kind of problem is of course not confined to cases in the Restrictive Practices Court. But it is a particularly sensitive area, since no criminal proceedings are involved. Not only do businessmen who have been mangled by Counsel feel disinclined to reappear in the Court whatever the merits of their case but expert witnesses also feel thus disinclined. Such an effect on expert witnesses obviously weakens the power and effectiveness of the Court procedure.

(i) *Defects of the 1968 Act.* Apart from the criticisms made above of the gateway (h) which was added in the 1968 Act, two other criticisms should be made of this Act. Firstly, Section 1 of the Act which allows the D.T.I. to exempt from the operation of competition policy agreements which it judges to be in the national interest is, as we have already argued elsewhere,[60] highly undesirable. It appears that it has only been used once. But that may very well be due to the demise of the I.R.C. and should this be regenerated or should the mercantilism of the late 1960s, which has never been wholly dormant, gather new strength, the power contained in this section of the Act could be seriously misused. Mr Brittan's strictures on 'pragmatism' are particularly relevant here. Other industries than the paper industry (which was the one successful in this instance) may have pleaded for exemption unsuccessfully. But 'pragmatic' policy could alter very sharply in the future. This is *par excellence* a provision which gives politicians and others the power to interfere with the normal operation of competition policy. Section 2 of the Act which allows for the exemption of agreements made under prices and incomes legislation has already been criticised in section (e) above under the heading of government intervention and there is no need to repeat the criticism here.

(j) *Defects in the Commission procedure*. Although there have been some high water marks in its operations, notably the report on Collective Discrimination, it seems undeniable that the Monopolies Commission, viewed as a major instrument of competition policy, has been remarkably ineffective. This is not so much because of the Commission itself which, despite some occasionally curious appointments, has done sterling work. Rather the blame must be laid at the door of the Board of Trade (D.T.I.) and successive ministers who have often been unwilling to refer industries to the Commission and (subsequently) to do anything about the Commission's recommendations. Moreover, the procedure which exists at the moment gives no real force to those recommendations. Orders giving force to them have rarely been issued by ministers and at the same time voluntary undertakings given by industries are not always taken seriously by those industries. So that whatever sterling investigatory work the Commission does (and it has done a very great deal) its efforts rarely come to full fruition.

Moreover, all this is quite apart from the extraordinary delays which have on a number of occasions manifested themselves between completion of a report by the Commission and its publication.

(ii) *Amendments to the Legislative Framework*
As a result of our study we felt that a number of amendments to the legislation framework were called for. These recommendations were written about eighteen months before the 1973 Fair Trading

Bill was published; and the best course of action seemed to be to let our conclusions stand and to comment on the new legislation in the light of them. We do the latter in Chapter 5.

(a) *General framework*. We would propose that the present dual system combining the Registrar and Court on the one hand and the Monopolies Commission on the other should remain. Despite criticisms made above there is no doubt that the judicial procedure, as independent of political decision, has shown enormous advantages over the system operated prior to 1956. Moreover, again despite criticisms noted above, the judicial characteristics of precedent and contempt are not only of the greatest assistance in operating competition policy expeditiously but are also of assistance to those affected by that policy. At the same time the Monopolies Commission has shown itself to be a highly effective method not only of investigating restrictive practices and positions of market dominance but also of uncovering the often relevant historical details of how these practices and positions were achieved. It has also proved a most valuable supplement to the enforcement procedure (of which more will be said below) of the Registrar's Office.

(b) *Main proposals on judicial procedure*. There can be little doubt that the results achieved by the Registrar and his staff in implementing the 1956 Act have been little short of dramatic, despite the typical quietness and intentional lack of drama with which this has been done. Through the efforts of the Registrar and his staff the whole climate of opinion in respect of restrictive practices has been changed very much for the better and awareness of their activities undoubtedly informs decisions made by business management. Nevertheless there are a number of areas where we felt that the framework within which they have to work needed improvement. Firstly, there seems little doubt that the procedure for registration of agreements needs tightening up. The main requirement here is the provision of an effective sanction to deter firms who do not register. An effective sanction only exists if the Registrar is sufficiently well informed of the activities of an unregistered agreement to obtain an order from the Court under the 1968 Act. This then brings us to our second recommendation which is that the powers of investigation of the Registrar need strengthening. We have seen throughout this study that industry has resorted to one stratagem after another to avoid the full impact of competition policy. Those who collude are often too sophisticated to use a device so crude as common pricing. It is therefore necessary that the Registrar's staff should have the power of descending unannounced upon firms. Coupled with this is a need for strengthening the powers of enforcement of all the decisions of the Court. But for the investigations by the Monopolies Commission of the battery and lamp industries these industries would have remained unscathed by the Act. There is also a need for strengthening Section 22 of the 1956 Act. This is particularly necessary as the Court was apparently doubtful of the extent of its powers to give the Registrar supervision over the Permanent Magnet manufacturers–details will be found in the full discussion of this industry. Indeed it is clear, particularly from the history of the cement industry which we give in our study that, if an agreement is to be allowed to continue, much more stringent safeguards are necessary than at present exist. This need might well be met by an extension of the powers of Section 22.

It is also important that the Registrar's staff should not be reduced now that the period of intensive Court activity is over. Rather, resources previously used in prosecution should be redeployed in enforcement.

The next recommendation is that the Court should concentrate on creating *conditions* for competition. This is important because the Court has shown itself notably deficient in the assessment of accounting data particularly in relation to profit levels. It is also desirable that the *sub-judice* rules should be enforced in relation to proceedings. Press handouts by industries in the course of defending agreements before the Court, predicting dire consequences should the Court find against them, are a highly undesirable way of bringing indirect pressure to bear upon the Court.

The precedent, dating from *In re Chemists' Federation Agreement (No. 2)*,[61] which allows, and indeed requires, the Court to ignore the *intentions* of those formulating an agreement should be removed by legislation. If the intentions of those formulating an agreement are not sincere in relation to its declared objects these are not likely to be achieved in the *long* run whatever may be done in the *short* run prior to the Court case.

In the light of what was said above about the effects of government intervention the Registrar should at least be kept informed of, and better still, be represented on, the various Little Neddies.

Price cutting as a 'predatory practice', particularly when used either to enforce price leadership or to achieve takeovers, should be made illegal and the enforcement of its ban should be made a responsibility of the Registrar. There is less evidence of such practices since 1956 because, on the one hand, it is easier for a ring than for one firm to finance such behaviour and, on the other, the main motive of such conduct used to be that of forcing competitors either into a ring or out of existence. But there are still some signs of this practice and control is needed. The same may be said of interlocking directorates; there is a case for, at the very least, control in this area and quite a strong *prima facie* case for prohibition. Export agreements should also come under the purview of the Registrar and here a degree of surveillance may not be out of place.

The recommendations of the Monopolies Commission concerning refusal to supply (Cmnd. 4372, July 1970) should be implemented; and pressure from established outlets to refuse supply to a new entrant should be made *per se* illegal. Again supervision should be the responsibility of the Registrar.

The final requirements for strengthening the legislation on the judicial procedure are that the legal loopholes noted above should be closed, that services should be included together with goods in the coverage of the restrictive practices legislation, that the gateways should be amended as suggested above, and that Sections 1 and 2 of the 1968 Act should be repealed. Price leadership should quite explicitly be brought within the ambit of the 1956 Act. That is although a price increase may be notified to customers before rivals, an arrangement may arise whereby other firms will always follow the announced lead. (The loophole in relation to the activities of trade associations and their recommendations could be closed by giving the Registrar power to apply to the Court for the imposition of a fine upon trade associations which had made such recommendations which were adhered to by their members despite the withdrawal of the recommendations.)

At the same time some modifications to the procedure from the point of view of those affected by the legislation are also desirable. Firstly, Section 22 of the 1956 Act should be amended so that it is quite clear that an *industry* can apply to have an agreement reinstated because of a change in circumstances. Thus the transformer industry was affected by the coming together of the Area Boards; yet it is far from clear that it could simply have applied to have an agreement already processed reinstated as distinct from registering a new agreement and going to all the expense, trouble and discomfort of defending it. Secondly, because of the expense involved in defending agreements, which not only encourages evasion of the law but also acts as a built-in bias against what might otherwise be justifiable agreements, the costs incurred in meeting anti-trust action should receive particularly favourable tax treatment. Thirdly, direction should be given to the judges of the Restrictive Practices Court on the degree of freedom which Counsel is to be afforded in that Court in examining both parties to agreements and expert witnesses.

(c) *Main proposals on Commission procedure.* The Monopolies Commission should be increased in size and allowed to work in small groups (even more than has been the case since 1965). It should have full-time members. In view of the unwillingness of Ministers and the D.T.I. to refer industries to the Commission, a Registrar of Monopolies and Mergers (who might be the same person as the Registrar of Restrictive Trading Agreements), should be appointed. The independence from day-to-day politics which has proved so invaluable in relation to initiatives to deal with restrictive practices under the 1956 Act would then be extended to monopolies (together with other concentrated situations and nationalised industries–see below). These three provisions should help to increase the speed and effectiveness of the Commission's work. Upon completion the Commission's report should be published immediately. Most importantly, its recommendations should have the same force as Statutory Orders, and the enforcement thereof should be the responsibility of the Registrar of Monopolies and Mergers. (Obviously this is inapplicable where legislation is required.) The relevant minister should have the power of vetoing a recommendation. This will reverse the present position in that under the proposed one, action will *normally* be taken and if it is not taken inaction will have to be justified in the House of Commons.

The Commission should concern itself with four main groups of situations. These are, firstly, monopoly situations; secondly, small-number oligopoly situations; thirdly, nationalised industries; and fourthly, mergers. It is our view that the one-third criterion (in the case of the monopolies and oligopolies) and the one-third and £5 million assets criteria (in the case of mergers) are too restrictive. A more flexible standard should be adopted which would enable investigations to take place below these limits. Thus in the case of mergers the Registrar would have the possibility of demanding justification (see below) of mergers which did not fall within the present criteria but which significantly reduced competition (Section 7 of the Clayton Act would be a guide here) or held out in prospect that such a reduction would ensue perhaps by merger matching. In examining monopoly and other concentrated situations the Commission should continue to be allowed to examine the way in which such a position has been built up. In the case of mergers, however, the historical material might well be considerably lightened in the interests of speed. In dealing with all four categories it should be able to make recommendations concerning tariffs. It should be quite willing to use its powers to recommend divestiture.[62] In looking at nationalised industries it should be able to investigate (in particular) cross-subsidisation within the industry and predatory practices by the industry.

The great area of expansion of the Commission's activities should be in relation to mergers. In the light of the volume of work which would be involved if the Commission were to be required to investigate even a substantial proportion of a year's mergers (which may total 1,000 or more) an approach similar to that operated in the United States might be followed; that is to say there might be a presumption that mergers are undesirable where there is any significant lessening of actual or potential competition. The role of the Commission would then be to hear representations by those who wished to achieve a merger and to judge whether or not the merger should be treated as an exception to the general presumption.[63] Normally the parties should have to justify the merger in terms of improved efficiency in resource allocation, quantifying such alleged benefits as economies of scale. However, in an industry with a number of firms going out of business, but taking a long time to do so and in the interim damaging investment, it should be open to the potentially merged parties to invoke a 'failing company' provision similar to that used in the United States. Thus the procedure would not seriously impede the selection mechanism. However, where the Commission finds that a merger is justifiable it should be empowered to follow up the effects of the merger and to see whether the alleged benefits have been realised. The mergers dealt with should not be merely horizontal ones but also vertical ones. Enough has been said in the course of this book to indicate that vertical mergers can have a severely restraining effect upon competition.

It could be argued that the machinery for dealing with mergers could, given the number of mergers in recent years, be swamped by applications to merge. Clearly the process of assessing the benefit of mergers is a time-consuming one, particularly since we propose that quantification, rather than mere assertion, of advantages would be called for. However, it by no means follows that the machinery would be swamped. It has to be remembered that the new approach would be radically different from that adopted under

o

the 1965 Act; there would, reminiscently of the 1956 Act, be a basic presumption against mergers. This might deter many from attempting to get a merger approved. Also, and again reminiscently of the 1956 Act, many mergers might be deterred if some of the early Commission decisions were to be founded on as strong a belief in the benefits of competition.

If, however, applications to merge still flowed in an embarrassing number then one of two courses of action might have to be contemplated. One would be to adopt a selective system–i.e. picking on the most important cases through reference by the Registrar. This does have the disadvantage of being highly arbitrary and discriminatory. We would therefore be driven, albeit reluctantly, to the alternative course of adopting a legal posture similar to that laid down in the Clayton Act. This would eliminate the time-consuming Commission stage.

(d) *Purchasing policy.* This discussion of policy proposals also provides a convenient opportunity to refer to some of the practical lessons which the various case studies have to offer for those engaged in purchasing. They apply equally to those in the private and public sectors.

As already pointed out the 1956 Act provided an impetus to the exertion of greater buying power. The exertion of such power was of little use when there was a common front on the production side. It was only when the Act opened up cracks in the once solid front that various devices for exerting buying power came into their own. Two lessons stand out in the case studies discussed above. Purchasers are likely to get better terms if they centralise purchasing; and they are likely to get better terms if they buy on a secret tender basis rather than off list.

It could be argued that this is a matter of redistributing the profit margin rather than increasing efficiency. There are two replies to this. The first is that if there is an imbalance of power which favours producers then the devices we have discussed seem eminently justifiable as methods of achieving a more equitable power balance. Secondly, pressure on profit margins could provide an incentive to increase efficiency. Moreover, centralising of purchases may be accompanied by a pruning of ranges of goods purchased and by the placing of regular bulk orders which can give rise to economies of scale at the production and distribution stages.

(iii) *Conclusion*

The proposals for amendments to the framework of competition policy contained in the previous section involve some fairly radical extensions of the existing framework. At the same time it should be emphasised that they are *extensions*; the basic framework has proved satisfactory but in the course of this study we have noted a number of defects. The task of those who have had to operate competition policy in this country has not always been very easy during the years since 1956 and what we have said is not intended to cast reflections upon them. Indeed it is surprising that so much has been achieved, given the shortcomings of the framework. That framework now needs strengthening and extending in the ways that we have suggested in order that competition policy may continue its valuable work in improving resource allocation by intensifying the stimuli to static efficiency, X-efficiency and dynamic efficiency.

REFERENCES

1 In respect of minor case studies where we have uncovered evidence of activities which contravene the law the names of the industries involved will not be revealed.
2 The market power of Leavers' lace producers was, however, limited by Schumpeterian factors. Leavers' lace is the traditional fancy dress lace which has a long history. But in recent years it has been increasingly displaced by Raschel lace which to the untutored eye is indistinguishable from the traditional variety. Raschel is based on the knitting process, which leads to economy in production–costs are said to be 50–75 per cent of the traditional product.
3 Not all case studies are cited since in some cases historical data is not available whilst in others (such as sand and gravel and roadstone) agreements were regional and no one figure is relevant.
4 It was put to us that, for example, A.E.I. was a member of every available ring. Almost certainly this did nothing to stimulate efficiency! The situation in heavy electrical equipment is a good but not perfect example of inclusion of the largest and best-known firms–e.g. Parsons were outside the turbo-alternator ring although they co-operated in respect of sales to the C.E.A. Then again Brook Motors was outside the relevant motor agreements. (A good example of inclusivity was chocolate and sugar confectionery where all the well-known names were parties to the so-called Five Firm Agreement which existed until 1956.)
5 Monopolies and Restrictive Practices Commission, *Report on the Supply of Sand and Gravel in Central Scotland*, 1956, pp. 56–7.
6 *Ibid.*, p. 57.
7 *Ibid.*, p. 57.
8 See Register R.617.
9 An old chestnut is that agreements having been signed parties made exits

from meetings for ostensibly natural reasons but actually for the purpose of passing telephone messages which enabled sales to be gained by anticipating the price increase.

10 In the case of standard metal windows it is interesting to note that attempts to provide a more satisfactory costing system appear to have owed their existence to the attentions of the Monopolies Commission.

11 See for example *Report on Sand and Gravel*, p. 48.

12 L.R.1 R.P., pp. 392, 459–62.

13 *Op cit.*, pp. 292–4.

14 They were in fact selected by reference to the *Report on Collective Discrimination* by the Monopolies Commission. Since this was made in 1955 the chances of other factors leading to abandonment are small.

15 Register R.619.

16 Watertube boilers was a case where the home and export aspects were not severed. Because of the impact of the agreement on the domestic market the agreement was referred to the Court and as it happens was upheld.

17 Register R.149.

18 Some carpet producers felt that although they lost the case the benefits of continued operation outweighed the legal and other costs incurred. We, however, feel that there may be an element of putting on a brave face in this attitude.

19 The four major case studies plus black bolts and nuts and watertube boilers.

20 One possibility is fibre rope. According to one large buyer no competition in tenders was experienced until October 1965; the *Galvanised Tanks* case occurred in May and June of that year.

21 Monopolies Commission, *Electric Lamps, Second Report on the Supply of Electric Lamps*, Part I, 1968, p. 16.

22 Nor were discounts in excess of those stipulated in the list to be granted.

23 There was some difference of opinion between the companies as to whether the understanding involved acceding to the views expressed at the meetings.

24 Register R.3061.

25 Private information.

26 We say 'In the main' because the arrangement of the L.M.F.A. probably only had a limited effectiveness since its membership covered about 65 per cent of total castings output.

27 L.R.6 R.P., pp. 58–9.

28 This is and has been quite a common form of informational arrangement in British industry and several examples have been cited by the reports of the Monopolies Commission – see for example Monopolies and Restrictive Practices Commission, *Report on the Supply of Tea*, 1956, pp. 35–6 and Monopolies Commission, *Report on the Supply and Processing of Colour Film*, 1966, p.21.

29 *Idem., Second Report on Electric Lamps*, p. 23.

30 *Report from the Select Committee on Nationalised Industries. The Electricity Supply Industry*, Vol. II, p. 134.

31 Register R.689.

32 Register R.2904.

33 Register R.3673.

34 D. P. O'Brien and D. Swann, *Information Agreements, Competition and Efficiency* (London, 1969) p. 169.

35 *Ibid.*, pp. 174–82.

36 The exception–or possible exception–is electric cables. The switch from

copper to aluminium was carried out by established firms. However, it has been put to us that it was the Area Boards which demanded the change; this puts a rather different complexion on this particular case.

37 Polyethylene, fibreglass and asbestos.

38 Industry has learnt that common prices are suspect – hence the use of cover pricing as in the *Electrical Sub-Contracting* cases of 1971. Price increases may also be introduced on a staggered basis.

39 In situations such as this the phrase 'combining business with pleasure' comes into its own.

40 Sometimes associations were abandoned when agreements were dropped. This was so in the case of the G.T.M.A. when its *information* agreement was terminated.

41 Price leaders are careful to see that all 'competitors' receive their price list.

42 This leadership related to off-list transactions as opposed to tender sales where competition remained evident.

43 It was reported that in 1970 one firm broke away and was willing to negotiate special discounts. Also in the five-gallon drum market Metal Box is apparently the leader.

44 This is evident in the case of general wiring cable where the number of producers helps to maintain a competitive environment.

45 Even industries with relatively large numbers of firms have an oligopolistic core – i.e. jute spinning and weaving.

46 New entry into an industry has not usually occurred in the section dealing with existing product and production technology. It has generally occurred in the area of Schumpeterian innovation – i.e. plastic baths and tufted carpets. Exceptions are Reliance Clifton in telephone cables and the roadstone industry.

47 G. D. Newbould, *Management and Merger Activity* (London, 1970) Ch. 3.

48 *Ibid.*, Ch. 4.

49 J. B. F. Earle, *A Century of Road Materials* (Oxford, 1971) p. 148.

50 *Ibid.*, p. 150.

51 This may be deceptively simple – mergers sometimes go sour.

52 There are of course a host of miscellaneous reasons for mergers – e.g. Hope and Crittall are said to have merged because together they would be less vulnerable to takeover. A forlorn hope as it happened!

53 It is necessary to draw attention to the fact that we have encountered a few (and we stress they are few in number) cases where cartels chose to compete for a customer's orders. It is necessary to set this point against our earlier analysis of trade association cohesion. These were not cases of backsliding but of agreement to treat certain customers competitively.

54 Events in 1972 did not give grounds for confidence that the D.T.I. would implement its merger powers vigorously. Thus it apparently was willing to accept the argument in the proposed Chloride–Oldham merger that membership of the E.E.C. would maintain competition; there is little evidence that economies of scale are such in this industry as to require such a combination. The merger was bound to reduce the number of competitors from what it would otherwise be within an E.E.C. framework with no apparent countervailing advantage. In the case of Glaxo–Beecham there was a remarkable dilatoriness which gave rise to considerable criticism. It was only the counter bid from Boots which precipitated action.

55 *Restrictive Trading Agreements, Report of the Registrar, 1 July 1966 to 30 June 1969*, Cmnd. 4303, 1970, pp. 1–8.

56 See *ibid.*, pp. 12–4.
57 S. Brittan, 'An Excess of Pragmatism' in J. B. Heath (ed.), *International Conference on Monopolies, Mergers and Restrictive Practices* (London, 1971) p. 59.
58 *Ibid.*, p. 60.
59 O'Brien and Swann, *op. cit.*, p. 240.
60 *Ibid.*, p. 241.
61 L.R.1 R.P., pp. 75, 104.
62 That is the power which exists under the 1965 Monopolies and Mergers Act.
63 It will be apparent that our proposal would involve a division of labour as between the Registrar of Monopolies and Mergers and the Monopolies Commission. The former would sift out those mergers significantly affecting competition. These would then be referred to the Commission for the appraisal process which we outline.

Chapter 5

THE FAIR TRADING
LEGISLATION, 1973

The preceding chapter was written towards the end of 1971 when our full study of the effects of the existing legislation had been completed. The recommendations in that chapter were, then, based upon what we had learned in our study. However eighteen months have elapsed during which publication of our study was delayed, and in the interim the Fair Trading Bill was published.[1] It will perhaps be helpful, then, if we summarise the legislation and compare it with our recommendations above.

I. CONTENTS

The Act, which replaces the 1948 and 1965 Acts and amends the 1956 Act, is difficult to summarise because these changes are only a part of its purpose. It not only sets out to amend the existing legislation on competition; it also attempts to provide legislation supplementary to that contained in the Trade Descriptions Act of 1968. It is then, in a sense, two Acts in one. Parts of it are not thus *directly* relevant to what we have been considering throughout this book although we will not ignore them entirely. This is not only for the sake of completeness, but also because any improvement in market transparency should increase the effectiveness of competition.

The Act creates the office of Director General of Fair Trading. It transfers to him the powers of the Registrar of Restrictive Trading Agreements, and also gives him a limited power to make monopoly references[2] to the renamed Monopolies and Mergers Commission (M.M.C.) as well as a watching brief (but little more) in relation to mergers. It also creates a Consumer Protection Advisory Committee (C.P.A.C.) which may investigate whether particular practices are detrimental to the interests of consumers, and which may be asked to approve orders suggested by the Director for the banning of particular practices.

The Act is divided into eleven sections. Part I provides generally for the Director to cover practices affecting consumers, and monopoly situations. Later in the Act we find that Clause 46 allows the Director to make references of monopoly situations to the M.M.C., but his freedom in this is limited by two considerations. First of all, Clause 13 allows the Secretary of State discretion over what is considered by the M.M.C. and what is considered by the C.P.A.C.; secondly, the Director is not free, under Clause 46, to refer for investigation either nationalised industries (as listed in Schedule 5 to the Act) or regulated sectors of agriculture (as listed in Schedule 7 to the Act). Nevertheless, these restrictions apart, the power to deal with concentrated situations is increased by a reduction from one-third to one-quarter in the market share of sales *or* purchases which qualifies for reference. Moreover the Director may also refer situations in which the U.K. market is not supplied at all, and export monopolies. He may also, under Clause 10, take account of local (geographical) monopolies and refer these for investigation. The latter may prove to be important. Under the 1948 legislation a monopoly in a substantial part, as well as the whole, of the U.K. could be referred. The word 'substantial' has now been removed which will enable the M.M.C. to investigate local monopolies. The Act also differs from the 1948 legislation by dropping its proviso (Section 3 (2)) that common action by firms as employers cannot constitute a situation about which a reference can be made to the M.M.C.

Parts II and III of the Act are concerned with consumer protection. The Director, or a Minister, may refer a consumer trade practice to the C.P.A.C. and ask it to report, although professional services are excluded[3] from this as they are (with some exceptions specified in Schedule 4) within the domain of the M.M.C., and the consent of the appropriate Minister is required if a nationalised industry is involved. The Director may propose orders banning particular practices, but these have to have ministerial approval, either as originally formulated or as modified by the C.P.A.C., before they can be laid before Parliament for final approval. However contravention of such an order approved by Parliament involves a fine of up to £400 on summary conviction, and a fine and/or up to two years imprisonment on indictment. Enforcement of such orders is the responsibility of the Weights and Measures Inspectors who are given power to enter premises and to seize goods and documents. Wilful obstruction of their investigation is itself an offence. Part III empowers the Director to take action against persons who persistently maintain, in their business activities, a course of conduct detrimental to consumers. He is first to attempt to get an assurance that the offender will desist. But if such an assurance is not obtained, or if it is obtained but not observed, then the Director can take proceedings in the Restrictive Practices Court to obtain an order banning such practices. (Presumably breach of such an order would constitute contempt of the Court, with all that that implies.) What seems to be desired is a flexible way of dealing with situations where, for whatever reason, the sanctions in the criminal and civil law have proved ineffective.

Part IV covers monopolies and concentrated situations. The Director is empowered to obtain statistical information to enable him to decide whether to make a reference, and it is an offence to fail to give him information or to mislead him deliberately. The form and nature of monopoly references are to be very much the same as under the old legislation, but the M.M.C. is to be allowed to concentrate on a particular aspect of a situation in order to speed its report. The reports and recommendations are to be in the same form as before and, as under the 1965 Act, the Minister can order divestiture in order to break up a concentrated situation.

Part V deals with mergers. This really covers exactly the same ground as the 1965 Act with two relatively small exceptions. Firstly, although the £5 million asset criterion is retained, the market share criterion is reduced to 25 per cent. Secondly, there is a novel provision (Clause 65, sub-section 3) allowing the Minister concerned to ask the M.M.C. to report on only one particular aspect of a merger proposal. (We will return to this below.) The Director has no power to make merger references although he is to advise the Minister on the desirability of such references.

Part VI deals with the reference of restrictive labour practices to the M.M.C. There is no power for a Minister to make an order, whatever the M.M.C. decides about a particular practice. The power is purely one of investigation.

Part VII empowers Ministers to censor reports of the Commission in order to protect individuals or the public interest. Part VIII comes nearer (Clause 79) to a definition of the public interest than any previous legislation and spells out the desirability of competition *per se*.

In determining for the purposes of this Act whether any particular matter operates, or may be expected to operate, against the public interest, the Commission shall take into account all matters which appear to them in the particular circumstances to be relevant and, among other things, shall have regard to the desirability—

(a) of maintaining and promoting effective competition between persons supplying goods and services in the United Kingdom;

(b) of promoting the interests of consumers, purchasers and other users of goods and services in the United Kingdom in respect of the prices charged for them and in respect of their quality and the variety of goods and services supplied;

(c) of promoting, through competition, the reduction of costs and the development and use of new techniques and new products, and of facilitating the entry of new competitors into existing markets;

(d) of maintaining and promoting the balanced distribution of industry and employment in the United Kingdom; and

(e) of maintaining and promoting competitive activity in markets outside the United Kingdom on the part of producers of goods, and of suppliers of goods and services, in the United Kingdom.

Part IX transfers the powers of the Registrar to the Director and extends the provisions of the 1956 Act to cover commercial (as distinct from professional) services. It also brings restrictive export agreements within the purview of the Director (though it does nothing more about them) and it also includes collective agreements to recommend or suggest (as distinct from enforce) resale prices. Another extension is the inclusion of patent pooling agreements within the coverage of the Act. In addition the range of persons who may, by order of the High Court, be examined on oath under Section 15 of the 1956 Act, where the Registrar suspects the existence of a restrictive agreement, is slightly widened. There are two other provisions of note in this section. Firstly, the powers of the Court to make orders against trade associations, and to make provision to see that these orders are carried out, are extended. Secondly, and perhaps significantly in the light of some of the delays which have occurred, the Director may now apply to the Court to make an *interim* order against a particular agreement.

Part X contains provisions relating to the method of dealing with commercial services. Registration of agreements relating to these services is to be on the basis of an Order designating the type of service, and this has, as in the case of orders for registration of information agreements under the 1968 Act procedure, to be approved by Parliament. The extension to commercial services covers not only explicit agreements restricting the supply of these but also information agreements.

Part XI, which contains miscellaneous provisions, provides for the Director to publish information and advice about consumer trade practices as well as an annual report on his activities. It also provides for relaxation of the patent laws where the M.M.C. has found that this would be desirable. Finally, amongst the schedules appended to the Bill there is a provision, in Schedule 8, for the M.M.C. to ban recommendations of resale prices.

II. EVALUATION

It is sad to discover that very few of the defects in the legislative framework which emerged during the course of our study are likely to be remedied by this Act. The merger situation remains as unsatisfactory as ever; and indeed in some ways it will become even worse than before, if the widely reported belief that the provision enabling the M.M.C. to examine only a particular aspect of a merger stems from official dismay at the condemnation by the Commission of both the Beecham and Boots bids for Glaxo although the Minister concerned had originally decided not to refer the Beecham bid to the Commission and only made a reference after the emergence of the Boots bid. This is all the more disturbing in the light of the recent example of one bid for a shoe company being referred to the Commission and the other not.[4] A degree of discretion, political discretion, is involved which simply makes competition policy unworkable in the area of mergers.[5]

It would have been better had the law been changed in such a way that mergers which significantly reduced competition were declared illegal–we are thinking here of the posture adopted in the U.S. Clayton Act. This point was made in Chapter 4 above. It is also worth mentioning at this point that several speakers in the debate on the Second Reading in the House of Commons[6] took the view that the law should be changed to require mergers to show benefit. The only good thing which can be said about the Bill's posture is the pro-competitive nature of the public interest criterion.

On the other hand there are several factors not directly connected with the legislation which point to a more hopeful state of affairs. Firstly, by requiring the Director to be fully appraised of the takeover situation in industry, the Act represents an improvement on the existing *ad hoc*, and necessarily speedy, investigation of actual merger situations when they occur, by the D.T.I. The Director's views on appropriate candidates for referral to the M.M.C. may well carry great weight when presented to the Secretary of State. Secondly, in pressing for further references to the Commission to an extent greater than hitherto the Director might well be aided by increasing public scepticism of the desirability of a further concentration of production in the hands of fewer companies. There are indications that the results of a study by the National Institute of Economic & Social Research have had a sobering influence in Government circles.[7] Work in the D.T.I. itself has also critically examined some of the allegedly beneficial effects of mergers.[8] Thirdly, the parallel pricing reference to the Monopolies Commission may bring a further critical eye to bear on the concentration process as achieved through mergers. Fourthly, the Government has declared itself ready to make full use of the 25 per cent definition of a monopoly which will also indirectly have an influence on horizontal bids for fairly large firms.[9] Fifthly, some recent merger references do accord with the view of the situation expressed in our research.[10] Nonetheless with all this said our criticism of the element of political discretion in respect of mergers policy does still remain a potent one. Moreover in view of the *very* small proportion of mergers investigated under the one-third criterion[11] the reduction in the level to one-quarter could also be viewed as being of doubtful significance.

There is no sign that tariffs are to be used as a weapon of policy. Nor is there any real recognition of the problems of trade association recommendations which are subsequently rescinded yet adhered to by the recipients, or of interlocking directorates. However it is true that some more notice (though apparently nothing more) is to be taken of restrictive export agreements; and, as a result of a decision of the Court itself, the device of joint marketing companies seems to have come to an end with the disentangling of the Schweppes and Lyons arrangement.[12]

The powers of enforcement and investigation possessed by the Director are only marginally greater than those available to the Registrar and the sanctions for non-registration are still extremely puny.[13] One cannot help contrasting the strong powers given to the Weights and Measures Inspectorate in enforcing the Trade Descriptions Act and the related sections of this Act with the enforcement powers relating to the other parts of the Act.

There is no real recognition of the difficulties associated with the conflict between government intervention in the economy, particularly in relation to the regulation of prices, and the operation of a competition policy; and the gateways in Section 21 (1) of the 1956 Act remain the same.

However the provisions of the 1956 Act have been extended to cover at least commercial services; and this is a marked improvement. Some move has also been made in the direction of dealing with the problem of the nationalised industries although, here again, political discretion is likely to be a potent impediment to the operation of competition policy.

Nothing is done about the defects in the Court procedure to which we have drawn attention above; and the defects in the Commission procedure remain, with the exception that the M.M.C. may be able to move a little faster in dealing with concentrated situations because of the provision for limited references. But there is nothing to remedy the delays in publication of reports and nothing to ensure that the recommendations are effective. The objectionable provisions in the 1968 Act, notably Sections 1 and 2, also remain unscathed. Although it is clear from the Registrar's latest Report that, for the moment, these are unimportant in their operation,[14] they need not remain so should political fashions change.

The Registrar has also drawn attention in his latest Report to the problem of refusal to supply.[15] The Commission in an earlier report felt that the problem was not serious,[16] but did make recommendations which are not implemented in the legislation. This is unfortunate because there is a potent barrier to entry involved here.

In favour of the legislation it should be said that it has succeeded in retaining the dual frame-work of Court and Commission which we judge to have been valuable, and it does hold out the potentiality of a more flexible and speedy Commission procedure. There is the possibility also that the Director could be independent, to a greater extent than successive Ministers, of day-to-day politics at least in his references of monopoly positions. Moreover the power of divestiture is again spelled out. In addition there are provisions to deal with difficulties which we did not encounter in our study but which may be important in some areas for all that; these are local monopolies (Clause 10), recommended prices (Clause 90), and patent pooling (Clause 91).

But making full allowance for these merits, the legislation is still markedly unsatisfactory. Control of mergers is a major problem facing government today; yet the legislation continues with a process of dealing with mergers which has been shown to be by turns impotent and arbitrary. It also (in Clause 79) again introduces employment as a criterion of competition policy, although, as we argued in Chapters 3 and 4, this is not a suitable inclusion. Clause 22 of the 1956 Act which clearly needed strengthening, as is further evidenced by the recent efforts of the Registrar in relation to the cement industry's agreement, remains unaltered.

A great deal will depend upon the way in which the Director goes about his task. It may be that he will proceed with the quiet efficiency of the former Registrar; but it may equally well be that he will prove as ineffective as the Department of Trade and Industry has been (and may continue to be) in dealing with mergers. The D.T.I. is of course in an impossible position, in that it has the dual role of acting as the voice of industry within government on the one hand and as the enforcer of competition policy on the other. But, precisely because of this difficulty, much more should have been removed from the area of political discretion than is being removed by this Act. In the light of our study we do not feel that the Act will meet the needs of the situation–certainly of the situation which existed at the time of our study.

REFERENCES

1 Bill 36, 1972.
2 The idea that there should in effect be a Registrar of Monopolies is not new. The Conservative Political Centre published a report in 1963 called *Monopoly and the Public Interest* in which it proposed such a change and in the White Paper *Monopolies, Mergers and Restrictive Practices* (Cmnd. 2299, 1964) the then Conservative government also proposed such a development but did not remain in office long enough to carry the idea out.
3 During the committee stage of the Act the government suffered a defeat in respect of its proposals relating to certain professions. In its Bill as published it had excluded legal, medical and dental services from investigation by the Director. The Standing Committee voted to delete Schedule 4 to the Bill which had provided for this exclusion. The government secured an amendment at the Report stage which restored the Bill to its original position. Nonetheless the considerable criticism that these and other professions should not be left without scrutiny led the government to announce the reference to the Monopolies Commission of some professional practices during the Report stage.
4 The bid for William Timpson Ltd by Sears Holdings was referred while that by United Drapery Stores–at a lower price–was not.
5 It is perhaps worth noting that in 1972 the Secretary of State indicated that he intended '. . . to make greater use of the Monopolies Commission in

major mergers, and if there is doubt as to whether a reference is desirable the balance is likely in future to be struck in favour of referring rather than not referring' (*Hansard Parliamentary Debates*, 24 November 1972, Vol. 846, c. 1829). Only time will tell whether this undertaking is really meaningful.

6 Most notably by Sir Tatton Brinton who argued strongly in favour of such a position during the Second Reading of the Bill. *Hansard Parliamentary Debates*, 13 December 1972, Vol. 848, Cols. 496–501.

7 See for example *The Financial Times*, 21 March 1973.

8 N. Owen, 'Competition and industrial structure: implications of entry to the E.E.C.', *Trade and Industry*, 22 March 1973, pp. 586–8.

9 Sir Geoffrey Howe told a Food Manufacturers Federation conference in April 1973 that certain food manufacturing industries would shortly be referred to the M.M.C. *The Grocer*, 7 April 1973, p. 5.

10 For example the bid by Glynwed for Armitage Shanks in 1972. As in other cases the bid was withdrawn following reference to the Commission.

11 See G. D. Newbould, *Management & Merger Activity, passim*.

12 Following the decision of Lord Justice Stamp Cadbury-Schweppes announced in March 1973 that they had acquired from J. Lyons the latter's minority interest in Rose Kia-Ora Sales Company Limited. At the same time J. Lyons had acquired the minority interest of Cadbury-Schweppes in O. R. Groves Limited.

13 However, the provision in the Act for investigating restrictive labour practices may help to persuade firms adversely affected by restricted agreements to co-operate with the competition policy authorities. Some industrialists apparently feel that there is a need to stick together and not assist the authorities while labour's restricted ability remains completely unimpaired.

14 *Report of the Registrar of Restrictive Trading Agreements, 1 July 1969 to 30 June 1972*, Cmnd. 5195, 1973, p. 15.

15 *Ibid.*, p. 6.

16 Report of the Monopolies Commission, *Refusal to Supply*, Cmnd. 4372, July 1970.

Index

(*R* = reference number on the page before this letter)

P

For Product Safety Concerns and Information please contact our EU
representative GPSR@taylorandfrancis.com Taylor & Francis Verlag GmbH,
Kaufingerstraße 24, 80331 München, Germany

Printed and bound by CPI Group (UK) Ltd, Croydon, CR0 4YY
01/05/2025
01858349-0004